WARFARE
IN THE ROMAN EMPIRE
AND THE MIDDLE AGES

WARFARE

IN THE ROMAN EMPIRE
AND THE MIDDLE AGES

HOFFMAN NICKERSON

DOVER PUBLICATIONS, INC.
MINEOLA, NEW YORK

Bibliographical Note

This Dover edition, first published in 2003, is a republication (unabridged, but with new page numbers) of "Warfare in the Roman Empire, the Dark and Middle Ages, to 1494 A. D." which comprised Part II of *Warfare: A Study of Military Methods from the Earliest Times* by Oliver Lyman Spaulding Jr., Hoffman Nickerson, and John Womack Wright, originally published by Harcourt, Brace and Company, New York, in 1925.

Library of Congress Cataloging-in-Publication Data

Nickerson, Hoffman.
    [Warfare in the Roman Empire, the Dark and Middle Ages, to 1494 A.D.]
    Warfare in the Roman Empire and the Middle Ages / Hoffman Nickerson.
        p. cm.
    A republication of: Warfare in the Roman Empire, the Dark and Middle Ages, to 1494 A.D., by Hoffman Nickerson, which comprised part II of Warfare, by Oliver Lyman Spaulding, Jr., Hoffman Nickerson, and John Womack, published in 1925.
    ISBN 0-486-43085-5 (pbk.)
    1. Military art and science—Rome—History. 2. Military art and science—Europe—History. 3. Military history, Ancient. 4. Military history, Medieval. I. Spaulding, Oliver Lyman, 1875–1947. Warfare. II. Title.

U35.N534 2003
355'.009376—dc21

                                    2003055402

Manufactured in the United States of America
Dover Publications, Inc., 31 East 2nd Street, Mineola, N.Y. 11501

CONTENTS

iii

LIST OF PLATES

ACKNOWLEDGMENTS

Plates 4–7 are reproduced from my book on the establishment of the Inquisition. Plates 8 and 9 are from Delpech. Plate 3 is from the hand of my friend Mr. Hilaire Belloc. I believe it to be the first contour map of the Hastings position ever published. My debt to Mr. Belloc is increased by his kind permission to reproduce Plates 1 and 10 from his "Warfare In England," and the maps of Crécy and Poitiers from his monographs on these battles.

CHAPTER I

THE IMPERIAL ROMAN ARMY

(FROM AUGUSTUS TO HADRIAN—29 B. C. TO 117 A. D.)

CÆSAR was assassinated (March 15, B. C. 44) almost exactly a year after Munda, and his death was followed by fifteen years of renewed civil war. Not until 29 B. C. was Cæsar's nephew Augustus the sole master of the Roman state.

That state was in imperative need of repose. After seventy years of foreign conquest and internal strife, no man alive in 29 B. C. could remember an era of political stability or of peace.

Augustus was himself a statesman rather than a soldier. In military affairs he depended upon advisers, particularly upon Tiberius who afterward succeeded him as Emperor. However, since Augustus was head of the state when the army reforms were put in operation, and since the army reforms themselves were a part of his general scheme of consolidation, it is fitting that they should bear his name. For the sake of brevity and convenience they can be treated as a single programme—if we remember that different items of this programme were conceived and applied at different times throughout Augustus' forty-three years of ascendancy.

First of all, what was the nature of the Roman state, and what was its general policy? From immemorial time the shores all around the Mediterranean had been covered with city-states each enjoying high civilization but without lasting political union between one city-state and another. Now one city—Rome—had conquered all the others and had carried the frontiers of civilization to the Atlantic and the Rhine. In this achievement the Roman governing class had been, and still was, sustained by the sense of a great mission. On the other hand the Roman temper was severely practical. The Roman had no silly love of conquest for its own sake. Hence he was utterly unwilling to invade territories whose subjugation would be of no material benefit to the

1

state. He would, of course, occupy small districts of barren
land when their pacification was necessary for the sake of public
order in rich agricultural territories near by.

With the purely political side of Augustus' arrangements this
book is little concerned. It is enough to note that his problem was
to replace the institutions normal to a city-state with others
fitted to administer so vast an empire, and that he solved it by
creating a centralized, bureaucratic, civil service taking its orders
from the commander-in-chief of the army. This commander-in-
chief or "Imperator," from which title our word emperor is derived,
was appointed for life by the Senate, and once appointed became
the lawful head of the government.

Only on one tiny fraction of its circumference did the Empire
border upon another civilized state. That was in northern Syria
where the Euphrates marked the boundary with Parthia. South
and southeast were deserts inhabited by a few nomads; north
were forests thinly peopled with shifting tribes whose small numbers, lack of organization, and total lack of national or racial soli-
darity made them contemptible antagonists. Still a certain slight
pressure was always to be expected from these outer barbarians in the way of raiding parties intent upon enjoying the fruits
of civilization, without the discipline which civilization must necessarily impose.

Since Mesopotamia (defended as it was by the far from contemptible Parthian army) was distant from the centre of Roman
power, and since there was practically nothing worth conquering
anywhere else, Augustus decided, in general, upon a defensive
policy. The war weariness of the community made such a policy
inevitable for the time being. Circumstances were to make it
permanent.

On the other hand, Augustus' policy, defensive though it was in
its general purpose, was by no means purely defensive. Indeed,
through its contrast with the strict strategic defensive begun by
Hadrian in 117, the period from Augustus to the death of Trajan
may be called the offensive phase of imperial strategy. In order
that the frontiers might be defended with a minimum of force they
must be established upon obstacles. Accordingly, the entire
southern basin of the Danube was conquered so that the river
itself, from its source to its mouth, was the frontier. A methodi-

cal attempt was made to advance the frontier from the Rhine to the Elbe—although the attempt was abandoned after the defeat of Varus in 9 A. D. That disaster (though it was rightly considered shocking and disgraceful) in no way threatened the existence or even the general well-being of the state. Rome thought of it somewhat as America thought of the Custer massacre, or as England thought of the fall of Khartoum and the death of Gordon. So much for the general military policy of Augustus. Let us now consider the army which was its instrument.

By 29 B. c. the Roman army had already become professional. Indeed Marius had taken the decisive step in this direction nearly eighty years before. Theoretically the old universal obligation to serve still remained, but it had become a dead letter. Ever since Marius' time the soldier had taken an oath to his general (i. e., "Imperator") as well as to the state, and had served for pay, booty, and a bonus or "donative" which he expected to get when discharged. The huge force of forty-five legions (from 162,000 to 270,000 men plus an equal or even greater number of auxiliaries) on foot at Augustus' accession had been recruited and paid in haphazard fashion. There was no definite term of enlistment or rate of donative (i. e., bonus) upon discharge.[1] In matters of organization all was chaos.

Augustus continued the professional army, but he greatly reduced its numbers and put the chaos in order.

Modern historians have shed so much ink in trying to prove that Augustus should have introduced conscription, universal service, and what not, that it may be well for us to consider the point. In general the situation was much like that of France after Napoleon or that of the United States after the Civil War and again in 1919: a large army in being, military problems of no great difficulty, and a thorough weariness of war. In the first place, Augustus was not an innovator except where innovation was absolutely necessary. The crying need of the time was consolidation and stabilization. In the second place, the thing would have been politically impossible. The whole force of public opinion would have been against it, for the community was sick and tired of the whole idea of military service, and a government much more strongly established than that of

[1] Dion Cassius: Bk. 55, sec. 23.

Augustus and the Senate would have had trouble in enforcing it. Finally conscription would have been both unnecessary and inexpedient; unnecessary because no formidable internal or external enemy threatened the Roman state (and no civilized community in all history has ever shouldered such a burden without the spur of evident necessity); inexpedient because the task of the imperial army was hardly more than constabulary work. For internal policing, and for campaigns in remote and thinly peopled theatres of war an army of short-term conscripts is an inefficient and enormously expensive instrument.

To-day the colonial troops of both England and France are professionals.

The one real military danger which menaced Rome—that of a general insurrection in some province—would have been all the greater if she herself had trained the mass of the provincials in arms. There was nothing she dreaded so much as internal disorder. In a third-century author, Dion Cassius (150–235), this factor of the problem is dwelt upon in the course of a discussion of the military policy put in the mouth of Maecenas, an Augustan statesman.[2] Altogether then, Augustus' decision to go on with a professional army is perhaps as nearly inevitable as anything in human affairs can be. So much for the pedants.

Augustus' most important step was the reduction of the numbers of the army. All slaves, freedmen and criminals were discharged. Of those with good records who were anxious to leave the service, great numbers were settled in "colonies" upon public land given them by the state. One account says there were as many as 120,000 so favoured. Only 25 of the 45 existing legionary organizations were continued.

The strength of the 25 legions which remained seems to have been fixed at 6000; plus a detachment of mounted men serving (in our own military phraseology) as "divisional cavalry." If we assume, as it seems we should, that this meant an increase in numbers per legion then that increase was provided for by raising the strength of the first and fifth cohorts to 1000 men each. At all events, the later distinction between quingenary ("quingenaria") cohorts 500 strong, and miliary ("miliaria") cohorts 1000 strong seems to date from this time. The possible

[2] Dion Cassius: Bk. 53, sec. 27.

change of formation involved in this change of organization will be discussed later.

I repeat that Augustus thought of himself as a consolidator, not an inventor. There seem to have been no changes in tactics or equipment. On the other hand, a regular training schedule was laid down and strictly adhered to, including strenuous practice marches three times a month in full field equipment. Sometimes the weight carried by the soldiers on these marches would be doubled—to increase their endurance.[3] Modern soldiers bitterly resent "dummy packs" and since the Roman soldier equally resented them [4] there is some question whether the practice was judicious. At any rate it indicates a high standard of training and discipline. Furthermore, Roman discipline was more brutal than ours.

Good order and discipline were particularly promoted by Augustus through reform of military finance. Rates of pay had varied scandalously and the worst sort of abuses had grown up in connection with the "donative," the bonus expected upon discharge. The Senate had played the fool by refusing to concede this bonus in principle, and then granting it over and over again when frightened by threats. Not to mention recent burning issues, our own Continental Congress had a similar experience with our Revolutionary army—and did about the same thing as the Roman Senate. Augustus now fixed a sum which the discharged soldier might lawfully claim. In the face of stubborn political opposition he created a fund, under control of the emperor alone and nourished by special taxes, from which all army expenses, pay, supply and bonuses, were met.[5]

The legions were usually stationed near the frontier. To serve as the Imperial body-guard and supplement the municipal police of Rome, ten miliary "prætorian" cohorts were raised.

Assuming 25 legions at 6000 per legion and 10 prætorian cohorts at 1000 per cohort, the total number of heavy infantry amounted to about 160,000 men. These troops were recruited from Roman citizens, who comprised the Italians plus the enfranchised com-

---

[3] Dodge, Cæsar, 775.
[4] Tacitus, Annals, Bk. 1, Sec. 20, for mutineers' resentment at heavy (probably dummy) packs.
[5] Dion Cassius: Bk. 55, sec. 23.

munities outside Italy, i. e., the descendants of veterans' colonies
and the cities or tribes to whom citizenship had been granted as
a favour. Whether enlistment was purely voluntary we do not
know. There may have been legal machinery for drafting men if
enough did not come forward. If so the draft must have borne
very lightly on the communities involved.

The soldier was expected to spend his entire life in the army,
which meant to leave him only "a little repose before old age
comes on."[6] Exactly how long the term of service was is uncertain.
The figure of twenty-five years given by some authorities is in-
consistent with the information that replacements were sought
every three years, unless we assume a one-year training period
before being assigned to a unit, the training period not counted
toward the enlistment. We know that there had been training
units (tirocinia) ever since Marius' time,[7] but a one-year training
period seems long. Maurice tells us in the "Strategicon"[8] that in
the sixth century A. D., recruits were called in the spring, trained
in the summer, furloughed home for the winter and assigned to
units in the following spring.

Besides the legions, the Roman army at Augustus' accession
comprised non-citizen forces at least equal and probably superior
to them in numbers. These troops, the auxiliaries, were recruited
from the more warlike of the unenfranchised inhabitants of the
Empire. Their units were incorporated in the Roman army
and served as cavalry and light infantry under Roman officers.
Although they were considered less important than the legions,
nevertheless an auxiliary contingent about equal in number to
that of the legionary troops formed a part of all armies. Without
auxiliaries and especially without cavalry the legions would have
been at a grave disadvantage.

Under Augustus the auxiliaries were supplemented by allied
units from the little states theoretically independent of but practically dependent upon the Empire. As time went on, however,
and these states in Morocco, Thrace, Northeastern Asia Minor,
and elsewhere in the East were one by one painlessly absorbed
by the Imperial system, their contingents were assimilated to
the other auxiliaries. For our purpose, therefore, we may treat
them as such from the first.

[6] Dion Cassius: Bk. 53, sec. 27.   [7] Boutaric, 20.   [8] Aussaresses.

The pay in the auxiliaries was less than in the legions. Nevertheless, since their recruiting ground was so much larger than that for legionary troops, and since the average level of culture in the populations from which they came was often lower than that of Roman citizens, their enlistment seems to have been entirely voluntary. One of the inducements to serve as an auxiliary was that such service carried with it the grant of full Roman citizenship to soldiers honourably discharged. The term of service, like that of the legionaries, was long, apparently twenty-five years.

There was no permanent auxiliary unit higher than the infantry cohort and the cavalry "ala" (literally "wing" as we should say "squadron"). In general such troops served with the equipment best suited to their capacity and local habits. Thus the Gauls were famous as cavalry, the Cretans and most of the Orientals were archers, etc. A sentence in Hadrian's speech to the army of Africa indicates that all auxiliaries were trained to use the sling.[9] Most had helmets although some had not. Some are represented with chain-mail or scale-mail shirts, which must have been lighter than the legionary cuirass of strap-metal, some with no armour at all. The greater number seem to have worn short leather tunics. Instead of the heavy legionary pilum they carried a light thrusting lance, to which the cavalry seem to have added a couple of javelins carried in a quiver slung on the back. On the other hand, in contradiction to the lightness of most of their equipment, the long broadsword, or "spatha" characteristic of all auxiliaries, was bulkier and must have been heavier than the short legionary thrusting sword or "gladius."

The tactics of the Imperial Roman army are known only in a general way. In battle, the legionaries were the chief arm and were used to deal the decisive blow. The auxiliaries, organized as cavalry and light infantry, were usually posted on the flanks. They might be used to begin an attack, for instance in working over difficult ground to which light infantry were particularly suited. The mobility of the auxiliaries, especially of the cavalry, made them useful in pursuit.

The legions were officered partly by young men of the upper classes, partly by promotion from the ranks. For the auxiliaries, officers were sometimes found among their own tribal chiefs.

[9] Cheesman, 132.

Sometimes an old legionary centurion would be promoted to command an auxiliary cohort or ala—we may reasonably guess that this was done when the troops in question proved hard to discipline. Usually the auxiliaries, like the legions, were officered by upper-class young men from civil life. What training these last received to fit them to hold a commission, we do not know.

Obviously, in the service of a world-state like Rome, no strong patriotism such as that inspired by the ancient free cities and (more fitfully perhaps) by our modern nations, could be expected of the rank and file. Morale was assured through *esprit de corps* and an elaborate system of rewards and punishments. *Esprit de corps* could easily be fostered, thanks to the permanence of the organized units, and rewards could be generously distributed, since, as in most professional armies, there was a large proportion of noncommissioned officers and extra-pay men.

Siege works were elaborate and skilful, and the number of catapults used in sieges was large; at the siege of Jerusalem in 70 A. D., the besieged had 340, which would be a high proportion of guns for a considerable force to-day.[10]

To what extent, if at all, catapult-artillery was used in mobile warfare we do not know. Indeed we know almost no details of the tactical method and the campaigns of the Roman Imperial army for over four centuries. On minor tactics we get only scraps, such as Josephus' statement that the legions marched in columns of sixes.[11] It so happens that from Cæsar's African campaign, culminating at Thapsus in 46 B. C., to Julian the Apostate's victory near Strassburg in 357 A. D., not one single account of a campaign in the field, written by a good military historian, has survived. We might be morally certain that a technical literature existed, even had its existence not been referred to by one of the historians of the time,[12] but the books which have come down to us (including that of the great Tacitus) do not pretend to interest themselves in the art of war as such. Even Cæsar's last campaign, in Spain in 45 B. C., has many obscure points: for instance, the site of the battle of Munda has been endlessly disputed in vain. From Munda to Strassburg we must content ourselves with outlining our subject

[10] Josephus: Bk. 5, Chap. 9.   [11] Josephus: Bk. 5, Chap. 2.
[12] Dion Cassius, H, 15, 6, and Lucian, De Hist. Conscrib., cited by Cheesman, 102, footnote.

and filling in the details within that outline only faintly and timidly because of our insufficient equipment in facts.

The first question to be asked of any military policy is, did it succeed? That is, did it avoid disaster at an expense in men and money which was reasonable in view of the problem to be solved?

Even if we take the entire Roman period, the Roman army succeeded. Leaving so general a statement for later discussion, let us (for the moment) confine ourselves to the period from 29 B. C. to 380 A. D. Throughout these four centuries, the Imperial armies suffered no general disaster at the hands of foes from without. Naturally through the chances of war over so long a period, there were severe local disasters, but they were surprisingly few, and in every case the general military position was soon re-established. These results were obtained at a minimum expenditure in men, and (as far as we can judge) at a cost in money not out of proportion to the budget as a whole. Unquestionably, therefore, the Roman Imperial army of the first four centuries succeeded.

While always willing to fight, the Romans were intensely practical. Accordingly, their strategy was that typical of a long-service professional army, that is of a highly trained force whose replacements can arrive only slowly and in small numbers, since those replacements take a long time to train and are expensive to hire. Such an army is a most keen and easily managed weapon. On the other hand, when opposed to great numbers it is, as it were, brittle like other highly tempered weapons; for its commander cannot undertake violent action which necessarily implies a high rate of wastage unless he can hope to get a decision at once. If he accept battle in the open field (or have it forced upon him) and then fail to finish off his campaign then and there, he may find himself impotent through the reduction of his numbers. It is true that under the ancient and mediæval conditions of short-range weapons the losses of the victor were usually small, whereas for want of artillery to cover a retreat the loser was usually wiped out unless he could take refuge in a near-by fortress. It is also true that the total population of the empire was much larger than that of its opponents. On the other hand, the numbers of the Roman army (as distinguished from population as a whole) were deliberately kept low to save expense, and because a comparatively small force possessed of civilized organization and traditions of war can usually defeat a horde of semi-savages.

Incidentally, all Rome's enemies were of this sort except the Parthians and the Persians, the successors of the Parthians, in the East. The army as reorganized by Augustus had two main weaknesses, the lack of a central reserve and the encouragement given to revolt through the military training furnished to those of the newly conquered peoples who enlisted in the Roman auxiliaries.

The prætorians could not act as an efficient reserve. Only 10,-000 strong, they were too few in numbers, and their duty as parade troops and metropolitan police was not calculated to make them efficient field soldiers. Indeed, prætorianism has come to be a name for the abominable tendency of unprincipled troops to bully the very government they should obey.

The danger arising from the want of a central reserve was recognized, and an attempt was made to meet it by improving the lateral communications inside the frontier. In particular, great roads were built over the Alps between Lyons and Turin and between, say, Verona and the newly founded city of Augsburg near the Danube, thus shortening the time required to transport an army between Gaul and the Danubian theatre of operations. Northern Switzerland seems then to have been too poor and barbarous to be a good lateral highway for armies. That more was not done was probably because the pressure on the frontiers was normally that of Roman upon barbarian rather than vice versa.

The other danger, that of revolts in newly conquered territories, was responsible for most of the serious military work of the offensive phase. The leaders would usually be men trained in arms as Roman auxiliary soldiers. On the other hand, such revolts were not inspired by anything like modern national patriotism. They were mere explosions of resentment against administration in an alien tongue, economic penetration, and the individual rogueries and villainies so frequent in modern colonial experience, plus personal ambition on the part of a few leading spirits. That these revolts were not more frequent and more serious, shows how large a part persuasion played in the building up of the Empire. Rome's political genius and power of assimilation have never been equalled in history.

Even so, revolt was a far more dangerous thing than the original occupation of a country. Thus the greatest peril Cæsar had had to meet in Gaul had been the revolt led by Vercingetorix in 52 B. C. six years after his first campaign.

Except Trajan's conquest of Dacia, all the chief military incidents of the first, that is the offensive, phase of imperial strategy were revolts. Let us take them in their chronological order.

First of all come the operations on the northern frontier during the reigns of Augustus and Tiberius. Before achieving supreme power, Augustus had already (in 35 B. C.) conquered Pannonia, the country between the Save and the Danube. In the following year he had put down a revolt in Dalmatia, between the Save and the Adriatic Sea. The operations had been economically profitable in themselves as they had brought in quantities of slaves, money and ships. In the first decade after his accession he occupied what is now Switzerland, together with southern Germany and upper Austria to the line of the Danube. By the year 13 B. C., although these regions still required military occupation and occasional punitive expeditions, nevertheless they seemed quiet enough to warrant attempting another enterprise. It was therefore decided to conquer Germany from the Rhine to the Elbe, partly because hope of German aid might encourage sedition in Gaul—the richest and most populous province of the West. The operation was methodically prepared. Since communications and supply were difficult in the savage densely wooded country, it was decided to have the fleet support the army by sailing up the rivers, and since the Romans feared open tidal water, a canal was dug from the Rhine to the lagoon which later became the Zuyder Zee. The occupation was a military success, but an economic failure, for the booty was small. No tribute could be had from the wild and undeveloped country, and the profits of its trade were a bagatelle compared with the cost of the army of occupation.

Nevertheless, the government of Augustus persisted, and in 6 A. D., eighteen years after the beginning of the operation, Augustus' general Tiberius was in what is now Bohemia stamping out the last embers of resistance, when he was recalled with many of his troops to meet a new danger. Angered at the heavy demands upon them for supplies and recruits for the auxiliaries, the Dalmatians and Pannonians revolted. The Roman garrisons and the traders were massacred, and the rebels increased their numbers until they were estimated at 200,000. Only Sirmium, the modern Mitrovitza on the Save, held out.

In Rome itself, the news produced a panic. The men whose ancestors two centuries before had shown such magnificent courage against Hannibal, whose grandfathers had kept a stiff upper lip in the face of Spartacus' slave insurrection, imagined the Pannonians to be marching on the city. Cohorts of freedmen were raised, and even slaves (freed by law for the purpose) were enlisted as so-called "volunteers." Grave risks were run in exacting tribute even from the poverty-stricken tribes of newly conquered Germany. It was proposed to recall Tiberius at once.

While sending for Tiberius, Augustus began preparations for moving against the rebels from all sides. The hodge-podge of newly raised troops from Italy were hurriedly pushed forward to Siscia, the modern Sisek on the Save, to cover Venetia. Meanwhile there were three legions on the lower Danube, in what is now Bulgaria. Augustus ordered two legions stationed in Syria to join them, and called upon the "allied" (i. e., dependent) king of Thrace for his contingent. The five legions and the Thracians, when concentrated, were to march up the Danube.

Meanwhile Tiberius had kept his head. He knew the revolted districts well, having often campaigned in them; and he correctly estimated the situation, judging that Italy was in no immediate danger. On the other hand, he knew that the revolt was dangerous because of the military training its leaders and many of their followers had enjoyed while serving as Roman auxiliary soldiers. He therefore began negotiations with the Bohemian chiefs and left for Pannonia only when he had come to a satisfactory understanding with them. On reaching Siscia early in the autumn, he was joined by the forces from the lower Danube who had just relieved Sirmium after hard fighting.

At Siscia he finally concentrated ten legions, seventy cohorts of auxiliary foot, ten "alæ" (i. e., squadrons) of auxiliary cavalry, the Thracian allied cavalry, ten thousand re-enlisted veterans and the scratch troops recently raised in Italy—all told his force was almost certainly well over 100,000 effective, possibly nearer 150,-000. Pannonia was a barbarous and barren country whose topography was little known in detail. Accordingly, supply was difficult and there was great danger of being ambushed upon the march. The troops from the lower Danube had already lost heavily in several ambushes. Tiberius' decision was worthy of the severely practical Roman temper at its best. We are reminded of Marius' operations against the Cimbri and Teutones. Instead of hunting for glory by trying for a pitched battle, he determined to distribute his troops in fortified posts, for like all barbarians the rebels were not good at sieges—they had not the necessary method and persistence. The Roman posts were therefore in little danger. Thus distributed, the Romans would be able to devastate the country systematically, and could, in the long run, starve out the rebels by making agriculture impossible. The commander-in-chief took upon himself the hard and tedious work of superintending the supply department.

Such measures did not suit public opinion in Rome, which had chopped around from panic to hopeful and excited demands that the war be ended at once by a great victory. In city populations of unmilitary temper such exhibitions are common, for instance "On to Richmond" in 1861, "À Berlin" in Paris in 1870, and the Londoners' delight in "killing Kruger with their mouths" in 1900. But in Romans such conduct is pathetic.

Tiberius, unmoved, stuck to his decision. In 7 A. D. resentment in Rome ran so high that a new commander, Germanicus, was sent out as his first lieutenant, or even his equal, so determined was the capital upon a striking victory. Opinion concerning Tiberius soon changed for the better, for Germanicus was ambushed and his command nearly cut to pieces on reaching the theatre of war. In the course of the year 8 A. D., the rebellion completely collapsed in Pannonia. The year 9 A. D. saw it stamped out in Dalmatia after a victory won by Tiberius there.

At the same time hostile feeling in Germany had been steadily rising. Only five days after the news of Tiberius' Dalmatian victory, word reached Rome that all Germany from the Rhine to the Elbe had revolted, that Varus, the Roman commander there, had been killed and his force of three legions wiped out.

Varus, who had previously shown ability in Palestine, had been completely taken in. Whether the fault lay chiefly with his intelligence service or in his own failure to estimate correctly the reports sent in, is not clear. We know that reports or at least rumors of coming trouble had reached him but that he utterly failed to estimate the situation. When he learned that his outposts to the northeast were being attacked, he moved forward with three legions, plus a proper proportion of auxiliaries, no doubt, to their relief. Mistakenly believing himself still in friendly country, he encumbered his column not only with masses of baggage but also with the wives and children of the army of occupation. Thus hampered, he was ambushed in passing through a dense forest, and his entire command was cut to pieces.

Tiberius, who was put in command, judged that the game was not worth the candle. War against poverty-stricken northern savages could not be made to pay as the conquest of Carthage, Gaul, and the populous and wealthy East had paid. Opinion in Rome had been disgusted even at his own recent Pannonian victories because they had emptied rather than filled the treasury. Accordingly, the greatest soldier of his time decided to withdraw the surviving garrisons. Five years later, when he himself had become Emperor, he authorized invasions of Germany in the three successive years, 14, 15 and 16 A. D. These operations, however, were little more than military promenades intended to put the fear of Rome into the hostile tribes. No further occupation was attempted, and the Rhine and Danube remained the frontier of civilization.

Two years after the last German campaign in 18 A. D., one Tacfarinus who had been trained in the Roman auxiliaries rebelled in Africa. The neighbouring allied king of Morocco remained loyal, like the king of Thrace during the Pannonian revolt, and furnished a contingent to the army which suppressed the revolt.[13]

Next in the order of time comes the conquest of Britain, but inasmuch as we know it in greater detail than any other operation of the offensive period of the Empire, let us postpone its discussion until the close of the period. Its crisis came in the revolt of Boadicea in 61 A. D.

In 69–70 A. D. occurred the Gallic revolt under Civilis. The Batavians, a poor but warlike tribe living around the mouth of the Rhine, had been exempted from Roman taxation on condition of finding a considerable number of recruits for the auxiliaries.

[13] Tacitus: Annals, Bks. 2, 3 and 4.

One of their chiefs, Civilis, had shown ability as an auxiliary officer but was a marked man because of repeated insubordination. In 69 A. D., Civilis saw his chance in the confusion and civil war which followed the death of Nero. He revolted, and was followed first by the eight Batavian auxiliary cohorts, and then by most of the Gallic and German auxiliaries serving on the Rhine frontier. With these forces, plus hordes of wild tribesmen, he defeated the two near-by legions and shut them up in Castra Vetera, the modern Xanten on the left bank of the Rhine opposite the mouth of the Lippe. The result of this action was a revolt which, for a moment, swept all Atlantic Gaul and was joined by the Roman troops stationed there. However, it collapsed as suddenly as it had sprung up, when Vespasian, having settled the civil war, moved vigorously against it. Civilis was defeated near Treves and disappears from history.[14]

While the revolt of Civilis was going on, the Roman troops in the East were also seeing active service in suppressing the rebellion of the Jews. These last were almost the only people in the Empire inspired by strong national patriotism in the modern sense. They resisted the Romans desperately, with the intense determination familiar to modern students of the Jewish character. On the other hand, their strategy was stupid, for after correctly deciding that they could not face the Roman army in a pitched battle in the open, they shut themselves up in cities and allowed themselves to be besieged without harassing the rear of the besieging troops by continuous guerrilla operations. Accordingly, their fierce resistance only made their agony longer and more bitter—while leaving the modern student without any account of first-century Roman methods in open warfare from the able pen of Josephus.

In the various sieges, especially of Jerusalem, pre-gunpowder position warfare may be said to have reached its climax. The army of Titus was composed of four legions, with a due proportion of auxiliaries, and possessed 340 catapults. Jerusalem resisted for about six months, the besieged suffering greatly from shortage of provisions toward the end. Titus threw up four huge banks or terraces to overtop the defences. One of Vespasian's battering rams weighed 100 tons, so that 1500 men were needed to swing

[14] Tacitus: History, Bks. 4 and 5.

it in striking against the wall. For transport it required 150 yoke of oxen or 300 pair of mules.[15]

The change in military policy necessitated by the western revolts will be discussed presently in connexion with the other changes during the offensive phase. Meanwhile let us consider briefly the operations of Trajan with which that phase ends.

In connection with the campaigns of Tiberius, I have already noted the poverty of the Danubian basin when first conquered by Rome. This poverty, however, was due not to the natural barrenness of the country but only to its lack of development. After a century, its natural fertility was apparent, and the Romans had found out that to the north of the river lay another highly fertile region extending to the Carpathians and comprising the plains of Hungary and the present territories of Rumania, including Bessarabia to the Dniester.

After six years' campaigning (101–107 A. D.), in which the Moroccan auxiliary cavalry particularly distinguished itself, Trajan conquered Dacia. The Carpathians and the Dniester made a defensible frontier, and the country was soon thoroughly Romanized.

Subsequently, in four years' campaigning (113–117 A. D.) against the Parthians in Armenia and Mesopotamia, Trajan advanced to the Caspian and the Persian Gulf. However, since the countries invaded were far from the centre of Roman power and possessed no good military frontier, most of them were promptly abandoned. Only certain districts on the left or east bank of the upper Euphrates were retained.

Insurrections among the Jewish colonies throughout the Roman East, particularly in Cyprus and Cyrenaica, probably helped to bring about the decision to withdraw. After over a million provincials and vast numbers of Jews had been massacred the insurrections were crushed. Nevertheless they must have added considerably to the military liabilities of the moment.

I have put off considering the conquest of Britain from a wish to end this summary of the chief military episodes of the Imperial offensive period with an account of one of those episodes at greater length. For this purpose, the conquest of Britain is well suited, for it is known in some detail and includes all the characteristic features of Roman occupations—especially the attraction of

[15] Dodge: Cæsar, 776.

rich agricultural districts, and the constant search for defensible frontiers.

The decision to invade Britain was made in 43 A. D., and its motive, we may reasonably guess, was a knowledge of the possibilities of agricultural wealth in England.

The force assigned to the operation included four legions, the II, IX, XIV, and XX, plus an equal or greater number of auxiliary light infantry and cavalry (including some Batavian horse) making a total of about 48,000 effective. It should be noted as an example of the extraordinary permanence of units under the Empire that two of these legions remained in Britain at least 364 years, until 410 A. D., the year of Alaric's mutiny! For the moment, however, the expeditionary force was most unwilling to move. The troops said that Britain was outside the known world, and probably (like most inhabitants of the Empire) they disliked and feared the sea, especially the Atlantic with its tides.

At this point the reader should fix in his mind that the chief Roman landing places in England were always on the coast of Kent. Later a secondary group of ports of entry was set up around Southampton Water. North of the Thames the length of the sea voyage seems to have prevented organized communication for large bodies of men.

Finally, Aulus Plautius, the commander of the expeditionary force, got his troops embarked (probably at Boulogne) and landed them in Kent. The Britons took up a defensive position behind the Medway, protected by forests and marshes. The Batavian cavalry, born and bred in exactly this sort of country, turned the position by swimming the river. The Britons then stood behind the Thames, but the Batavians swam its lower reaches and turned the British left. The Britons now retreated to the marshes of Essex, which held up the Romans, whereat Aulus Plautius asked for reinforcements and for the Emperor Claudius in person. The operations in Essex may have been a check, and Plautius' request a confession of weakness; or (more probably) the Emperor was asked to take the credit of a campaign already virtually won, and the reinforcements were needed only to replace the wastage incidental to active service.

Claudius concentrated the replacements for the British expeditionary force at Ostia. Among his contingent were some war-elephants. The private comments of his transport officers when directed to move such huge beasts from Italy to Gaul must have been worth hearing.

Pyrrhus had moved elephants across the Straits of Otranto and Hannibal had done the like along the highly civilized Mediterranean shores and over the Alps as well. Even so, to get the great beasts across Gaul and then across the Channel must have been a business.

Starting in 44 A. D., the troops went from Ostia to Marseilles by sea, made their way across Gaul, crossed the channel and joined Aulus Plautius, who was holding the general line of the Thames. The Britons had concentrated at Colchester. They were defeated somewhere in the neighbourhood of that place, and with the minor operations which reduced what is now Norfolk and Suffolk, the first stage of the conquest was completed.

The territory in Roman hands was bounded from northeast to southwest by the Welland, the Avon, the lower Severn, Exmoor and the lower Exe. Of course, near their headwaters the Welland and the Avon were not serious military obstacles, but it is probable that at that time the gap between the points at which each stream began to have military value was not much more than 30 miles wide, from near Coventry on the Avon to near Ashley on the Welland. About thirty miles in rear of the centre of that gap, a permanent fortified station was established at Towcester. From this the garrison, in a single day's march, could strike any force which had passed the gap and was moving south or east. The first-class engineered road known as the Watling Street which started at Canterbury (the road-centre for the Kentish harbours) and went on through Rochester to London, was continued northwest to Towcester. Three cities, London, Colchester, and St. Albans, were colonized with veterans and established as fully organized Roman municipalities. The choice of the three points shows clearly the systematic way the conquest was organized; London the lowest crossing of the Thames, the most important road centre in the island and its natural capital, Colchester the centre of resistance to Claudius in 44 A. D., and St. Albans, 25 miles—a long day's forced march—northwest from London on the Watling Street leading to Towcester, the advanced G. H. Q. of the army of occupation. The whole southeast, the most fertile and most densely inhabited part of the island was thus rounded off and secured to the Empire.

The four legions of the original expeditionary force remained

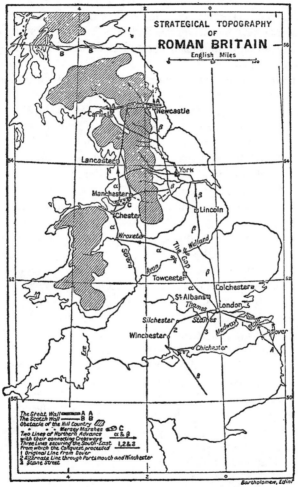

PLATE 1.—STRATEGICAL TOPOGRAPHY OF ROMAN BRITAIN.

in the island. The IX legion, based upon Colchester, held the right. The XIV and XX composed the centre, whose axis was the Watling Street from London through St. Albans to Towcester and the gap. On the left stood the II, based perhaps upon Cirencester.[16] The auxiliaries were stationed in advance of the legions and were usually brigaded in groups of three or four cohorts or alæ.[17]

Rome was not long content to stand still. Her authorities in the island were tempted by the fertility of the unoccupied Midlands northwest of the Avon-Welland line, and annoyed in a military sense by raids based upon the Welsh hills to the west and the Pennines to the north of the Midlands. The occupation of the northwest Midlands was begun in 49 or 50 A. D. and garrisons were pushed forward to Wroxeter and Lincoln. From thence the Romans found themselves compelled to move against Wales and the southern Pennines, just as every conquerer finds himself compelled to coerce " . . . . districts which, while exterior to those it is worth his while to occupy, furnish reservoirs of discontent and opposition; hill-places to which the defeated rulers of the fertile plain can retire and fastnesses of little value to commercial development, but of indefinite military value as a reserve whence attack can proceed." [18]

A Roman general, Ostorius, marched to the mouth of the Dee, broke an attack from the north and then (turning east) subjugated the greater part of Wales.[19] Master of Wales, the Roman provincial government saw before it the island of Anglesea, the centre of the British religion, which was naturally the chief inspiration of the islanders' resistance. In 60 A. D., Suetonius Paulinus, then Roman commander-in-chief in Britain, determined for the sake of the moral effect to wipe out the population, and especially the Druid priests of Anglesea. The original four legions were still in the island and had maintained their respective positions, but by this time they had all moved forward. In the east the headquarters of the IX legion was Lincoln. The XX, based upon Chester, was operating northward. The II was in the Severn valley; its headquarters may have been already as far forward as Caerleon-on-Usk. The XIV legion was based either upon Chester or upon Wroxeter, two days' march to the south; at any rate it was operating westward against North Wales, and

[16] Haverfield, E. B., Vol. IV, 583.
[17] Cheesman, 105–107. See Plate 11.
[18] Hilaire Belloc: Warfare in England, 70.
[19] Tacitus: Annals, Bk. 12.

was chosen as the legionary component of the force which was to advance upon Anglesea.

In itself the operation against Anglesea was a complete success, but under the political conditions of the moment the decision to undertake so distant a march proved a most serious politico-military error. Eastern and central Britain was angry at the overbearing attitude of the Roman colonists. Various cruelties and outrages on the part of individual Roman officials (especially the scourging of Boadicea, the queen of the Norfolk tribes, and the ravishing of her two daughters), had aroused resentment. Seizing her chance while Suetonius was far away in Anglesea, Boadicea revolted and carried the whole country with her. She began by attacking Colchester. When the IX legion advanced to relieve the place, she defeated and almost destroyed it, its commander being killed in the action. Colchester then fell, and after it St. Albans and London. Tacitus tells us that they had been better provided with handsome public buildings than with defences. Boadicea massacred their inhabitants and the entire Roman and non-British population, about 70,000 in all.

Upon hearing of these disasters, Suetonius moved eastward from Anglesea to Chester, where he was joined by a considerable detachment of the XX legion. Why, in the face of this awful peril he did not take the whole XX with him is hard to say, for if his small force had failed to crush the rebellion, the troops left behind at Chester would almost certainly have been cut off and massacred. However, it is justifiable in a military sense to detach troops if their presence in a subsidiary theatre of war serves to keep a greater number of the enemy out of the principal theatre, and it may be that the units of the XX near Chester were keeping northern hostiles at bay while Suetonius was dealing with Boadicea.

From Chester the Roman general moved on London which he reoccupied. He had sent an order to the II legion in the southwest, but that order (which was probably to concentrate on Suetonius himself) was not obeyed. The commander of the II may have been panic-stricken and considering escape by sea, or his disobedience may have been only excessive caution and slowness in joining—we do not know. At all events, Suetonius could not for the moment count upon the II. If there was anything left of the IX, the remnant must have been far to the northeast around Lincoln, separated from the commander-in-chief by the whole strength of the rebellion. The forces under his hand, therefore, were only the XIV legion and the detachment he had taken from the XX, plus certain units of auxiliary cavalry and light infantry, about 10,000 effective in all. Nevertheless he took counsel of his courage and determined to meet Boadicea in the field.

In some unknown locality, probably in the neighbourhood of London, Suetonius found a defensive position with cover of some sort for his flanks, a wood in rear, and an open field of battle in front—in which he could not be ambushed should he advance. He formed his troops with the legionaries in the centre (as usual) and in close formation, and the auxiliaries on the wings, the auxiliary cavalry in front of the foot and concentrated on either wing. The Britons came on in enormous numbers, so confident that they ringed in their own flanks and rear with wagons from which their wives and children were to see the battle as if in a theatre. At the beginning of the action the Romans stood fast. Then, when the British supply of missiles was exhausted, the legionary troops counter-attacked in "wedge" formation, the auxiliaries conforming to the movement. The Britons were broken. Ringed in by their own wagons, nearly 80,000 of them were massacred, the Romans losing only about 400.

The back of the revolt was completely broken, as might well have been expected after such a smash. Boadicea took poison, and the disobedient commander of the II legion, in his envy and chagrin, stabbed himself with his own sword.[20]

In connexion with this campaign there are a number of points worth noting. First there is the large extent of country which the Romans were not only invading but also (a much harder task) attempting to hold with forces probably less rather than more than 50,000 strong. Second, the high professional standard throughout the army of occupation (even the suicide of the delinquent commander of the II testifies to this). Third, the willingness of the commander of the IX and afterwards of Suetonius to accept battle with a contempt for numbers like that of Clive and Wellesley in India. Fourth, the neglect of fortification.

[20] Tacitus: Annals, Bk. 14.

Finally, an interesting and difficult tactical point is raised by Tacitus' description of the formation in which the legionaries delivered the decisive attack as a "wedge" (cuneus). The word itself suggests a triangular figure, but in practice it is hard to see how a triangle with a true apex could have brought good results. If we assume that it means a dense deep column, the objection at once appears that neither the short sword nor the pilum (which last could hardly have been worth much as a pike) would have been effective in such a formation. The difficulty therefore remains.

After Boadicea, Britain never again required any considerable military effort on the part of Rome. The garrison was at first kept up to the same strength in legionary troops (i. e., four legions) by the arrival of the VI in the eastern sector of the island to replace the annihilated IX. In 67 A. D. it was even possible to withdraw to Pannonia the XIV legion, which had been stationed either at Wroxeter or at Chester. However, the same causes which had formerly made for expansion were still active, represented by the desire to control near-by fertile lands (in this case Lancashire and the Carlisle district on the west of the island, together with the great plain of York on the east) and the corresponding necessity of cleaning out hill brigands (i. e., those of the Pennine hills). Accordingly, some time in 70 A. D. or soon after, the legionary garrison was again brought up to four legions by the arrival of another legion bearing the number II, plus the title "Adiutrix" to distinguish it from the old II legion known as "II Augusta." With these forces, undoubtedly accompanied by their due complement of auxiliaries, a new decade (70–80 A. D.) of advance began. First the permanent headquarters of the VI were moved forward to York. Then the fertile Scotch lowlands south of a line drawn across the narrowest part of the island from the Clyde to the Firth of Forth were occupied and held. This occupation, in the inevitable sequence of Roman imperialism, led to a punitive expedition against the Scotch highlanders in 85 A. D., and a victory over them somewhere north of the Forth at an unknown place called Mons Graupius. Agricola, the commander in this last advance, talked of invading Ireland, which he said could be conquered and held by a single legion plus auxiliaries; but he was recalled by Domitian's government at Rome.[21] At the same

[21] Tacitus: Agricola.

time Legio II Adiutrix was ordered away from Britain to Pannonia—the same province to which the XIV had been sent in 67 A. D.[22]

The recall of this legion, together with that of Agricola, ended Roman expansion in Britain. The permanent defensive organization of the province is best considered in connexion with the defensive phase of imperial strategy—more especially since Hadrian, whose accession in 117 A. D. marks the beginning of that phase, gave his name to the Great British Wall. Meanwhile I shall end my account of the offensive phase with a few words on the obscure subject of Roman minor tactics during the first century and on the changes in the recruitment of the army which had taken place by the end of the phase.

It is possible, but by no means certain, that the legions were usually formed for battle in two lines of five cohorts, instead of in three lines as ordinarily in Cæsar's time. The chief argument for the two-line idea is that the 1st and 5th cohorts (which would stand upon the flanks of a front line of five cohorts), were the two cohorts to be raised to 1000 men each.[23] Still the question is not worth the ink spilt over it, for any army kept supple by frequent field operations on a large scale is able to vary its formations to suit the requirements of each particular case. Cæsar's lieutenant, Crassus, being short of troops, had formed in two lines against the Aquitanians in 56 B. C. Cæsar himself had used four lines at Pharsalia and one at Ruspina during the African campaign.

There are indications that the men were sometimes placed closer in ranks than formerly. Tacitus expressly says that this was done against Boadicea, and the "wedge" with which that action was won strongly suggests a close order formation. On the other hand, pilum and gladius could scarcely have been wielded freely in anything but a skirmishing order, and we know beyond question that they were continued as the weapons of the legionary.

During the entire offensive phase, both legions and auxiliaries were ready to take the field at a moment's notice. The garrison of Britain, for instance, was not only on a war footing but actually in the field almost every summer from 43 to 85 A. D. The legions would often lie in pairs, as the XIV and XX were doing in 60 A. D. and in the same way, two, three or four auxiliary cohorts

[22] Dion Cassius: Bk. 55, sec. 24.   [23] Dodge: Cæsar, 772.

or alæ were usually grouped, or "brigaded," as we should say, under a single commander. A cohort of 500 infantry was supposed to require a camp of five acres, and the winter camps of the period which have been excavated run from ten, thirteen or fourteen acres up to thirty-five. Winter camps were fortified, but only with a stockade and ditch not much more elaborate than those of the nightly camps when in the field. When an army went into winter quarters it threw out towards the enemy a line of observation composed of single auxiliary cohorts in separate little camps each about one and one-half acres in area.

Each legion may or may not have had certain auxiliary units more or less permanently assigned to its support. The weight of evidence seems a little against it.

Tactically, the legions were still the chief arm, the core of a defensive action, in attack used to deal the decisive blow.

We hear of no major action decided by a cavalry charge as under Alexander or by the fire power of archery as at Crécy and Poitiers.

On the other hand, cavalry (while still subordinate) was growing in relative importance. In part this growth resulted naturally from the regular organization of the army as a whole, in contrast with the haphazard system of the later republic, for the chief weakness of republican armies had been inferior cavalry. Hannibal had consistently profited by this weakness until Zama. That action was the first in which the cavalry of the Roman side had not been driven from the field by the great Carthaginian's mounted troops. The great smash of Carrhæ had been directly due to cavalry inferiority. One of Cæsar's narrowest shaves had been at the Ruspina. Any intelligent war department might be expected to take steps towards ending such a situation. It is true that we have no direct evidence of the existence of an Imperial War Department but inasmuch as the Roman Empire never had less than 300,000 men under arms, spread out all around the Mediterranean basin, it is impossible to believe that such a force could have been used intelligently without some well-staffed central agency.

To return to the matter of cavalry, the problems set before the imperial armies were such as to give cavalry a chance to shine and thereby strengthen itself still more by attracting energetic and ambitious officers and men. The distinguished service of the

Batavian horse in the original invasion of Britain and that of the Moors in the invasion of Dacia, are examples. Obviously in frontier defences against raids (which was after all the chief task of the Imperial armies even during the offensive phase) mounted troops are of more use than foot.

Still, the growth in importance of cavalry was as yet only beginning. Far more significant were the changes during the first century in recruiting.

Under Augustus, the higher officers of the whole army and the enlisted men of the legions were still mainly Italians, while the auxiliaries were tribally recruited bodies, serving in the general neighbourhood of their homes, fighting more or less in their own traditional manner, and partly officered either by their own chieftains or by legionary centurions promoted to field rank as a reward for distinguished service. By the time of Trajan, the repeated revolts of the first century led the government to remove the auxiliary units from the neighbourhood of their homes, and to destroy their tribal character by keeping them up to strength by means of recruits from the provinces in which they happened to be stationed. Naturally, after this change we hear no more of tribal chiefs as field officers—or indeed in any capacity in the regular auxiliaries. It is not so clear why the practice of promoting centurions to field rank was stopped, but toward the end of the offensive phases such promotions had become exceedingly rare. On the other hand, the increasing Romanization of the provinces was depriving the officers' corps of the entire army and the enlisted personnel of the legions of their distinctly Italian character. A few years as a field officer of a legion, or in command of an auxiliary cohort or ala, was becoming the customary introduction to a career in the imperial civil service. Finally, the very success of the imperial policy in assuring internal peace and civic order was beginning to contract the recruiting ground of legions and auxiliaries alike to the frontier provinces. There the level of civilization was a trifle less high, and the presence of the army kept the soldierly spirit alive.

The second-century change in status of the auxiliaries from tribal bodies to mere units in the cosmopolitan Imperial army resulted in the raising of a new category of troops, the Numeri. The reader will remember that among the reasons why the Imperial government of the first century valued the auxiliaries were first that their tribal patriotism helped to build up *esprit de corps* in their units, second that the lower level of wealth and culture among the peoples from which they were recruited made them easier and cheaper to raise than troops from more highly civilized districts. Of these two advantages the first was now completely destroyed by the new practice of filling the gaps in the original auxiliary cohorts and alæ by replacements from any neighbourhood in which they happened to be stationed. The second was in a fair way to disappear through the Romanization of the provinces, a process which was to culminate in Caracalla's grant of citizenship to all inhabitants of the Empire (212 A. D.). The second-century Empire was now in touch with new tribes especially among the Moors, the Germans of Dacia, and the Orientals. Accordingly units were recruited from them, and these units were not incorporated as auxiliaries but were known as "numeri" and placed on a separate footing in order that they might serve the special purposes for which the original auxiliaries had been raised. Instead of being subjected to the uniform imperial training they were encouraged to keep their tribal methods of fighting and even their dialects and outlandish war-cries. The fact that the commanders of numeri ranked below those of auxiliary units together with the small camp space allotted to each numerus in the German forts, may indicate that numeri were only two or three hundred strong. Smaller than that they can hardly have been as we find them divided into "centuries" and the cavalry into troops (turmæ).[24]

It would be interesting to know what training the officers of the entire army received and what was the organization of the higher command and of the War Department. The practice of appointing only men of the "equestrian order," i. e., men of some wealth, to field rank, and still more that of appointing none but men of "senatorial" rank, i. e., millionaires, to serve as general officers, suggest careful staff training for such appointees as well as for their chief assistants. Unfortunately the supposition is mere inference—like that of the existence of a War Department. Nevertheless—given an army over 300,000 strong and so widely distributed in space—it is hard to see how operations could have been carried on without some sort of staff training. The fact that Claudius, in

[24] Cheesman, 88.

44 A. D., concentrated at Rome the reinforcements intended for Britain, seems to imply that Rome was the centre at least of transport and supply department. But all that we can certainly say is that there was a centralized pay department located there, and that the "Prætorian Prefect," the supreme commander under the Emperor of the whole army, spent most of his time in the capital.[25]

[25] Haverfield, E. B., Vol. 23, 474.

CHAPTER II

THE IMPERIAL ROMAN ARMY

(FROM HADRIAN TO THE DEATH OF CONSTANTINE—117-337 A. D.)

THE accession of Hadrian in 117 A. D., marks the adoption of a new military policy for the Empire, that of a strict strategical defensive. In this chapter I shall first consider the phase of successful, rigid, frontier defence beginning with 117 and ending with the assassination of Alexander Severus in 235 A. D. In order to understand the phase of confusion which begins in 235 and ends with the pacification of the Roman world by Diocletian in 297 A. D., a brief discussion of the causes of the decline of ancient civilization will then be necessary. After this, the military events will appear symptoms rather than causes of the decline. There will then follow a description of the Roman army as reorganized by Diocletian and Constantine, who abandoned the policy of rigid frontier defence and substituted for it one of elastic defence, supporting the frontier troops by means of field armies composed of the crack units of the service. The chapter will end with a word on Roman tactics about the time of Constantine's death in 337.

What then were the reasons for Hadrian's decision to adopt a defensive on all frontiers? First of all, it was emphatically not a case of severe military pressure from without, for there was no such pressure. Unless the reader thoroughly grasps that fact he will utterly fail to understand the military position of the Empire.

The reasons undoubtedly were: first, that the Romans were no longer tempted forward by districts at the same time fertile and easily defensible, lying just outside their frontiers; second, that they were beginning to feel the difficulty of administering so vast an empire without the aid of modern mechanical means of rapid transport and communication.

Let us consider this second point for a moment. From Lisbon to the Euphrates is nearer three than two thousand miles as the crow flies. From Carlisle to Wadi Halfa in upper Egypt is even more.

What this meant in terms of time is shown by the extraordinary effort made to convey to Galba in Spain, the news of Nero's death in Rome. From Rome overland to Clunia, somewhere in the district of Burgos, south of that city and east of Valladolid, is about 1100 miles as the crow flies—in actual road distance not less than 1400 miles. Nero's death was announced to Galba by mounted post in seven days, which must have been about 200 miles a day, and the feat was considered almost a miracle.[1] To get a legion over the same space and bring them in fresh enough for action without a long rest would certainly have taken three nearer than two months. From Durazzo to Constantinople by the great Egnatian road was nearly 500 miles. Allowing 15 miles a day as a high average for infantry, would mean over 27 marching days for the distance. From Belgrade to Constantinople would be about the same, and from Constantinople to Antioch rather more. Therefore we must allow over 2 months as the minimum time required to get a legion from Belgrade or Durazzo to Antioch, a little less time between Belgrade and Treves, and a month between Treves and York. In the unheard of event of a legionary march from York to Antioch, six months would be breakneck speed. The reader must remember that these time estimates are absolute minima, for the average length of a day's march was not 15 miles but somewhere between 11 and 12, as we shall see, for instance, by the spacing of the camps or "mansiones" on the Stane Street;[2] and furthermore, not every day of a long march is a marching day. Obviously such distances were a standing temptation to ambitious local commanders to mutiny and make a throw for empire. In themselves they explain well enough Hadrian's decision to advance the frontiers no further.

This decision boiled down the problem of the Roman army to policing the frontiers. Leaving out of account, for the moment, the changes produced in that army in adapting itself to its new and restricted mission, let us consider the enormous engineering works undertaken to facilitate its work. There were, first of all, the erection of artificial obstacles to supplement the natural obstacles, i. e., unfordable first-class rivers, upon which the frontier reposed throughout most of its length, and, secondly, the improvement of the road system over which the troops must move.

[1] Young, Vol. 1, 172.   [2] Belloc: The Stane Street, 114–139.

The problem of defending a frontier covered by continuous obstacles reposes upon permanent military principles. Allowing for the differences in weapons and communication, what the Romans did is what modern armies would do to-day. First of all they maintained an intelligence service with agents in the near-by unoccupied territory, so as to be warned against threatening attacks. Wherever they could—for instance on the lower Rhine—they obtained the firm friendship and co-operation of the tribes just outside the frontier. Where they could not—for instance on the middle and upper Rhine and in Britain—they devastated the country, making a No Man's Land a day's march wide in front of the frontier obstacle to prevent surprise. Where that obstacle was a river, its course was patrolled by flotillas of guard-boats. The legions were stationed on the near bank in great fortified camps from 50 to 60 acres in area, and the auxiliaries strung out between them in smaller fortified posts.

When the frontier rested on the desert, as in Africa and in Syria south of the Euphrates, chains of permanent works were arranged in depth along the natural lines of approach to Roman territory. Many of these desert outposts are astonishingly careful and solid in construction. Naturally, the more advanced works were garrisoned chiefly by cavalry.[3]

Where there was neither river nor desert, continuous walls were set up. Two such walls were permanently held, the German "limes," between 250 and 300 miles long from the Rhine near Neuwied to the Danube near Ratisbon, and Hadrian's wall in Britain, 73 miles long from the Solway Firth to a point on the North Sea coast just north of Newcastle-upon-Tyne. In Germany the obstacle was an earthen mound for half its length crowned by a solid oaken palisade and by a rough stone wall for the other half. In Britain it was originally of earth but was afterwards (in Septimius Severus' time, 193–211) strengthened by a wall of good masonry 8 feet thick and 16 feet high.

Noting the elaborate nature of these walls and their ditches, unmilitary scholars have assumed that they were meant to be defended, and have puzzled over the fact that their earthen banks are generally more steeply scarped on the Roman side. Naturally, in pre-gunpowder fortification it was of the utmost

[3] Cagnat: Frontière Tripolitaine.

importance to have a steep escarpment which the assailant must climb. The fact is, of course, that the Roman walls were completely indefensible because they were never manned by anything remotely like the number of troops necessary to defend them, as I shall presently show. They served as screens behind which patrols could march in comparative safety, thus keeping the whole line under constant surveillance, and especially as obstacles not only against the advance of a raiding party, but also (which was perhaps even more important) against its retreat. The raiders, as they clambered over the obstacle, would have to leave their horses behind. To stay and break it down would take time which they could not afford to waste since their approach would have already been announced far and wide by smoke signals, and the nearest Roman detachments would be coming up. Many if not most of these detachments would be mounted and therefore far more mobile than the dismounted raiders. Furthermore, if they succeeded in driving off cattle, or in retreating with any heavy plunder, they would again find themselves in difficulties as they recrossed the obstacle. Indeed, this would be the most critical stage of the operation, from the point of view of the raiders. Byzantine military writers, treating of very similar conditions on the Saracen border in Asia Minor, recommend that the defenders should then make their main effort.[4]

This system is familiar to us now, having been applied in almost exactly the same form though on a smaller scale, by the Spanish in Cuba. Their "trochas" were largely of barbed wire, and their No Man's Land much narrower. The same general idea appeared in the British blockhouse system in South Africa.

The garrison of the wall itself was composed of auxiliaries; in Britain they were stationed in fortified permanent camps upon the wall itself, and in Germany usually close behind it although sometimes as far back as three or four miles. Each camp held a single ala or cohort. In Britain the auxiliary garrison has been estimated at 6000 cavalry, 2125 mounted infantry (a branch of the service to which I shall return in the summary at the end of this chapter) and 20,875 infantry, a total of 29,000. Since the front to be defended was 73 miles long, if all these troops were concentrated upon it they would give just under 400 men per mile,

[4] Oman, Vol. 1, 211, 214, quoting Nicephorus Phocas: "Border Warfare."

or nearly 4½ yards per man! Even if we take these figures as minima, especially in cavalry, they dispose absolutely of the theory of a formal defence of the entire wall. Between the camps, small camps about 50 feet square were dotted along the wall at intervals of about a mile, to serve as guard-houses and observation posts, and between these "mile castles" there were watch-towers about every 100 yards.

The auxiliaries were well able to deal with any ordinary raiders. For raids in great force the provincial commander would call upon his legionary troops. These lay concentrated in permanent fortified camps covering from 50 to 60 acres, not in pairs, as in the offensive phase, but singly.

Turning from obstacles and camps to the troops which manned them, let us first consider the question of numbers. From about 117 to 161 A. D. it is possible to establish a fairly complete list as follows:

Britain. Legions: II. Augusta (Isca Silurum, now Caerleon)
      VI. Victrix (Eburacum, York)
      XX. Valeria Victrix (Deva, Chester)
  Auxiliaries: 6,000 cavalry, 2,125 mounted infantry, 20,875 infantry, total 29,000.
Lower Germany. Legions: I. Minervia (Bonna, Bonn)
(Lower Rhine)   XXX. Ulpia Victrix (Vetera, Xanten)
  Auxiliaries: 1,500 cavalry, 250 mounted infantry, 1,750 infantry, total 3,500.
Upper Germany. Legions: XXII. Primigenia (Moguntiacum, Mainz)
      VIII. Augusta (Argentorate, Strassburg)
  Auxiliaries: 1,500 cavalry, 1,125 mounted infantry, 9,275 infantry, total 11,900.
Rhætia. No legion in the province before Marcus Aurelius (161–180) raised III Italica and stationed it there.
  Auxiliaries: 3,500 cavalry, 500 mounted infantry, 8,500 infantry, total 12,500.
Noricum. No legion in the province before Marcus Aurelius (161–180) raised II Italica and stationed it there.
  Auxiliaries: 1,000 cavalry, 3,000 infantry, total 4,000.
Upper Pannonia. Legions: X. Gemina (Vindobona, Vienna)
(Danube to Semlin) XIV. Gemina (Carnuntum, Petronell)
      I. Adiutrix (Brigetio, near Komorn)
  Auxiliaries: 3,500 cavalry, 875 mounted infantry, 4,125 infantry, total 8,500.

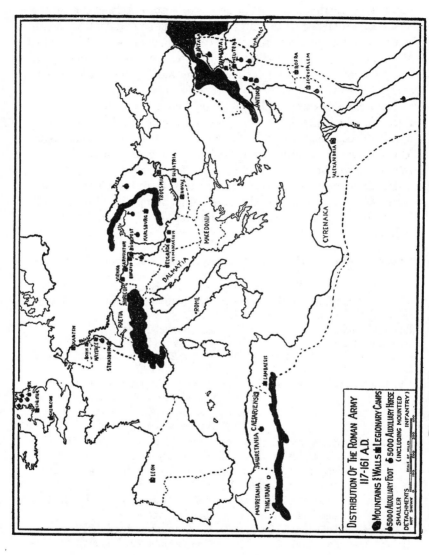

PLATE 2.—DISTRIBUTION OF THE ROMAN ARMY, 117–161 A. D.

Lower Pannonia. Legions: II. Adiutrix (Aquincum, near Budapest)
Auxiliaries: 3,500 cavalry, 1,875 mounted infantry,
9,125 infantry, total 14,500.

Dalmatia. Auxiliaries: 250 mounted infantry, 1,250 infantry, total, 1,500.

Upper Mœsia. Legions: IV. Flavia (Singidunum, Belgrade)
(Middle Danube)   VII. Claudia (Viminacium, Kostolac)
Auxiliaries: 500 cavalry, 250 mounted infantry, 3,250
infantry, total 4,000.

Lower Mœsia. Legions: I. Italica (Novæ, Sistov)
(Lower Danube)   XI. Claudia (Durostorum, Silistria)
      V. Macedonica (Trœsmis, Iglitza)
Auxiliaries: 2,500 cavalry, 250 mounted infantry, 4,250
infantry, total 7,000.

Dacia (now Transylvania). Legions: XIII. Gemina (Apulum, Karlsburg)
Auxiliaries: 6,000 cavalry, 1,125 mounted
infantry,   18,175   infantry,
total 25,300.

Macedonia. Auxiliaries: 500 infantry.

Asia Minor (Cappadocia). Legions: XV. Apollinaris (Satala, Armenian frontier)
XII. Fulminata (Melitene, on upper Euphrates)
Auxiliaries: 2,000   cavalry, 1,875   mounted
infantry,   7,125   infantry,
total 11,000.

Syria. Legions: XVI. Flavia (Samosata, upper Euphrates)
IV. Scythica ⎫
VI. Ferrata ⎬ (near Antioch?)
III. Gallica ⎭
Auxiliaries: 4,500 cavalry, 2,375 mounted infantry, 9,625 infan-
try, total 16,500.

Judea. Legions: X. Fretensis (Jerusalem)
Auxiliaries: 1,500 cavalry, 125 mounted infantry, 6,875 infantry,
total 8,500.

Arabia. Legions: III. Cyrenaica (Bostra)
Auxiliaries: Unknown.

Egypt. Legions: II. Trajana (near Alexandria, a disorderly city)
Auxiliaries: 2,500 cavalry, 750 mounted infantry, 5,950 infantry,
total 9,200.

Cyrenaica. Garrison unknown.

Africa. Legions: III. Augusta (Lambæsis)
Auxiliaries: 1,000 cavalry, 500 mounted infantry, 2,700 infantry,
total 4,200.

Mauretania. Auxiliaries: 4,000 cavalry, 250 mounted infantry, 5,950
(Cæsariensis)   infantry, total 10,200.

Mauretania. Auxiliaries: 500 cavalry, 125 mounted infantry, 1,375 infan-
(Tingitana)   try, total 2,000.

Spain. Legions: VII. Gemina (Legio, Leon, in N. W. Spain)
    Auxiliaries: 1,000 cavalry, 250 mounted infantry, 2,250 infantry,
        total 3,500.
Unlocated Auxiliary Units. 1,000 cavalry, 375 mounted infantry, 5,125
        infantry, total 6,500.

In the adjoining map, interior provinces whose garrisons are not mentioned in the text are left blank. Frontier provinces with legions stationed within their borders may be identified by the legionary camps. For the sake of clearness, only the names of those provinces mentioned in the text as garrisoned solely by auxiliaries are shown on the map.

The above list establishes the following totals:

Prætorian Guard.. 10,000
Legionaries...168,000
Auxiliary Cavalry................................ 47,500
Auxiliary Mounted Infantry....................... 15,250
Auxiliary Infantry.............................131,050

    Total Auxiliaries......................................193,800

        Grand Total....................................371,800

Cheesman, from whom most of these figures are taken, considers that a complete list of the auxiliaries would show about 80,000 for the cavalry plus mounted infantry, and 140,000 for the infantry. This would give a grand total of 398,000, almost 400,-000 men. To this again must be added the numeri, the personnel of the navy (including the crews of the sea-going fleets and those of the river flotillas so important in the scheme of frontier defence), the cavalry of the Imperial Guard, and the six "Urban Cohorts" which helped police some of the larger cities.

But even after making generous allowance for all possible omissions, still the striking thing about the list is that the grand total is so small considering the territory administered. We should remember that in 1914 one small poor province, Serbia, could mobilize 225,000 trained men.

On the other hand, we note that the Augustan military establishment of 300,000 has been increased by more than a third. This undoubtedly indicates an increase in the difficulty of the military problem which the Empire had to meet. In this connexion it is reasonable to suppose that the wild tribes of northern Europe would gradually become more formidable due to increasing military knowledge and improved armament derived from intercourse with Rome, that is with civilization. But when we remember that the Empire now included not only the territories ruled by Augustus but also England and the Scotch lowlands, Morocco, the Hungarian plain and Rumania, Thrace, Northeastern Asia Minor and Armenia, and also the Sinai Peninsula, it is plain that the numerical increase is not quite as formidable in comparison with the increased territory to be administered as it at first appears.

The heaviest concentration was just where we should expect it, that is on the narrow frontier between the impassable mountains of Armenia and the equally impassable Palmyrene desert, since here alone the organized forces of a civilized state were to be confronted.

It should also be noted that sometimes the legionary camps were upon the frontier itself, i. e., on the Danube and the Rhine, sometimes in the interior near unusually turbulent communities such as northwestern Spain, Palestine with its Jews, and the cosmopolitan city of Alexandria.

It would be interesting to know why new legions were designated with the numbers of legions already on foot plus the suffix "Adiutrix" (assistant) or "Gemina" (twin) but there seems to be no evidence on which to base a judgment.

The distribution of legionary troops in Britain is a little out of the ordinary for the VI at York was over 80 miles south of the east end of the wall, and the XX at Chester was a good 100 miles south of the western end. Of course the reason for this was the intervening north-and-south obstacle of the Pennine Hills, to which we shall return in connection with communications. The fact that the II was held at Caerleon-on-Usk probably means that the Welsh hillmen would still stand watching—although it is also true that the II stayed there long after all fear from the Welshmen must have been at an end. Were we dealing with modern governments, this matter might be explained by the desire to continue to utilize the large military reservation at Caerleon. Rome, on the other hand, was as ungrudging in military expenditure as she was economical in man power. She was, moreover,

practical and supremely direct in all her measures, so the anomaly
of leaving the II far off to the southwest in Caerleon remains
unexplained.

Considering the Empire as a whole, the obvious weak point of
the defence was the same as that of the original establishment
under Augustus, i. e., the lack of a central reserve. Such a state of
things would have been intolerable had the system been intended
to resist a severe strain. Even in the face of the slight pressure
which was all that the northern barbarians could exercise, it was
thought worth while to lessen the danger by spending great sums
on improving the lateral communications not only between legion
and legion along the border itself but also between province and
province.

The extreme care given to communications may be illustrated
by examples taken from the province of Britain. The obstacle
of the Pennines running north and south through the area between
the wall and the legionary camps at Chester and York, was crossed
from east to west by at least three lateral roads suitable for troops.
The main crossing, about 70 miles from the wall and therefore
level with York, left the great eastern road at Tadcaster, went
over the Ilkley-Skipton gap, descended the Ribble valley and met
the western road at Ribchester. About 20 miles due north of the
Ilkley-Skipton line was another crossing from the Tees Valley at
Bowes to the headwaters of the Eden near Kirkby Stephen.
Twenty-five miles, or one day's forced march, south of the Ilkley
gap another metalled road ran east from Manchester across the
hill country. And in addition to all this there seem to have been
several ways east and west over the Peak district itself.

Britain can also show great Roman causeways. One carried the
western road over the marshes of the Mersey to Manchester.
Another carried the great eastern road between London and York
over the marshes of the Ouse and the Welland at Stamford.

Finally Britain has, in the Stane Street, a remarkable instance
of strategic road building far behind the frontier to facilitate the
movement of troops from province to province—in this case between Gaul and Britain. I have said that London was the chief
city in the island and the centre of its road system, also that the
chief approach to it from the Continent was across the straits
of Dover and through Kent, but that an alternative approach was

later arranged from Southampton Water. This alternative approach originally reached London by way of Winchester, Silches-
ter and Staines, about 72 miles from, say, Southampton to London.
For the sake of cutting the distance by not much more than 16
miles, one long day's march for hardened troops, the Roman
government was willing to build 56 miles of metalled road from
Chichester through Dorking direct on London.[5]

Although the existence of such a road abundantly proves that
its builders expected that there would be times when a day saved
in moving troops from province to province would be highly important, still the calculation underlying the Imperial military
policy was that such times would be rare. A man assigned to a
legion would usually know that it had not changed station since
his great-grandfather's time, and the great-grandchildren of that
man might count on finding it there still. An auxiliary soldier
would find himself even more strictly localized. Since his ala or
cohort would constitute a link in the chain of front-line defence
along the frontier he might expect to spend practically his entire
military life—25 years—patrolling the four-mile intervals between
his own and the next two auxiliary camps. Naturally each sta-
tionary unit built up for itself the strongest kind of local associations. For instance, married quarters (or what were virtually
married quarters—for the auxiliary soldiers, denied the right of
contracting legal marriages, formed permanent attachments
recognized by custom and legalized upon discharge) grew up
around every station. Besides married quarters there were baths,
temples, shops, and the cottages of discharged veterans who
wished to live near their old comrades.

Although efficient for its mission of frontier defence, such a system was obviously ill-adapted to the rare emergencies of an
invasion in force, for the legions of his province constituted the
only concentrated field army under the orders of the provincial
commander. The only way of getting reinforcements was to
borrow from the next province. Owing to the local associations
formed by the troops, and to the fact that each unit called away
left a gap in the frontier defence in its own province, the custom
grew up of answering requests for aid by dispatching, not perma-

[5] For Roman military roads in England, see Belloc: "Warfare In England,"
and "The Stane Street."

nent units, but temporary commands formed by detachments from a number of such units. These detachments were called vexillations (from "vexilla," the Latin for a standard). One cavalry vexillation serving against the Parthians under Trajan was drawn from no less than 5 alæ and fourteen "mounted cohorts." [6] The practice was sometimes followed during the offensive phase—the vexilla is expressly mentioned by Tacitus as accompanying the detachment of the XX Legion taken by Suetonius Paulinus to help him fight Boadicea. During the second century it hardened into a set custom rarely departed from, if at all.

Any soldier, or even any man of common sense, will agree that such scratch formations are inferior to permanent units taking the field as such. They can have no *esprit de corps*. The fact that the system was workable at all is the strongest possible testimony not only to the skill of the Roman command but also to the high standard and especially the uniformity obtained in the training of units. And yet the fact remains that the system did its work well.

How it worked may be illustrated by an outline of the crisis surmounted under Marcus Aurelius. In the first place the Parthians invaded Cappadocia in 162 A. D., won a decisive general action in that province, and devastated Syria. A field army was organized by drawing heavily on the Danubian troops for vexillations and the tide of battle was turned against the enemy. All this was not outside the Roman experience. The shuttlecock of war had been batted to and fro across the Euphrates ever since Crassus' time. Meanwhile the Roman intelligence service gave warning of coming trouble from the tribes around what is now Bohemia. By this time the Parthian war was nearing its end. With tenacity which reminds us of Tiberius' conduct in 6 A. D., the government of Marcus Aurelius decided not to recall the vexillations which the Danubian troops had sent to the East until a decision had been obtained there. In so doing they deliberately ran risks on the upper Danube, where the storm broke in the year 165 A. D. It does not seem certain that these tribes knew of the Parthian war and most improbable that they should have intentionally synchronized their attack with it. That it was necessary to fight on two fronts was

[6] Cheesman, 113.

only an unhappy coincidence for the Empire. On the upper Danube, the local Roman commanders, weakened by the absence of their numerous vexillations in the East, were unable to hold the frontier. They therefore set themselves to delay the barbarians' advance and postpone the crisis of the campaign until their vexillations could return. In the course of the year 165 the Parthians made peace and the vexillations started westward. It would take at least two weeks to get a courier from Venetia to Antioch, assuming that the Emperor was at the headquarters of the troops covering Italy so that no time need be lost in consulting him. When the vexillations had left Antioch, it would be another two months, and probably nearer three months, before they would be ready to go into action in Bosnia. When at last they arrived, the Roman command would have been able to act vigorously had it not been for a second unhappy chance which upset all calculations. The vexillations from the East brought the plague with them. The mortality was heavy and the army was badly demoralized in consequence, so that the barbarians overran what is now Switzerland, together with the country between the Save and Danube. Still the Save seems never to have been crossed, nor was Italy ever invaded. In 168, three years after the original loss of the Danube line, the frontier was re-established. In 169, the war was renewed but its theatre was now the neighborhood of the Danube, and after three years the two chief barbarian tribes were decisively defeated, one of them being wiped out in an attempt to retreat across the river.

Certainly it seems that the whole trouble came from the deliberate economy of the government in men.

How far the Roman art of war and the fighting power of the army were affected during the period of frontier defence, if at all, is hard to say. It seems as if the restriction of its mission must have brought about some decline, as the service gradually forgot that it had ever been a field army, and more and more came to think of itself as a constabulary rooted to particular spots of ground. And yet we must not exaggerate, but remember that, after all, the Roman army of the defensive period did its job and remained superior to all opponents.

In the army list, mounted infantry appears. Strictly speaking, this is a separate arm, mounted for transport and dismounted for action. It is sometimes resorted to by services which must increase their proportion of mounted men, but are content with half measures in so doing, since it is easier to convert infantry into mounted infantry than into cavalry. Some auxiliary cohorts were partly horse and partly foot—an arrangement which shows clearly how far the army had become a mere frontier patrol, for such a body could never act as a true tactical unit. There was a camel corps in the East. The importance of cavalry was increasing, and toward the end of the century cavalry units with the riders and forward parts of their horses completely covered by scale mail began to appear.[7]

Marcus Aurelius (161–180 A. D.), increased the establishment by adding two new legions which he stationed, one in Rhætia (Switzerland) and the other in Noricum (upper Austria). Toward the end of the phase, Septimius Severus (192–211 A. D.) sick of the turbulence and inefficiency of the Prætorians, broke the entire corps and arranged for their future recruitment by promoting distinguished officers and men from the frontier legions. The same Emperor added three more new legions, two for Mesopotamia and one in central Italy in reserve.[8] Throughout the second century the numeri were constantly being increased until there were scores of them. The additions and the crews of the fleets must have raised the total number of men in the imperial service to more than 400,000 at the beginning of the third century.

Although the army organization as a whole remained unchanged, certain changes in recruitment, discipline and morale can be traced. I have already said that neither the masses of the civil population nor the rank and file of the army itself could be expected to feel any strong patriotism for so huge a state. The mere idea of civilization is too abstract to kindle the least devotion in the average man. This want of patriotism naturally became more and more glaring as the achievements of civilization came to be thought commonplace, and no serious peril appeared to threaten its life. Furthermore, the very success of the Roman professional army, by removing even the idea of war from the minds of the great civilian majority, increased the unwarlike character of the masses. The ever-increasing wealth and peace of the provinces continued to tell in the same direction. Thus the recruiting ground of the

[7] Cheesman, 28, 30, and 128.   [8] Dion Cassius: Bk. 55, sec. 24.

army tended still more to contract to the neighbourhood of the frontiers.

A certain decline in discipline and in professional spirit seems to be indicated by two new developments which appear early in the third century. The first of them concerned that permanent problem of long-service professional armies—married quarters. Augustus had forbidden soldiers to marry. But with a term of service of over twenty years, not even Roman discipline at its best could enforce the spirit of such an order. Accordingly the custom had grown up for many of the men to enter into what a modern would call "common-law marriages" which were fully legalized upon their discharge. Now Septimius Severus (193–211) gave the men leave to marry.

The same Emperor permitted or encouraged the special-duty men of each legion, i. e., the regimental clerks, artificers, ordnance personnel, musicians, etc., to form associations known as "colleges." [9] How far these colleges were autonomous, voluntary associations we cannot tell. The development coincided in time with the multiplication of colleges composed of men exercising similar economic functions in civil life. Certainly, if the military colleges were autonomous "soldier committees," the effect upon discipline must have been bad.

In any event, it is certain that about the time these innovations were introduced, civilization in general began to decline.

All sorts of explanations have been given for the internal decay of the ancient world. Even the ridiculous suggestion that sexual immorality was a chief cause has been seriously made! Perhaps the most reasonable guess, and the only one which has any bearing on the military phase of the subject (with which alone we are here directly concerned), is that in all life there is a rhythm, a flux and reflux of energy. According to this idea, the effort involved in the maintenance of a high civilization is too great to be indefinitely pursued. After it has gone on for a certain time there must be repose. The human mind must lie fallow in barbarism, or an approach to it, until its energy return.

But if the underlying cause of the slackening energy of the ancient world is obscure, the symptoms are clear enough. From

[9] Cagnat: Lambese, 36–47.

235 to 297 A. D. is a phase of confusion. A series of Roman civil wars gives the barbarians many temporary successes. The immediate cause of the decline of ancient civilization was this third-century epidemic of civil wars.

Inasmuch as the civil wars were fought between groups of the Roman army acting in the interest of generals seeking the Empire, it has been assumed that they were caused by some weakness or fault in the army itself. The fact is otherwise; these civil wars were the cause of a certain decline in the discipline and professional spirit of the army, but they themselves were due not to military but to political weakness in the structure of the Empire itself.

Certainly the Roman army cannot be blamed for conquering the known world and thereby making patriotism impossible for the mass of mankind. If Augustus (acting wisely enough according to his lights) set up a centralized monarchy which repressed local initiative both military and civil, pretending meanwhile to preserve the republic and therefore failing to provide an adequate legal method of succession to the Empire, none of these things were done by the army which Augustus commanded and to which he owed his throne.

If the reader thinks I dwell too long on these political matters, let him remember that they alone explain the character of war from the third to the ninth century, and that the difficulty as to succession explains the Roman civil wars which began the decline.

The Senate, which had the sole legal right to replace a dead emperor, could no longer command respect for its decisions.[10] Indeed the vastness of the political unit, the repression of local civic initiative, and the relegation of all military work to a small professional army, all combined to make the "consent of the governed" within the Empire, a more and more passive thing. Hence there was no moral authority competent to prevent the legions of the East, or of the Danubian, or the Rhenish command, from proclaiming their general Emperor and marching on Rome against the Emperor there.

The reader may object that it was the duty of the army to resist the outer barbarians. The Roman army would have answered

[10] Ferrero: The Ruin of the Ancient Civilization and the Triumph of Christianity.

that these barbarians were a nuisance rather than a peril. It was impossible to think that they could ever destroy civilization, and as a matter of fact the northern barbarians never did. To be sure, if in order to make your general emperor you withdrew any considerable number of troops from any one section of frontier, the barbarians might break in and ravage. But they were not good at taking walled cities, and as soon as the regrettable unpleasantness over the imperial succession was cleaned up, these same barbarians would have to run for their lives over the border to escape being cut to pieces, as they invariably were if they could not get away.

War is always and necessarily destructive, but the Roman civil wars of the imperial epoch did not involve widespread destruction of property or intentional interference with the population. It has been metaphorically said that they were fought "over the heads" of the citizens. Even the barbarian raids, although far more serious in this respect, were limited as to the harm they could do, because (1) their aim was plunder rather than systematic destruction, (2) they could seldom take a walled city, (3) like all the rest of the world before the invention of gunpowder, they possessed no means of demolition except fire and human muscle. Even so they were bad enough and the harm they did was exaggerated in the public mind by contrast with the centuries of unbroken peace the interior Roman world had enjoyed.

The obvious palliative for such conditions was fortification. Septimius Severus (192–211 A. D.) supplemented Hadrian's earthen wall across Britain by a continuous wall of stone. Most of the cities of the Empire walled themselves in. Aurelian (270–275) went so far as to fortify the city of Rome itself, which had seen no enemy for nearly 500 years and was to see none for over a century more.

The interesting passage already referred to in the last chapter, from the third-century author, Dion Cassius,[11] shows that the weakness of the professional army system without reserves was understood. Dion makes Mæcenas, a first-century statesman, remark: ". . . if we check all military activity on their part (the Provincials), we shall run the risk of finding nothing but raw and untrained troops when we need a contingent for our assistance."

[11] Bk. 53, sec. 27.

Nevertheless he makes Mæcenas go on to argue against universal training because such training would make sedition more formidable, and against hastily raised troops because of the great distances to be traversed.

Despite this passage, it is probable that during the third century the Imperial government could not possibly have found time (in the intervals between civil wars and the assassinations of emperors) to overhaul the military system as a whole. No emperor tried it, but all did what they could with the means at hand. The abler emperors, "sweeping together household troops and fragments of the broken frontier armies and enlisting thousands of barbarian mercenaries,[12]. . . strove to keep a concentrated force at their disposal which they moved constantly backwards and forwards across the empire as each internal or external crisis demanded. It was this field army which shared in the imperial triumphs and received such rewards as the exhausted finances could bestow. In comparison with it such units of the old frontier troops, legions and auxilia alike, as maintained their old positions (and many did so) sank steadily in prestige and importance." [13]

These same abler emperors, Claudius II, Aurelian, Probus and Carus, tried to keep up discipline by savage punishments. Carus affected an extreme soldierly simplicity of dress and personal habits. Such measures could not fully remedy the evils of continuous political instability and the standard of discipline and training unquestionably declined. Probus was assassinated in an unpremeditated mutiny of the troops enraged at the efforts he personally required of them in "land reclamation," i. e., draining a marsh.

Incidentally, it should be said that the civil wars within the empire are of little interest to the military student. Indeed, this is true of most civil wars, because the base and political backing of neither side is as firm and definite as in wars between regularly constituted political units. Therefore the political rather than the military factors in war tend to predominate, and thereby rob the operations of strategic interest. To this general rule the American Civil War is an exception, for it was a war between two

[12] In numeri, not in the old auxiliary cohorts and alæ.
[13] Cheesman, 136.

sections almost as definite, in a military sense, as two separate countries. But almost all civil wars, for instance, the Wars of the Roses in England, the 16th century Wars of Religion in France and the 17th century civil wars in England, help to prove the rule. Two points of tactical interest drawn from the civil wars will be considered in connexion with Vegetius and the 4th century Roman army.

Finally, I would remind the reader that the period of confusion saw not one definite lodgment effected by force within the boundaries of the empire. The nearest thing to it was Aurelian's voluntary abandonment of Dacia and retreat to the line of the lower Danube.

Throughout the phase of confusion the Roman military system did not break down. It is true that Decius (249–251 A. D.) fell in battle against the Goths and that Valerian (253–260 A. D.) was taken prisoner by the Persians, but these unprecedented disasters to the person of the Emperor were balanced by corresponding victories. Claudius Gothicus (268–270 A. D.) massacred 50,000 Goths at Nish in modern Serbia, and Carus (282–284 A. D.) temporarily swept the upper and middle Tigris-Euphrates region as no Emperor since Trajan had done, driving the Persians before him and capturing their capitals of Seleucia and Ctesiphon.

But although the Roman army did not collapse under the strain of the phase of confusion, the units which composed it became hopelessly disjointed and mixed up. We have seen that these units had become localized during the preceding phase of successful frontier defence and that when large field armies were called for they were formed, not by the removal of permanent units as such but by temporary bodies known as vexillations, each vexillation being drawn from a number of units. Now, after more than half a century, the vicious system of vexillations had brought matters to such a point that fragments of the same legion were to be found serving all over the place.[14] The old legion, 6000 strong, had broken up as a tactical unit. Many of the old auxiliary cohorts and alæ had disappeared altogether, for (in spite of the two centuries of tradition which might be behind it) such a unit did not have the same prestige as a legion and detachments from it were much more apt to lose their identity. Prob-

[14] Oman, Vol. 1, 7, and Cheesman, 140–141.

ably any intelligent officer in the entire service whose position permitted him to appreciate the situation of the army as a whole, would have told you that the first sufficient interval of peace and political stability would be used to overhaul the entire organization of the Roman army.

Such a lull was provided by Diocletian, who became Emperor in 284 A. D. and had consolidated his position throughout the entire Roman world by 297 A. D. For our purposes we may neglect the customary spasm of civil war between Diocletian's abdication in 305 and the beginning of Constantine's universal power in 314, and may consider as a whole the army reforms bearing the names of both Diocletian and Constantine.

With Diocletian's establishment of absolutism and with his changes in the civil administration, we are not concerned. His division of the Empire into four groups reduced the distance which a messenger must travel to and from Imperial Headquarters. In general it may be said that from Diocletian's time to the final breakdown of centralized administration there were usually at least two legitimate Emperors at a time. On the other hand, this division was purely administrative. In civilization and in feeling, the Roman world remained one thing. Indeed it might even be said that uniformity was carried to excess.

Besides the attempt to divide the administration of the Empire itself, Diocletian completely changed the mechanism of the Roman higher command. Formerly the Prætorian Prefect had been, under the Emperor, Commander-in-Chief. Now each and every Emperor had under him two "Masters of Soldiery," one Master of the Infantry and the other of the Cavalry,[15] incidentally indicating the increased importance of the cavalry arm. The titles suggest those of the Chiefs of Arms existing in so many contemporary armies, Chief of Infantry, of Cavalry, etc. Of course the "Magister Equitum" of the fourth century and after has no connexion with the temporary Magister Equitum, or Lieutenant Dictator of the early Republic.

Perhaps the most revolutionary of the fourth-century army reforms was the reorganization of permanent field armies, composed of the best troops in the service. These field armies were

[15] "Magistri Militum," one "Magister Peditum," and the other "Magister Equitum."

composed of three categories—the Palatine, Comitatensian, and Pseudo-Comitatensian troops. The Palatines took their name directly from the Palatia (Palaces), which were the official seats of the Roman government in every province, and indirectly from the Palatine hill in Rome from which the first Emperors had governed. They were not the personal escort of the Prince—that duty was performed by smaller bodies known as the Domestic or Scholarian troops. The Palatines were the crack troops of the new field armies, and it was significant of the way things were going that there were both Palatine legions and Palatine auxiliaries. Next after the Palatines came the Comitatenses, whose name means comrades or household troops and is derived from the same root as that from which we get our word "comrade." After them came the Pseudo-Comitatenses who were ranked lower than the Comitatenses and much lower than the Palatines but higher than the surviving frontier troops to whom we shall come in a moment. All told, the total strength in legionary soldiers belonging to these three categories amounted to about 33% of the strength in legionaries of the entire establishment. The field armies were held concentrated well behind the frontier, near large cities which were also road centres.

Conservative people found fault with the arrangement because it exposed the troops to the corruptions of city life and exposed the city people to the rowdyism of the soldiers.[16] This situation is one that is familiar to us all; the troops and the people being distinct, each wants the other for its own purposes, and at the same time each knows its own good points and fears degeneration through the bad influence of the other.

Meanwhile the remaining 66% of legionaries, together with a proportion of auxiliaries difficult to determine, were held in their old stations as Riparian or Limitanian (frontier) troops, continuing to enjoy, or endure, the fixed local ties which almost all their units had had for two centuries and many of them for a century before that. Service in the frontier troops was now hereditary in law as well as in fact—the son of a soldier was bound to enlist.[17] Indeed such procedure was now commonplace outside the army, for ever since Septimius Severus (192–211 A. D.)

[16] Ammianus Marcellinus: Bk. 22, ch. 4.
[17] Codex Theodosianus, VII, 22, quoted Cheesman, 137.

the Emperors of the decline had tried to stiffen the crumbling civilization over which they ruled by a whole series of laws compelling the sons of free handicraftsmen and even small business men to be about their fathers' businesses.

Naturally, the sons of soldiers could not, by themselves, be expected to fill the gaps caused by active service. Accordingly, we find in the fourth century a system of conscription of a sort which foreshadows the feudal armies of all mediæval Europe, inasmuch as the unit called upon to furnish a man to the colours is not a unit of population but a landed property of a certain size.[18] For the purposes of conscription, landed properties not large enough to be compelled to furnish a recruit would be lumped together until the required acreage was made up. The owners would then be compelled to furnish recruits in rotation. By modern standards the conscription was very light, for the number of troops to be raised in proportion to population was small. Furthermore, men were not always held for the full legionary term of service. When the needs of the service permitted, they were discharged after 15, 10, or even 5 years. Nevertheless the service was unpopular, soldiering often is; for instance it is unpopular to-day in large sections of English and American opinion. The English army of the 18th century was sometimes filled from the jails. In the 4th century the unpopularity was so great that fraud and even self-mutilation were often used to avoid it. The soldiers were branded like criminals to prevent their deserting.

Service in the legions was even more unpopular than in the auxiliaries, for the equipment of a legionary was heavier, the work more exhausting, the discipline more severe and the promotion slower.[19] It is possible that the new conditions of mobile warfare, which may have made it necessary for the soldier to carry more on his person than the localized troops of former times had done, helped to make it hard to get the men to carry the heavy legionary arms and armour. We know that, in the 16th century it was chiefly the necessity for increased mobility which caused armour to be laid aside.[20] At all events, the 4th century dislike for legionary

---

[18] Boutaric, 21 *et seq.*, quoting Codex Theodosianus, VII, 13, together with laws of Valentinian and Valens.

[19] Vegetius: Bk. 2, ch. 3, quoted in Boutaric, 25.

[20] Dean: Helmets and Body Armour in Modern Warfare, 45–52.

service made it easier to get good men for the auxiliaries, and correspondingly lowered the spirit and efficiency of the legions.

Another change, only less striking than the organization of the field armies, was the reduction of the legions serving in those armies to 1000 men. Most auxiliary cohorts and alæ had been 1000 strong ever since Trajan's time, so now to make the permanent legionary unit of the same strength assured a greater measure of tactical uniformity by having the units all of the same size. Another change was to give the name " vexillation " to permanent cavalry units. We find the old name "cuneus" (wedge) also applied to 4th-century cavalry squadrons.

To make the legions in the field armies consist of no more than 1000 men did not mean a reduction in the total number of legionary soldiers. On the contrary, it seems that the number was considerably increased. The numbers of the 4th-century Roman army may be estimated, partially and very roughly, as follows: [21]

33 Limitary legions at 6000 each	198,000
132 Field Army (i. e., Palatine, Comitatensian and Pseudo-Comitatensian) legions at 1000 each	132,000
Total legionary soldiers	330,000
108 Units of Palatine Auxiliaries at 1000 each	108,000
91 Units of Cavalry at 1000 each	91,000
"Domestics," i. e., personal escort of the Emperor	15,000
	214,000
	544,000

In part this total is too high, for we know that some legions formerly stationed on the frontiers were assigned to the field armies and have therefore been twice counted in the foregoing figures. On the other hand, it is certain that the grand total of the entire Roman service was far above the figure of 544,000 since the above figures do not include any auxiliaries but the Palatines. Now we know that there were many non-Palatine auxiliaries. Probably 200,000 is a conservative estimate of their numbers. The Roman service also included great numbers of numeri together with a new kind of barbarian auxiliary known as Federati. It included

[21] Compare Hodgkin, Vol. 1 ,Part 2, 628–631; Gibbon, Vol. 2, 294; Young, Vol. 1, 404.

also the crews of the fleets which controlled the seas and the great boundary rivers. Pausing for a moment to ask the reader to remember the word "Federati" to which I shall return in connexion with Theodosius, I give it as my own opinion that the total number of men in the 4th-century service may have amounted to three quarters of a million, a larger disciplined force than afterwards existed down to the Wars of the French Revolution and the largest professional army the world has ever known.

In view of the various civil wars in the phase of confusion, it would not be surprising to find that the standard of training and discipline had been lowered. On the contrary we are surprised that so large a measure of discipline was still in force. There is a story which is told, with variations, of many of the mutinies with which civil wars would begin; of mutineers murdering centurions nicknamed "hand me the other" from the habit of calling for a second switch with which to beat a soldier for some military offence, when they had already broken the first one over his back! The surprising thing is not that such centurions were murdered in the frequent mutinies but rather that they existed at all. Evidently the Roman noncommissioned and company officer was often of such a temper that he was willing to risk his own life in his effort to keep up discipline in his own cohort.

As to equipment we find a vastly increased number of cavalry units with both man and horse so well protected by scale mail, that the barbarians at Strassburg (A. D., 357) thought the only way to bring down such monsters was to slip under the belly of the horse and stab him from below.[22] In the opposite direction there was the tendency on the part of an increasing number of the infantry to give up both helmet and body armour and to rely more and more upon archery and other forms of fire action. This tendency Vegetius condemns as part of the degeneracy of his contemporaries [23] although it was probably a natural development of the time. An army whose main business is chasing raiders must be able to move fast and to skirmish and, in the rarer case of an invasion in force, the usefulness of the new field armies must have depended a good deal on the speed they could make over long distances.

[22] Ammianus Marcellinus: Bk. 16.
[23] Vegetius: Bk. 1, sec. 20, quoted Oman, Vol. 1, 18.

In 312 A. D., Constantine, whose power was then based chiefly upon Gaul, was threatened by Maxentius, Emperor of Italy. Although Maxentius had 200,000 troops to Constantine's 80,000, Constantine determined to invade Italy. Crossing the Alps, he met near Turin a large part of Maxentius' army. Finding himself inferior in cavalry, he drew up his infantry in two lines with a considerable distance between them and wide intervals between the units of the front line. When Maxentius' cavalry charged they were permitted to pass through the intervals. The first line then wheeled about, attacking their rear, while they were engaged in front with Constantine's second line, and almost destroyed them. What happened to Maxentius' infantry we are not told, which makes it seem that they made no effort to retrieve the defeat of their cavalry.[24]

The manœuvre of Constantine's first line indicates a high degree of discipline, control, and tactical flexibility. This may have been due to the personal excellence of Constantine, but at any rate it indicates that tactical flexibility was not yet unknown to the Roman infantry.

[24] Young, Vol. 1, 375.

CHAPTER III

THE IMPERIAL ROMAN ARMY

(FROM THE DEATH OF CONSTANTINE TO THE DEATH OF JUSTINIAN—337–565 A. D.)

THE Roman Empire never fell and the tradition of civilization was never broken. It is true that with the civil wars of the third century there began a long period of decline in population, in wealth, and in the arts, including the art of war; but the decline was due to internal causes far more than to external ones. Its outstanding feature was not successful invasion from without but an internal change in the Roman army which stood sentinel over the civilized world. That army, while remaining (in general) faithful to its trust and successful in discharging that trust, became predominantly barbarian in blood. As the internal decline continued to weaken (and especially to impoverish) the central government, at last the reality of power in the West was taken over by the provincial commanders-in-chief, barbarian-born men friendly to the civilization they served but incapable of administering successfully a civilized state because of the limitations of their minds.

Throughout the period covered by this chapter, the Roman army remained a highly trained, professional force, and continued to conduct its operations according to a doctrine of war suitable to such a force. Many of the identical units raised by Augustus and his immediate successors can still be traced into the early fifth century. This professional army remained successful. Although the internal decline of civilization continued, nevertheless the military victories of its defenders outnumbered their defeats and in the second half of the sixth century the greater part of the Roman world was still directly administered by the Imperial government from its new capital, Constantinople.

In the second half of the fourth century, within the Roman service (and in spite of the intense conservatism and strong traditional feeling of that service) a momentous tactical revolution took place. Cavalry replaced infantry as the chief arm.

The supremacy of cavalry determined tactics for over a thousand years. It resulted in part, but only in part, from the general internal slackening of the energy of the declining ancient world. Special military conditions also helped to bring it about.

The first point to consider in connexion with the decline of infantry is the relaxation of Roman discipline which began in the confusion of the third century. The second point concerns equipment. By the fourth century the heavy legionary javelin, the pilum, was no longer carried. It had been replaced by a pike. As far as we can tell, the pike was usually light enough so that it could be hurled as the pilum had been.

This change in equipment helped to cause a loss of flexibility and offensive power on the part of infantry. The sword, or for that matter, the modern bayonet, as the chief close-quarters weapon of infantry, tends to produce an attack in skirmish line, with intervals and distances sufficient to permit a degree of individual fencing. The large, dense columns of the later Napoleonic period are not a true exception to this rule since it is not clear that they ever did much serious hand-to-hand fighting but were expected to act chiefly through the moral effect of their massed approach. On the other hand, the use of the pike required close formations and strict alignment. Any serious break in alignment admits the enemy because the pike must be levelled in order to be used, and when levelled cannot be traversed without first being raised upright, thus leaving the pikeman defenceless. Accordingly a body of pikemen is formidable for passive defence, as a hedgehog or porcupine is formidable, but its attacking power is limited. It can attack only slowly, and the troops must be brought to a remarkably high state of drill and discipline in order to be able to do even that. They must have good ground to advance over. Dislocation in their ranks is fatal; they are then like the porcupine unrolled, with his naked belly opposed to the claws and teeth of his destroyer.

Very few armies of pikemen have ever been able to attack successfully. Much of the offensive power of Alexander's army was developed by the cavalry. The Swiss (after their original startling successes in their native mountains) are always found acting as a part of armies whose other parts supplemented their work. All mediæval warfare illustrates the truth that a body of pikemen, not disciplined and drilled to perfection, must stand rigidly on the defensive or be destroyed.

Indeed the difficulties of delivering an attack with pikemen are so great that the Romans seem never to have attempted it. In an attack the pike was hurled as the old pilum had been and the attackers then fell to with the sword. The pike was undoubtedly needed because the discipline and instruction of infantry could no longer be depended upon to get them to stand firm before charging cavalry unless they were packed in dense formation and furnished with a weapon capable of keeping the horseman at a distance.

In this matter discipline is all important. Belloc's "Poitiers" [1] has an admirable discussion of it as follows:

The strength of an armed body consists in its cohesion. When the whole body is in peril, each individual member of it wants to get away. To prevent him from getting away is the whole object of discipline and military training. Each standing firm (or falling where he stands) preserves the unity, and therefore the efficacy, of the whole. A few yielding at the critical point (and the critical point is usually also the point where men most desire to yield) destroy the efficacy of nine times their number. Now, one of the things that frighten an individual man on foot most is another man galloping at him upon a horse. If many men gallop upon him so bunched on many horses, the effect is, to say the least, striking. If any one doubts this, let him try. If the men upon the horses are armed with a weapon that can get at the men on foot some feet ahead (such as is the lance) the threat is more efficacious still, and no single man (save here and there a fellow full of some religion) will meet it. But against this truth there is another truth to be set, which the individual man would never guess, and which is none the less experimentally certain—which is this: that if a certain number of men on foot stand firm when horses are galloping at them, the horses will swerve or balk before contact; in general, the mounted line will not be efficacious against the dismounted. There is here a contrast between the nerves of horses and the intelligence of men, as also between the rider's desire that his horse shall go forward, and the horse's training, which teaches him that not only his rider, but men in general, are his masters. . . .

To teach infantry that they can thus withstand cavalry, instruction is the instrument. You must drill them and form them constantly, and hammer it into them by repeated statement that if they stand firm all will be well. This has been done in the case of men on foot armed only with staves.

[1] Belloc: Poitiers, 112–114.

Now from all the circumstances of the 3rd and 4th centuries, and especially from the fact that popularity with their troops was all-important to the candidates for Emperor in the innumerable civil wars, we know that it was harder to bring the discipline of infantry to a point which would enable them to withstand the anguish of being charged by cavalry. Dense formations and the replacement of the pilum by the pike which would hold the cavalryman at a greater distance were therefore the natural expedients with which to meet such a situation.

Let us now consider in their chronological order the important general actions of Mursa (351), Strassburg (357), and Adrianople (378), noting how each of the three seems to mark a stage in the process we are considering.

The Diocletian-Constantinian reforms failed to check the internal decline of ancient civilization, and soon after Constantine's death the recurrent plague of civil wars, palace conspiracies, and assassinations of Emperors broke out again.

One incident of these civil wars was the hotly contested battle of Mursa, the modern Essek on the Drave. In 351 A. D., the Roman army of the East was opposed to that of the West and especially that of Gaul. The Emperor of the East—Constantius—was superior in light and heavy cavalry and also in archers. He had stirred up the tribes beyond the Rhine to invade Gaul and so retain as much as possible of the Roman army in Gaul to defend that province. Nevertheless, the Western troops at Mursa seem to have been superior in legionary infantry and also included a large force of German and Frankish auxiliaries without body armour. Constantius' troops attacked in oblique order, left in front, and succeeded in overlapping and rolling up the right of the Westerners. Meanwhile the unarmoured Germans had suffered severely from the fire of the Eastern archers, so that when the invulnerable Eastern lancers finally succeeded in breaking into the formation of the Gallic legions the Eastern light horse were easily able to complete the victory.[2]

The conditions under which the battle of Strassburg was fought in 357 A. D. spring directly from the campaign of Mursa six years before. The German barbarians stirred up by Constantius had pushed back the Roman frontier from the Rhine to about the

[2] Gibbon, Vol. 2, 368–369.

Meuse. In 355, Constantius appointed his cousin Julian to the office of Cæsar of the West to go into Gaul to handle the situation. At the same time Constantius treacherously and secretly ordered the Roman commander in Switzerland (who was his own appointee) not to support Julian properly. Meanwhile a rebellion of the Roman army north of the Seine temporarily increased Julian's difficulties. The local commander there, learning that he had been falsely accused of treason, set himself up as Emperor in the hope of saving his own life, which he lost a month later by assassination.

In the campaigning season of 356, Julian failed to accomplish much. Moving eastward from Reims, he lost two legions, wiped out in a barbarian surprise attack, and although he was able to advance to Cologne he could not maintain himself there, but felt it necessary to retreat and winter at Sens.

The year 357 opened badly. The Roman commander in Switzerland, who was supposed to co-operate with Julian's eastward movement by northward attack against modern Württemberg and Baden, intentionally failed to do so. Indeed he was so slack that he failed to destroy a barbarian raiding force which crossed the gap of Belfort, pushed down the Doubs and Saône to the gate of Lyons and returned safely. Nevertheless, Julian pushed forward to Saverne, or Zabern, established a fortified post there, and prepared to strike with his little army of 13,000 against the enemy 35,000 strong concentrated near Strassburg.

The barbarians had felled great trees across the hilly roads, but Julian was able to advance with his cavalry (including fully armoured lancers and also horse-archers) on either flank of the infantry marching column. Since Saverne is nearly 25 miles as the crow flies from Strassburg, we may assume that it must have been on the second or even the third day out that (in the afternoon) contact with the enemy was established. Then followed an incident that throws a vivid light on the 4th-century Roman army. Julian assembled most of his troops and made a speech to them saying that he meant to halt for the night and attack in the morning. The troops in their eagerness gnashed their teeth and clashed their shields loudly to express dissatisfaction. Whereat Julian consulted his generals, who told him that discipline might suffer if the opinion of the army was not consulted and an immediate attack was ordered!

Both sides drew up in dense formation. Julian put most of his cavalry on his right and the barbarians placed their own cavalry opposite them, mixed with light armed men who were to try to crawl under the Roman horses' bellies and stab them from below—that being almost the only part of either horse or man unprotected by armor. The Roman cavalry disgraced themselves by stampeding at the very beginning of the battle and would have swept away the infantry had these last not stood firmly in their dense formation. Julian rallied the flyers but we do not hear of their accomplishing anything until the pursuit. The decisive phase of the action was a long stand-up fight between the opposing infantry, the Roman troops apparently doing most of their fighting by thrusting with the sword. Once the barbarians, with their superior weight and strength, broke deeply into the close ranks of the Roman "testudo" formation. But reserves were brought up, especially the Batavian auxiliaries under their "Reges" or tribal chieftains, and the battle was renewed. Their high training made it possible for the Roman troops to fight on hand to hand until at last the barbarians could stand the losses no longer and broke. Six thousand of their dead were counted on the field, and many thousands were drowned in trying to cross the Rhine which cut off their retreat. The Roman army lost only four officers and 243 soldiers.[3]

In this action we find the infantry still doing most of the work, but doing it in dense formation, which can hardly have been flexible enough to permit manœuvring.

An interesting example of the conservatism of the Roman service and its intense desire to preserve tradition is furnished by the use of the word "testudo" to describe the new, dense, battle formation. Literally the word testudo meant a turtle. Ever since early republican times it had been used of the close siege or escalade formation, with shields interlocked overhead to keep off missiles from the walls and thus resembling the turtle's shell. We now find it carried over to describe the new close formation, apparently for the express purpose of giving that novelty a traditional flavour.

Two other points connected with the aftermath of the battle are worth noting. Julian sent certain Frankish prisoners to the court of Constantius far away in the East, and Constantius

[3] Ammianus Marcellinus, Bk. 16.

promptly enlisted them in his own personal bodyguard. Then, when Gaul had been cleared of barbarians, it was thought a great thing that Julian was able to persuade his auxiliaries to help his legionaries rebuild the ruined cities. Finally the names of Julian's general officers, Dagalaif, Rhœmetalces, Hormisdas, Fullofaudes, Vadomar, Merobaudes, Davitta, Immo, Agila and Malarich show how many barbarian-born men were to be found even in the highest ranks of the Roman service.

After Strassburg, the next important Roman campaign was that of Adrianople. It was serious from the very first because when it began the Visigoths were already inside the Danube barrier with its Roman river fleet and its line of fortified strong points garrisoned by Riparian troops. The Visigoths were a border tribe, attracted like most border tribes by Roman civilization and therefore essentially friendly to the Empire, whose "allies" they had been for a century. They were being converted to Christianity. Naturally when attacked from the northeast by the Mongol Huns in 376 A. D., they asked to be received inside the Roman border with their families. It was finally granted on the severe conditions that they should give hostages and be disarmed.

The local Roman officials oppressed the wretched Goths, grafted and profiteered on their food supplies, and failed to disarm them. They stood this for over a year but finally revolted, the revolt beginning at Marcianople, the modern Shumla in Bulgaria west from the port of Varna. From there they moved on Adrianople, failed to rush its walls and began pillaging the countryside. The Emperor Valens was in the East fighting the Persians. He sent some of his generals against the Goths, and Gratian the Western Emperor sent reinforcements from the Gallic command. The imperial troops won several minor actions but failed to get a decision and the war swayed to and fro from Thrace to the Dobrudja where we hear of a Roman attack in the close testudo formation upon a Gothic wagon camp.

The campaign of 378 opened well enough with the destruction of a Gothic detachment in a surprise night attack delivered by a far smaller body of Roman troops. About midsummer, Valens was in Constantinople with a large army at his back, peace having been made with the Persians. Meanwhile Gratian, the Western

Emperor, had smashed his local barbarians at Colmar in Alsace and was moving eastward. The position of the miserable Goths now became highly critical. They had merely been drifting about, pillaging, and had failed to make any solid lodgment in Roman land because of their inability to take walled cities. At their back they had the strong line of the Danube with the garrisons of its fortified posts and its river fleet. Valens marched to Adrianople, whereupon the barbarians concentrated in the neighbourhood, entrenching themselves in one of their great circular or oval camps, ringed about with wagons like a Boer laager.

Valens might have waited for Gratian, of whom he is said to have been jealous, but instead he decided to force a battle at once. His intelligence service underestimated the number of the Goths, and even had they not done so he knew that Roman armies were usually able to beat vastly superior numbers of barbarians not under Roman discipline. Drawing up his troops, legions in the centre, light infantry in front, and cavalry on either flank, he prepared to attack the wagon camp. It was about two in the afternoon of August 9th. The troops had marched from Adrianople at dawn, they had not been properly rationed, and they were suffering from want of water under a blazing sun.

It seems that Valens' intelligence officers, besides estimating the total number of the barbarians far too low, had also failed to find out that a very large detachment of mounted men were out of camp, foraging in the neighbourhood. On top of this, Valens neglected to throw out proper security patrols and covering detachments, at least on his left. The barbarians played hard for delay, sending messengers offering to surrender and meanwhile setting fire to the grass to hinder the Roman deployment.

Valens did not have his troops in hand; while negotiations were still going on his light infantry, without orders, made a premature attack on the wagon camp and failed to push it home. Thereupon the Roman cavalry on the wings attacked, although the left wing was not well concentrated. It had come up fast but had left behind it many stragglers and even lost units on the roads over which it had advanced. About the time that such of its units as had come up were committed to the attack on the wagon camp, the great mass of barbarian horsemen who had been out foraging suddenly appeared and charged their exposed outer flank. Naturally the cavalry of the Roman left were driven off the field, and their flight exposed the left of the Roman infantry. Julian's legions at Strassburg thirty years before had been able to meet such a situation but Valens' troops could not. Men and units got so jammed together that no effective resistance could be made. The Batavian auxiliaries of the reserve took to their heels, the Emperor was killed, and only a third of the army escaped.[4]

Even after such a disaster the barbarians utterly failed to consolidate their position within the Roman border. They could not so much as take the city of Adrianople, but merely went on drifting to and fro, ravaging. Philippopolis and Sofia also held out. Gratian, who had by this time reached Belgrade, appointed an able general—Theodosius—as Emperor of the East. Theodosius made his headquarters at Salonika. Then the two Emperors went to work on the problem much as Tiberius had gone to work in Pannonia nearly 300 years before. While refusing battle, they forced the Goths to keep concentrated in order to be able to resist them; they worked steadily to lessen the area subject to loot and they were always rounding up or massacring Gothic detachments. One particularly successful surprise attack was delivered by a lieutenant of Theodosius named Modar, himself a Goth but an orthodox Christian. Theodosius had been crowned in January, 379. By the end of 380 there was not a Goth alive south of the Danube who had not been captured and sold as a slave or else had consented to enlist in the Imperial Army. Six years later, when another Gothic force tried to cross the river, Theodosius' generals tricked them, the Roman river fleet rammed their light canoes, and the miserable barbarians were drowned by thousands.

The importance of the campaign of Adrianople is not its immediate consequences, which as we have seen were local, temporary and slight. The point is that after that campaign the Roman army was reorganized in a form big with consequences for the future.

In the first place, the tactical revolution in the relations between cavalry and infantry was now complete. Cavalry was now the chief arm. Vegetius seems to have written shortly after Adrianople, and in Roman tactics as he describes them it is the cavalry who (in all normal cases) are called upon to deliver the decisive attack. The light infantry would prepare and support the attack

[4] Ammianus Marcellinus, Bk. 31.

by their fire. But the heavy infantry were expected merely to stand firm "like a wall" behind their great shields, not stirring from their place for fear of breaking their strict alignment. Their immovable mass was the pivot of a defensive action, and in such an action they still played the chief part, for the light infantry could not, unaided, withstand the hostile shock and could not stand on the defensive at all—they must charge, skirmish or flee. Obviously a decision can seldom, if ever, be obtained without taking the offensive, and on the offensive the rôle of the Roman heavy infantry was now virtually limited. to standing in reserve ready to repel hostile counterattacks should the Roman cavalry be repulsed.[5]

It is impossible to exaggerate the importance of the tactical revolution which made cavalry the chief arm.

I repeat that normally, for the most part because of the fear of men in general felt by horses, infantry is and must be the chief arm. Well-disciplined, unshaken infantry can not only stand off a superior number of cavalry; they can advance despite the opposition of that cavalry. Sometimes they can even break its cohesion, as Cæsar's legionaries broke the Pompeian cavalry at Pharsalia. Besides their tactical superiority, they have the economic advantage of being far less expensive to maintain than an equal number of cavalry.

But although the importance of the fourth-century supremacy of cavalry cannot be exaggerated, and although that supremacy was, in part, due to a certain decline in the discipline of infantry, still the reader should remember that there was another powerful force at work.

Besides the enormous moral effect of its charge, cavalry has also this advantage compared with infantry, that it is far more mobile. Now we have seen that for four centuries the task of the Roman army had been chiefly the repulse of frontier raids. Ever since Trajan's time it had been almost exclusively that. For raiding and the repulse of raids, cavalry was obviously better than foot because of its mobility. Naturally, the cavalry arm became more important on both sides of the frontier. Cavalry would see more of active service and therefore energetic and ambitious men would prefer a career in this arm, which would still further increase its

[5] Delpech, Vol. 2, 130–134, copiously quoting Vegetius.

importance. This was a natural and, under the conditions, an inevitable process; our own regular army when dealing with the Indians of the Great Plains or with Philippine insurrectos found that much of the work had to be done by mounted troops. Therefore the supremacy of cavalry from 380 to, say, 1500, was not due to folly but was brought about by virtue of special military conditions and partly by a decline in the discipline and instruction of infantry.

The reader must not think of the tactical revolution and the new preponderance of barbarian personnel as abrupt breaks in the traditions of the Roman service. It was no more than the culmination of a long and gradual development. Afterwards there were still many important elements of permanence. For instance there was the general doctrine of war. After the tactical revolution the fourth-century Roman army continued to maintain its traditional doctrine adapted to the nature of a professional, long-service force without large organized reserves and without an abundant and rapid supply of replacements. We find in Vegetius such maxims as the following: "No man is to be employed in the field who is not trained and tested in discipline" and correspondingly, "It is better to beat the enemy through want, surprises, and care over difficult places (i. e., through manœuvres) than by a battle in the open field."

As far as possible the idea is to win without fighting! Such doctrine is that of almost all professional armies everywhere, especially when they are opposed, as the Roman army was usually opposed, by forces more numerous but far less highly organized than itself. We have seen it successfully used not only since Tiberius' time but ever since Marius' campaign against the Cimbri and Teutones in 102 B. C. Nevertheless it is dangerous to the state that practices it and particularly dangerous if the citizens of that state (like the fourth-century Roman empire) are unwarlike and lacking in patriotism.

Still we must not exaggerate, for a civilized force is always superior to an equal number of barbarians and usually superior to a far greater number. Adrianople is the one example of a great disaster inflicted at barbarian hands. The effects of that disaster were local and temporary and in any case it is counterbalanced by the splendid succession of victories.

Besides completing the tactical revolution, Theodosius' reorganization brought about another fundamental change. It made barbarian personnel predominate over native.

Ever since early Republican times the Roman army had had in it non-citizen elements. By Constantine's time these elements, originally subordinate, were about equal in importance with the citizen elements, as is proved by the existence of numerous Palatine auxiliaries among the crack troops of the service.

Such a development was natural enough. I repeat that in so vast a community there could be no patriotism except in the tiny minority immediately concerned with public affairs. Familiarity with the comforts of a high civilization disinclined men to military service then as now. Accordingly, recruitment from within the Empire became increasingly difficult in spite of the infinitesimally small proportion of troops to population. The Imperial Government was forced to meet the difficulty by the same expedient which we see to-day in the Colonial armies of England and France—that is, by the employment of barbarians. These barbarians were in no way hostile to the civilized society which they policed; as long as they were paid they were tractable enough, and under Roman commanders imbued with a long tradition of civilized warfare, they would cheerfully cut to pieces many times their number of hostile barbarians from outside the frontiers. Nevertheless, as time went on the disinclination of civilized Romans for military service increased until the officers as well as the men gradually became largely barbarian in blood. The easiest way to enlist men was to accept in block the personal following of barbaric chieftains willing to serve as officers.

After 380, it was in no way an innovation that Theodosius enlisted or pressed into the Roman service great numbers of barbarian horsemen. The ominous new thing was that he paid them higher than the regular Roman troops and showed them greater consideration.

Moreover, these new auxiliaries were given a new status, that of "Federati," different both from that of the original auxiliary units and from that of the numeri. It seems that the Federati were technically allies, not subjects of the Empire; therefore their legal status resembled that of the allied contingents which had served in the armies of the Republic and of the early Empire.

In practice they seem to have differed from auxiliaries and numeri not only in that the commander of a federate unit was usually the tribal chief of its original personnel, but also in that he seems to have had considerable liberty in appointing his subordinate officers. Of course this patronage increased the independence and potential political importance of these commanders. On the other hand, there is nothing to show that such a unit continued to be tribally recruited as it was moved about from province to province.

The predominance of barbarian over native personnel in the Roman army determined the manner of the loss of centralized government in the West in a different way from that in which the thing is presented by many popular historians of the recent past. It is true that after Theodosius' death in 395 A. D. no Emperor effectively ruled the entire Roman world, and that the centralized administration in the West soon afterwards showed signs of breaking up. But this change did not come through successful attack from without. It was the result of the increasing decline of civilization from internal causes. In no battle did barbarians from the outer darkness defeat a Roman army and permanently appropriate to themselves Roman land. To this general statement, only two local exceptions appear. A narrow belt south of the upper Danube was overrun, and in Britain small heathen pirate settlements on the south and east coasts cut off the Romanized Britons from communion with Christendom.

With these two exceptions, the chieftains who set themselves up as local governors in the provinces of the West, although most of them were indeed barbarian in blood, obtained their power not bcause of that fact but because they were commanders of auxiliary units in the Roman army. Their units had come to feel loyalty for them as their immediate commanders rather than to the Roman state they nominally served, but the numbers of those units were tiny compared to the populations they policed. For instance, Clovis' less than 8000 "Franks" came into a Gaul of millions.[6] Moreover it is highly doubtful whether any of the auxiliary units which installed their commanders as local governors were still tribally recruited or retained any tribal consciousness whatsoever. Their tribal names seem to have become mere regimental desig-

[6] Gregory of Tours' "Historia Francorum," quoted in Fustel de Coulanges: L'Invasion germanique et la fin de l'empire, 480.

nations. Before establishing themselves as provincial governors their chiefs engaged in civil wars between claimants for the title of Emperor, but we never hear of such a chieftain seeking the Empire for himself. They sometimes fought one another for more territory from which to collect taxes, but their taxes were the Roman taxes and were collected by the traditional Roman civil service. With two exceptions, no commander of auxiliaries ever made war upon an Emperor. The exceptions were first, the Vandal chief who looted Africa and then set up a dynasty which lasted for a century there, and second, Alaric in his brief and somewhat pardonable mutiny when the impoverished Imperial government failed to pay him as it had contracted to do. In general, the new provincial governors acknowledged the authority of the Emperor of the day; and he on his side apparently made no effort to make them pay him taxes.

There were invaders from without but those invaders were either destroyed like Radagaisus or beaten back like the Mongol Attila. Radagaisus raided Italy in 406 with 200,000 men at his back. His great following was opposed by a far smaller Roman force under the command of a general of barbaric blood—Stilicho the Vandal. It was hemmed in by means of entrenchments (much as Cæsar had hemmed in Vercingetorix at Alesia) and was wiped out.

The troops at the command of the Visigothic chieftain in Spain, the Vandal in Africa, the Herul or Ostrogoth in Italy, continued to be organized as they had been when units in the armies of the centralized Empire. That is, they were heavy cavalry armed chiefly with the lance and light infantry who were mainly archers. They were recruited from the descendants of the original unit, plus such newcomers, either barbarian or native, as that body chose to admit. Such admissions were rare, for the warband constituted a rich and highly privileged body. With one great exception—to which we shall come in a moment—there seems to have been no recruitment of provincials on a large scale, not because the local governors would have been unwilling to have their help (could they have obtained it without breaking down the exclusiveness of the privileged body upon which they depended for support) but because the provincials themselves were unwilling to serve in armies commanded by men heretical in religion.

Where there was no racial difference (as in the case of the Huns) the politics of the Dark Ages turned not upon the distinction between provincial and barbarian as such, but upon points of religion. The reason why the local governors of 5th-century Africa, Italy, and Spain could not recruit provincials was that the provincials were Catholic and the Governors Arian. To this state of affairs the great exception was northern Gaul. The Frankish chieftains were Catholics and their auxiliary forces were supplemented by troops recruited from the Roman population, equipped (and presumably organized) in the traditional Roman manner.

In view of the fundamental religio-political difference between Gaul and the other states governed by barbarian chieftains, and in view of the survival of infantry as the chief force in the Frankish armies, it will be convenient to leave Gaul on one side to be considered in the next chapter. Meanwhile we should remember that the declining population of the entire Roman world continued to think of itself as Roman. The various new local governors preserved a theoretical allegiance to the Emperor at Constantinople and that Emperor directly administered the Eastern half of the Roman world.

In the 6th century we have the restoration of direct imperial government throughout Africa, Italy and Southern Spain. This restoration was brought about by arms. Its campaigns, together with the contemporary episodes of the perpetual border war on the Persian frontier constitute our only detailed knowledge of the warfare of the time.

Justinian (A. D. 527–565) on becoming Emperor, inherited an army in which a determined effort had been made by Leo I (A. D. 457–474) and Zeno the Isaurian (A. D. 474–491) to reduce the relative importance of barbarian as compared with native personnel. This had been done by enlisting large numbers of Isaurian mountaineers from southern Anatolia who were apparently granted pay and privileges equal to those of the barbarian federate auxiliaries.

In the century and a quarter preceding Justinian, the total numbers of the Roman army of the East had fallen heavily. In 527 he effectively ruled the Balkan peninsula, Anatolia, Syria and Egypt, and commanded from 150,000 to 200,000 soldiers, whereas, in, say, 400 A. D., these same provinces were garrisoned by about 350,000 men. The cause of this decline was the continuing decline of civilization itself, of which the symptoms were depopulation, financial decay, and corrupt administration. This last reached such a point in Justinian's old age that he is said to have had a paper strength of 645,000 men and only 150,000 in reality to police his original dominions plus Africa, Italy and part of Spain.[7] The diminished Roman army of the East was still organized, as prescribed by Diocletian more than two centuries before, into "Palatine" (i. e., Field Army) and "Limitary" (i. e., localized frontier) troops.[8] The tactical unit is still known by the old name of "numerus" translated into Greek as "katalogos" but all the other old names for units, legion, cohort, ala, etc., seem to have disappeared. The independence and patronage of the generals which we have discussed in connexion with the Theodosian reorganization had continued to increase, so that now native-born Roman generals as well as barbarian chieftains had great military households of personal retainers. That of Belisarius at the climax of his career was nearly 7000 strong.[9] Units were no longer designated with a number or regimental title but only with the name of their commander.

In equipment and tactics, the tendencies of relying upon cavalry rather than infantry, and also the increasing importance of archery fire had worked themselves out to their logical conclusion. As has been previously shown, these tendencies were due in part to a decline in the discipline and instruction of infantry and in part to special military circumstances, especially the use of the army as a constabulary. They were also fostered by the fact that the Eastern provinces had always been great cavalry and archery countries. There was still heavy armed infantry in Justinian's armies, but in all the battles of his reign we hear of only one feat of arms which it performed. That was the stand in the testudo formation with interlocked shields (and doubtless with the spear butts resting against the ground and the right foot as prescribed by Vegetius) backed up against the river Euphrates and confronted by the whole Persian army after the defeat at Sura in 531. Even this, however brilliant, was only a negative success. The Isaurians

[7] For these figures, see Young, Vol. 2, 205 and 322. Also Bury, E. B., Vol. 23, 523.

[8] Bury, E. B., Vol. 23, 523. Also Aussaresses, 9.

[9] Young, Vol. 2, 246.

were mostly foot archers. The flower of the native army were the heavy cavalry, fully armoured in scale mail and equipped as archers, with a sword, a little shield strapped to the upper left arm, and usually a lance as well. There were also lightly equipped horse archers, many of them Mongols, and barbarian heavy cavalrymen from the north armed with the lance.

At first glance one would think that the East-Roman heavy cavalry, with their lances and bows as well, were not organized on sound lines. Since fire delivered mounted must necessarily be inferior to infantry fire with a similar weapon, it seems as if foot archers ought easily to have obtained fire superiority over them. If this was so, then why not concentrate on shock tactics instead of losing time from training with the lance in order to practise shooting? A similar case is that of the 16th-century German mounted pistoleers whose fire was inferior to that of dismounted musketeers while they were usually routed by a vigorous charge of mounted lancers.

I think that the answer in both cases is to be found in the characteristics of the infantry which the late Roman and the early modern cavalrymen had to meet. In both cases the infantry in question was instructed to resist cavalry by arraying itself in masses of pikemen so dense that it necessarily lacked mobility, was clumsy in its formations and could not develop effective fire power. Heavy cavalry equipped both for fire and shock could ride down light infantry armed with missile weapons or drive them behind the heavy infantry where their fire would be ineffective. Then the cavalry would circle around the heavy infantry and fire into the fine target offered by its dense masses. The fact that the ancient light infantry were archers or slingers, and the ancient cavalry were archers, whereas the early modern light infantry were musketeers and their cavalry pistoleers, merely illustrates the similarity of the principle involved in both cases.

On the other hand, armoured cavalry equipped for both fire and shock must not be confused with light cavalry relying upon fire alone, such as the horse archers who defeated Crassus and gave the Crusaders so much hard work. There the principle is different inasmuch as this last kind of cavalry cannot close while their opponents retain any cohesion whatsoever.

There were in Justinian's day men of an antiquarian school of military thought who still deprecated archery and kept praising the old type of hand-to-hand fighting legionary of whom they read in their books, but their contentions were without effect. The practical soldiers of the time despised them as pedants, and insisted upon the variety of weapons, and especially the complete armour, enjoyed by their heavy armed horse archers.[10]

East-Roman generals could afford to take great liberties with their opponents, because the hostile armies were never flexible and lacked the power to manœuvre on the battlefield. With armies of anything like equal manœuvring power, Napoleon's maxim—"Beware when trying to outflank your opponent that you are not outflanked yourself"—comes into play; and yet the three great victories of Justinian's reign were all won by variations on the device of defensive envelopment from a concave formation!

At Daras in upper Mesopotamia in 530, Belisarius had 25,000 men against 40,000 Persians. The Persian infantry of that day fought behind great cumbrous wicker shields like their ancestors of 1000 years before. The Persians put their cavalry, their only striking force, on the wings. Belisarius refused his infantry centre and advanced his cavalry wings, covering his whole front with a non-continuous trench. The Persians, being unwilling to advance into his trap, made contact only on the wings, and were defeated by Belisarius' ability in using the superior tactical flexibility of the Roman cavalry units. A turning movement by a small body of 300 men, culminating in a surprise charge launched from behind the cover of a hill against the Persian left, contributed to the success.[11]

At Taginæ in Italy in 552, Narses had the unusually large force of 60,000 men but seems to have had no Roman infantry of the line with him.[12] Therefore, in order to have a pivot or core for the defensive action which he proposed to fight, he dismounted his heavy armed barbarian cavalry armed with the lance, and threw forward obliquely his wings of Roman foot archers and cavalry. The Ostrogoths, who were mostly mounted lancers and foot archers, could not co-ordinate the work of their two categories of troops. Their horse charged, bull fashion, against the Roman

[10] Procopius: "De Bello Persico," Bk. 1, sec. 1, quoted by Oman, Vol. 1, 25–26.

[11] Oman, Vol. 1, 27–29.

[12] Young, Vol. 2, 297.

centre but failed to break it and suffered severely from the Roman arrows. Meanwhile a detached body of cavalry on the extreme Roman left was threatening the Gothic archers and preventing them from co-operating with the attack. Finally, the main body of the Roman horse charged the disordered Gothic cavalry, broke them, and decided the day, for the wretched Gothic foot failed to make any sort of stand.

The next year, in 553, Italy was invaded by a huge marauding band of Alemanni plus Frankish hotheads who had joined the expedition on their own account without authorization from their government, 75,000 or 80,000 in all.[13] This great force split in two columns one of which marched down each side of the peninsula. They lost heavily by disease and by sudden attacks of the imperial garrisons, but these last were too few to stop them, and the eastern column escaped northward over the Alps in the Autumn. The other column wintered in the South.

In the Spring of 554, Narses concentrated 18,000 near Rome, moved south and met the marauders near Casilinum, the modern Capua.[14] The Alemanni were 30,000 strong, all infantry, armed solely for shock and protected only by shields without helmets or body armour. East-Roman generals were accustomed to study their enemy. On reaching Italy, Belisarius' first care had been to size up the Gothic equipment and tactics—so we are not surprised to find Narses familiar with the crude tactics of the Alemanni who were accustomed to ploy into a single deep column or wedge without manœuvring power.

Accordingly he prepared to fight a delaying action with his centre and envelop their mass with his wings of horse archers. Against these last the wretched Alemanni were helpless because of their fire inferiority and their lack of defensive armour. They were able to push back the Roman heavy infantry in the centre but when enveloped by the horse archers they could do nothing and were wiped out. It is said that only five escaped!

The small numbers of the armies which fought Justinian's wars illustrate not only the high standard obtained by the Imperial troops but also the flimsy character of the Arian local governments of the West. The original Vandal chieftain, with his mixed horde at his back, had been originally invited into Africa over a century

[13] Bury: Later Roman Empire, Vol. 2, 414.   [14] Hodgkin, Vol. 5, 38.

before Belisarius landed in arms. The fertile territory governed by the descendants of this horde is over 115 miles broad and nearly 950 miles long. And yet, when invaded by an Imperial expeditionary force of only 15,000 men, we find the Vandal state bursting like a bubble; worse still, only 5000 of Belisarius' force were cavalry and both actions of the Vandal war were cavalry fights.[15]

Obviously such figures show that the numerous civil population in whose territory the war was fought, remained completely passive. Half a thousand years of unbroken reliance upon a professional army had firmly convinced the masses throughout the Empire that in no war could they be expected to play an active part. The same thing is shown by Justinian's campaigns in Italy and Spain. But before considering these campaigns I digress to record an African incident which throws light upon the conditions of the time.

After the collapse of the Vandal state, the survivors of the army which had formed a privileged class in that state were given the chance to enlist in the Imperial army. Since their alternatives were slavery or death the poor devils naturally accepted and were embarked for Constantinople *en route* for the Persian frontier. Those who arrived seem to have served obediently enough inasmuch as we hear of no mutiny. Indeed they had little choice as they had no chance of getting home. The prospect of deserting to the Persians cannot have appealed to them. But 400 of them turned their ship about at Lesbos and returned to Africa with a favouring wind. On landing they found that half the Imperial garrison was in mutiny for arrears in pay. Moreover, the mutineers had been joined by that permanent component of Roman anarchy —runaway slaves. The 400 Vandals joined them and the mutiny dragged on for some time before being finally put down.[16]

Justinian's conquest of Italy, although a longer business than that of Africa, was achieved by campaigns of the same sort. As in Africa, the population was friendly to the Imperialists but inert and passive in the war. The disproportionately small number of regular troops, when compared with the large area to be conquered, is even more striking. The flimsy Ostrogothic state (its dynasty was still Ostrogothic and its small, highly privileged military caste may still have contained traces of its far-off Ostro-

[15] Hodgkin, Vol. 3, 598.   [16] Hodgkin, Vol. 4, 27–37.

gothic origin) controlled not only Italy and Sicily but also south-eastern France to the Rhone together with Dalmatia, Croatia, Switzerland and lower Austria to the Danube. Belisarius success-fully attacked in 536 with less than 9000 regulars.[17] One is re-minded of the collapse of the Neapolitian Bourbons before Gari-baldi.

It is true that there was another Imperial army operating east of the Adriatic, but that force was even smaller—3000 or 4000 men—and it was Belisarius' attack from the south that was the main blow.[18]   The Goths were not much more numerous; they could muster only 15,000 to besiege Rome when it opened its gates to the East-Romans, not enough to surround and contain the place.[19] By this time the wastage of campaigning, plus the tiny garrisons left in Palermo and Naples, had reduced Belisarius' numbers to 7500, but by great diplomatic efforts he persuaded some of the citizens to do guard duty on the walls and tormented the besiegers so much with sudden sallies of his regulars that they raised the siege.

That the war dragged on for nearly twenty years was entirely Justinian's fault for insisting upon a divided command and for losing touch with military affairs altogether and absorbing himself in theological speculation. In the first four years when Belisarius had a free hand he so reduced the Goths that they held only a few points and those north of the Po. Most of the fighting was position warfare, i. e., sieges. Italy was full of citadels, and whichever side had the upper hand would try to peg out a larger area of occupa-tion by throwing forward tiny garrisons, or by besieging the en-emy's advance strong points. When in 552 Justinian for the first time raised a large army, Narses promptly broke the back of the Goths for him in the following year at Taginæ.

Of Justinian's conquest of southern Spain we know very little. It was undertaken by local troops from the province of Africa and the operations seem to have been like those in Africa and Italy.[20] Andalusia, the richest and most thickly populated part of the pen-insula, was garrisoned, and although we hear of no further expedi-

[17] Young, Vol. 2, 217.
[18] Hodgkin, Vol. 4, 2.
[19] Bury: Later Roman Empire, Vol. 1, 392. Hodgkin's high figures can-not be reconciled with the events of the siege.
[20] Bury: Later Roman Empire, Vol. 1, 415.

tionary forces being sent out, nevertheless some cities held out against the feeble Visigoths until about 623 A. D.

Up to Justinian's death in 565 the Roman armies had never fallen back before military pressure. We have seen that the original loss of centralized administration in the West (except for the east coast of Britain and perhaps the upper Danube country) had come about through political rearrangement and not through military defeat. Now Africa, Italy, Dalmatia and southern Spain, a good half of the western Provinces, had been returned by arms to the direct control of the Emperors. The army which had been the instrument of their recovery was still incomparably the finest in the world.

CHAPTER IV

THE EAST-ROMAN ARMY

(AFTER THE DEATH OF JUSTINIAN, 575–1079 A. D.)

AND THE DARK AGES IN THE WEST, 451–1000

In the last three chapters we have considered the transformation of the Roman professional army from Augustus to Justinian. I now propose to follow that army down to the loss of its corporate tradition, and to discuss the change of military system in the West from professional to feudal forces.

Soon after the death of Justinian in 565, the Roman Empire enters upon a period of shrinking frontiers. It is true that, until the beginning of the Mohammedan conquests in 634, the underlying cause of the shrinkage was financial rather than military weakness. If the loosely organized Visigothic state was able successfully to besiege the Andalusian cities one by one, it was because Constantinople could not afford to raise and transport armies to relieve them. If the Lombards were able to spread themselves over much of Italy, it was for the same reason. The same thing is true of the Slavic occupation of the interior Balkans except that the early Slavs were quite willing to do homage and pay tribute to the Empire. Moreover, both Lombards and Slavs entered depopulated provinces where there was land enough and to spare, so that newcomers were welcome. The population of the Empire had long been on the decline and in Justinian's time a severe epidemic of plague made matters worse. This depopulation had helped produce the financial shortage which was aggravated not only by Justinian's far-flung campaigns but also by his passion for building. Religious troubles had increased Justinian's military tasks. He had to keep large forces in Egypt, in order to hold down the heretical Monophysites of the turbulent city of Alexandria. Finally, there was increased pressure upon the Persian frontier, always the chief military liability of the Empire, and this pressure continued throughout the reigns of Justinian's successors, so that there was no chance to get together a surplus in the exhausted treasury.

There is need here to repeat the discussion as to whether the Romans would have done better had they relied upon larger, short-service, armies. I have already said that, given the whole nature of their state and their great distances (as measured in the time required for troop movements), a professional long-service army was necessary to them. Axiomatically, such an army is more efficient than an equal number of short-service troops, and is therefore a smaller drain on the man-power of the community. But it is equally axiomatic that it is far more expensive in money than an equal, or even a considerably larger, number of conscripts need be. In deciding for a professional long-service force, the Roman Emperors deliberately accepted the comparatively high expense per man that such an organization involves. Down to the seventh-century Mohammedan invasions, the Roman troops were still the best in the world. If Visigoths, Lombards and Slavs were winning land from the Empire it was not because they were equally good soldiers. It was because the Roman treasury was no longer able to pay, equip and transport armies to take the field against them.

Towards the end of the sixth century the Roman army, whose long and glorious history we have reviewed, took its final definite form.

It so happens that we have from this period a sort of Training and Field Service Manual, the Strategicon of the Emperor Maurice (582–602), probably written about 579 when he was still only a General.[1] The Strategicon shows that the Roman army was still, man for man, far superior to its opponents. From it we learn that the Imperial Government was working to lessen the quasi-feudal tendency of the soldiers to attach themselves to particular generals rather than to the state and to remedy that main weakness of all long-service armies—the lack of trained replacements.

The Strategicon is a complete military manual. Its name is derived from "strategos" the Greek for "general" and might be translated "Manual for General Officers"; or from "strategeia" which would mean a Manual of Troop Leading. It embodies the correct principle that military instruction should begin at the top

[1] For the date, see Oman, Vol. 1, 173. The account of the Strategicon is from Aussaresses.

and radiate downwards throughout the army, and that it is supremely important that the higher officers should know their job. After beginning with intelligence studies of the usual enemies of the East-Romans, it takes up the civil laws concerning military service and recruitment, the different qualities of recruitment, the organization of the army in its different subdivisions—administrative and tactical—and the various staff departments charged with administration and supply. It next deals with cavalry and infantry training, then with field service, including intelligence service in the field, espionage, and counter-espionage, etc., and finally with tactics including both the morale and the mechanics of combat.

The author recommends that the conduct of war should be adapted to the tactics and organization of the enemy against whom it is waged. Thus against the Avars of the lower Danube, who were Tartar horsebowmen, the Roman commander should force the fighting, taking care meanwhile to protect his flanks and rear and above all to prevent surprise. Against the Lombards and other Western peoples he should do exactly the opposite and never willingly accept battle except under peculiarly favourable circumstances, for these peoples are fierce fighters. On the other hand they are careless as to their flanks and against surprises; their supply departments are ill-organized so that if the campaign be spun out they are likely to go home in disgust. Maurice describes the Lombards as mounted lancers. The Slavs who are all infantry are formidable only because of the difficult nature of their country. They can easily be beaten if the Roman army be not ambuscaded or surprised in a wooded defile. Against the Persians, the most dangerous enemy of all, the Roman commander should put forth all his skill. Whenever he can he should support his cavalry with good infantry.

The section dealing with recruitment tells us that the old theoretical liability to universal military service was still maintained as it had been ever since Augustus. The army was conscript as it had been at least since the fourth century. The various units are of unequal value and it seems almost certain that at least some of the crack corps are still barbaric in recruitment. However, the author bases no hard and fast distinction upon this, but solely upon military value. In any case, the barbarian element was less important than formerly. The crack units were privileged in many ways, particularly so with regard to the number of camp followers or armed personal servants allowed them. The Bucelaries, as the personal escort of the Generals were called, were allowed as many of these as they chose. The cavalry of the line had one follower for every seven soldiers. All told, an army of 20,000 cavalry would have between four and five thousand followers.

The chief administrative and tactical unit is the "tagma," that is the company or troop. This unit is evidently the successor of the "numerus" as it is sometimes called "arithmos," the Greek translation of "numerus." It is also sometimes called a "band." Each tagma is divided into platoons of 100 and squads of 10 men. The fact that Maurice makes it only 300 strong, whereas the old numeri numbered 1000 men, may perhaps be explained by the decline of the total numbers of the Roman army. By Maurice's time the actual tagma may well have remained far below its original paper strength for so long a time that it seemed best to him to reorganize on the smaller basis.

Whereas in Justinian's time we hear of no echelon of command intermediate between the numerus and the army commander, Maurice organized a system of higher echelons (brigades and divisions we should call them). Previously the numerus or regiment, 1000 strong, had been the highest organized unit. Now command in the field was to be facilitated by an organization of three or more troops or companies in brigade, and three brigades in division at the outbreak of war. Justinian's arrangement reminds us of the pre-Revolutionary eighteenth-century armies, indivisible tactically. It should be noted, however, that Maurice does not recommend permanent higher units but assumes that the general will organize them upon the outbreak of war. It is interesting to find that Maurice recommends a practice afterwards followed by Napoleon, i. e., making the higher units unequal in strength so as to make it harder for the enemy to calculate the numbers of the whole army.

Still more important were the reforms in personnel. Maurice saw clearly the danger of too high a proportion of barbarian auxiliaries and that of the undue independence of the higher officers with their large bands of personal retainers. Therefore, although he did not do away with the auxiliary or federate troops, he counterbalanced them by the encouragement of re-cruiting among hardy peoples within the Empire. He took away from the general officers their power of patronage by retaining in the hands of the Emperor himself the appointment of all officers above the rank of centurion—as we should say, of all field officers. Undoubtedly it was these measures which gave the East-Roman armies the cohesion necessary to preserve Anatolia by halting the Saracen on the line of the Taurus Mountains. Junior officers were appointed from a cadet corps, the Spatharies, of whom a contingent served in the field with the headquarters company of each general.

In equipment only one new thing is to be found, the use of stirrups. Before Augustus' time the ancients all seem to have ridden on a mere blanket and surcingle. The cavalry of the early Empire had a shaped saddle with a high pommel and cantle but before the loss of pictorial record in the fourth century we have no indication of the use of stirrups. At some time during the fifth or the first three quarters of the sixth century, stirrups began to come in, just when it is impossible to say.

The tactical importance of stirrups is self-evident. Without them the ancient horseman was always liable to be pulled off his horse by any infantryman who could seize him by the foot. With them cavalry were far more formidable.

The passages dealing with the administrative staff sections show that the East-Roman Army had highly organized supply depart-ments, medical and ambulance service, chaplain's department and pay department. The lives of the soldiers were so highly prized that the mounted ambulance men received increased pay for every seriously wounded man whom they rescued. The sections on cavalry and infantry training are interesting and thorough. They begin with recruit training and the school of the soldier and go upwards through the school of the company, the battalion, and the regiment or brigade, to that of the army.

The Field Service Regulations outline a sound service of security both on the march and in camp, together with a system of espionage and counter-espionage, rules for the examination of prisoners and for estimating the enemy's numbers. Field works and the fortification of the nightly camp are also considered.

The section dealing with combat recommends careful attention
to the supply services during action. The morale of the troops
is to be encouraged by all possible means. For Maurice, the
typical engagement is a cavalry fight. He particularly insists
on the greater mobility of cavalry and remarks that if necessary
they can dismount and fight well on foot. When infantry are
present their action is usually subordinate to that of the horse.
The reader should note, however, that it is particularly in dealing
with the Empire's strongest enemy, the Persian, that he recommends infantry support for the cavalry. He insists upon the importance of supports and reserves, of attacks upon the enemy's
flank, and of security for the Roman flanks and rear. Whenever
possible he recommends that the decisive attack should be
launched from behind cover such as that of a ridge of land. In
fact all supports and reserves are best kept out of sight until
wanted.

The infantry was definitely an auxiliary arm. Only in a country
so difficult as to hinder the movements of cavalry were the footmen
expected to play the leading rôle. Nevertheless their organization
and tactics were as carefully thought out as those of the cavalry.
Their discipline and cohesion must have been high, for we hear of
their delivering night attacks.

The tactical and administrative unit was the band or tagma,
the successor of the old numerus. Its strength was nearer four
than three hundred. Each infantry band was divided between
heavy and light troops, very much as the sixteenth-century battalion was divided between pikemen and musketeers. The East-
Roman light infantry were archers and javelin men.

In a mixed force of infantry and cavalry, if the proportion of
infantry was high they would usually stand in the centre with
cavalry on the wings and in reserve. If the proportion of infantry
was low they would be held back and would be expected merely
to stand fast and repel the enemy's counterattack if the Byzantine
cavalry charge failed.

The offensive tactics of the East-Roman heavy infantry seem
to imply the same contradiction already noticed in connexion with
Julian the Apostate's victory at Strassburg in 357—an attack with
sword and axe and yet that attack delivered in close order. We
are distinctly told that the formation was a line of close columns,

sixteen deep, with the shields of the rear ranks raised overhead as in the old siege testudo. And in the same breath we are told that the lances were hurled just before contact, like the old legionary pilum, and that the actual close fighting was with sword and axe. This contradiction vanishes if we assume that, after hurling their spears, the front ranks then deployed as swordsmen with the necessary intervals and distances. This is much what the legionaries of the republic and the early empire did after hurling their pilum. On this assumption the tactics in question, although a much more cautious, defensively minded system, nevertheless appear as a normal development, or deformation of the earlier practice. Since neither Ammianus nor Maurice mention such a deployment it remains mere assumption but an interesting and possible one. The line of columns instead of a single heavy line is also interesting. In the general conduct of war we find Maurice following directly the age-long traditions of the Roman professional army. For him the ideal of generalship is to win campaigns without fighting battles. When the decision to attack has been made, it is better to make partial rather than general attacks, and above all, to use stratagem and try to effect surprise. During sieges, when the Romans are besieging they are not to be in a hurry to assault. When they are the besieged they should beware of wasting men in sorties. Obviously such procedure tends to postpone the decision. Still it must be remembered that against most of their enemies, if the Romans could gain time, their loosely organized opponents would either commit some folly which would permit of attacking them under favourable circumstances or else, (owing to their imperfect organization) would find themselves faced with the alternative of retreat or starvation. Whereas on the other hand, a bull-headed immediate attack might involve the destruction of the Roman army if the enemy were superior in number, which was usually the case.

Within thirty years of Maurice's death, the Roman army reorganized by him had to face the Mohammedans.

As a sort of curtain-raiser to this titanic struggle, the long Roman-Persian war entered its last and most extensive phase. During the centuries of war to and fro across the Euphrates, the Romans had three times, under Trajan (98–117), Carus (281–284) and Julian (361–364) occupied Mesopotamia, while the Persians had never gone beyond Antioch. Now, however, the political position in the Eastern provinces had gone against the Imperial government. That government was orthodox-Catholic and many Syrians and Egyptians had become heretical in religion. In Egypt, matters were so bad that there were said to be only 30,000 orthodox in the province opposed to a solid mass of five or six million heretics. Since the modern mind is unfamiliar with the idea, it can never be too often repeated that from the 4th to the 17th century, politics hinged on points of religion. That the Persians, in 608–618 were able to overrun Syria and Egypt, to cross Asia Minor (which was not heretical), and besiege Constantinople was partly due to the incompetence of the reigning Emperor Phocas (602–610) but was chiefly due to heresy (and consequent disaffection) in Syria and Egypt. Heraclius (610–641) ousted them in a series of brilliant campaigns (622–628) full of stratagem and hard fighting, too. Sailing from Constantinople he landed his army in Cilicia and worked his way further east than any Emperor before or after him, dictating peace on the Iranian plateau in 628. Unfortunately the details of his campaigns are unknown. The mere geography of them proves his great ability and energy. More unfortunately still, Heraclius' reign is memorable not so much for the victories of his middle life as for the defeats inflicted upon the Empire in his invalid old age when he could no longer take the field.

Mohammed, dying in 632, left behind him a united Arabia, and a people at a white heat of enthusiasm for the conquest of the "infidel" world. His successors, the Caliphs, found Rome and Persia exhausted by recent war. In the case of Rome, there was also long-standing financial weakness, plus heresy in Syria and Egypt, the provinces nearest Arabia.

The Mohammedans, being originally desert men, preferred fighting on horseback. It had been their custom to skirmish but they now learned to charge home with the same extraordinary fanaticism which, in modern times, has made them such formidable foes in the Soudan and Afghanistan. In the apostolic age of Mohammedanism its warriors fought with the deliberate intention of seeking death. It was this spirit, and not the shortcomings of the forces opposed to them, which gave them their unbroken series of victories. It is hard enough to oppose such men with modern high-power weapons. In pre-gunpowder warfare it was even more difficult.

Besides their extraordinarily high morale, the early Mohammedans had in their favour high mobility and superior numbers. Their desert breeding and the fewness of their wants helped them to move rapidly. The fact that they were volunteers serving from religious enthusiasm and not for pay, made it possible for Arabia, in spite of its poverty, to outnumber the armies which Rome was able to mobilize. Furthermore, the early Mohammedans, like the Romans of the great conquering time, could persuade. In heretical Syria and Egypt their enthusiasm was contagious and they made converts right and left. The nearest historical parallel to the early Mohammedan conquests is the Revolutionary and Napoleonic period in France. Here again we find rapidly raised armies defeating professional troops by means of the same three factors of superior mobility, numbers, and enthusiasm. However, even the most sincere admirer of the French Revolutionary spirit must admit that the democratic theory has never aroused in men the same utter contempt for death found among the early Mohammedans and occasionally, though rarely, among their successors to this day.

The details of the early Mohammedan conquests are not clear, but the astonishing fact is that the Romans were unable to win a single battle. At the Yarmuk, the decisive action in Syria, the Romans had the upper hand all day through the superior fire power of their Armenian archers. It was near evening, when the Armenians' ammunition had run low, that at last the Moslems were able to close and get a decision.[2] Within nine years of Mohammed's death in 632, his followers had conquered the entire Near East, north to the Taurus Mountains and west to include Tripoli. Persia was entirely subjugated. It is greatly to the credit of the East-Roman military system that (after the heretical provinces of Syria and Egypt had been conquered) the rest of the Empire was able to put up so good a fight. It took the Mohammedans over fifty years to win North Africa. They did not finish the job until 709. In Asia Minor they could never get a foothold. They attacked Constantinople by sea in 672, and besieged the place for five years before they were beaten off. They besieged it again

[2] Young, Vol. 2, 443.

in 717. This time their fleet was supported by an army which was able to cross Asia Minor and the whole expedition was on a larger scale than before. Nevertheless they were forced to raise the siege in the following year, saving only a small remnant of their forces.

The two defeats before Constantinople were the real turning points of the defence of Christendom against Islam. From a military point of view, they are interesting because of the great part played in them by the new invention of Greek fire. This was either a sort of low-power explosive or else crude petroleum from Baku. It was so efficient a combustible that by its use the Christians succeeded in destroying the Saracen fleet. Tubes furnished with plungers were mounted on the forecastles of the Christian ships and from them the liquid fire was squirted upon the Saracen vessels. The fire may also have been used in catapult projectiles.

After the disastrous failure of the second Saracen siege of Constantinople in 717–718, the military position of the East-Roman Empire stabilized on the line of the Taurus Mountains. The pressure was still that of Mohammedan against Christian rather than vice versa. As late as 806 and 838 the Saracens made determined efforts to conquer Asia Minor. But with the decline of their original fanaticism, the better military system of the East-Romans became able to cope with the superior numbers and high mobility of their enemies. Each of the last two invasions, after taking an important city, found the Christian resistance so stubborn that no attempt to hold the isolated conquest was made. Saracen attacks, no matter how great the numbers of the attackers, tended to become mere raids, and two could play at that game. Nevertheless the diminished Empire maintained a force of about 120,000 men—only 30,000 less than Justinian's army.[3]

Meanwhile, the interior Balkans and most of the remaining Imperial possessions in Italy were lost. Indeed there was very little resistance there, for the entire available strength of the Empire was absorbed in the desperate effort to stand off the Mohammedans. In the Balkans the feeble Slavs were accordingly allowed to occupy all but the coast lines and to live half in vassalage to the Empire, half in independence or even in fitful hostility to it. The

[3] Bury: Eastern Roman Empire, 226.

city of Rome, and with it the greater part of Italy, were lost not through military defeat but through a political quarrel, based upon religion. The able Emperor, Leo the Isaurian, who had commanded the successful defence of Constantinople, tried to banish all statues and pictures from the churches. Opinion in Italy ran so high against any such Judeo-Mohammedan innovation that the Italian domain of the Emperors rapidly shrank to the extreme south plus the district of Venice. When later Emperors returned to the traditional use of images, the harm had been done. The Popes had tasted independence and had no intention of giving it up.

As in the case of the sixth-century conquests of the Lombards in Italy there was still another reason for the gains made by the sixth- and seventh-century Slavs in the Balkans—depopulation. In the Imperial provinces the number of the inhabitants had been going down hill for centuries. It is clearly impossible to expect stubborn resistance to invasion from districts in which, after all, there is land enough and to spare for invaders and invaded alike. The newcomers dispossess almost no one.

The foregoing paragraphs should reconcile the reader's mind to the paradoxical fact that the East-Roman Empire, confined as it was to Asia Minor and the coasts of the Balkan peninsula, together with scraps of land in Dalmatia, Venetia, and Southern Italy, possessed incomparably the best military system then existing in the world.

The question naturally suggested by this statement is why the Empire of the eighth, ninth and early tenth centuries did not use its unequalled military machine for purposes of conquest. The answer is to be found in the social and economic conditions within the Empire itself.

The level of East-Roman or, as it is now possible to call it, Byzantine civilization and of wealth was higher than anywhere else in the world. This in itself was enough to cause outside pressure upon the Byzantine state. The nature and sources of that wealth were such as to leave little reasonable motive for aggression. The great wealth which the Empire enjoyed through the Dark and early Middle Ages was not primarily agricultural but commercial and industrial. It came from superiority to the rest of the known world in arts and crafts, and also through possession of Constantinople, the world's centre of commercial exchange. These economic factors determined the military policy pursued by East-Roman statesmen. Since so great a part of their enormous riches was industrial and commercial in origin, they were far less concerned than other contemporary princes with attempts to enlarge their boundaries. Constantinople must be strategically secure and a sufficient amount of agricultural land must be held to make the Empire independent of foreign and therefore doubtful foodstuffs. But when these two ends had been assured, it was enough to hold the most defensible natural frontier, and folly to borrow trouble by attacking one's poorer neighbours. Thus understood, the cautious and unenterprising Byzantine strategy, at which the historians of yesterday were accustomed to sneer, appears reasonable enough.

The army which was the instrument of the defensive Byzantine policy was almost unchanged from the days of Maurice. Barbarian recruitment, already lessening in importance towards the end of the sixth century, had now ceased altogether. The temporary higher units described by Maurice had now become permanent, localized bodies distributed in depth. But with these two exceptions no important change can be recorded.

The army was still a permanent, professional, highly trained force, as Roman armies had been since Augustus about the beginning of the Christian era, or ever since Marius a century before that. It was still recruited by the same light conscription [4] based upon property in land which had existed at least since the fourth century. Rich men were keener to serve as officers than they had been during the later centuries of the old, universal dominion. That was only natural as the Empire grew smaller and more homogeneous, and as the old sense of world-wide security disappeared.

Except for his stirrups (which were already in use in Maurice's time) the East-Roman cataphractos, or heavy cavalryman, had not changed from his predecessors in the Imperial Army as early as the end of the second century. Like them he was fully armoured in scale mail, and like theirs his mount was armoured on the head, chest and shoulders. Only in the gravest emergencies, when there was a serious shortage of equipment, the scales of the armour might

[4] Leo the Wise: Tactica, Bk. 4, sec. 1, quoted in Oman, Vol. 1, 189.

be made of horn instead of metal, or even heavy leather shirts might be worn.

Like his predecessors in the Imperial service ever since the fourth century, the mail-clad Byzantine horseman was the chief reliance of armies. His tactics were exactly what they had been at least as early as the second half of the sixth century under Maurice. In fact, given the conservatism of the Roman service and the high level of intelligence throughout the Empire, it seems probable that Maurice's tactical method was already old in his day. With its provision for successive shocks, combination of frontal and flank charges, general elasticity and suppleness, it could hardly have been improved. Ambuscades and concealed turning movements were especially cultivated. There was a regular service of security in camp, on the march and in combat. The administrative and staff sections were unchanged since Maurice's time; and the signal service introduced, or perfected, under Justinian, was now carried so far that a Saracen raid in the Taurus, 400 miles straight away, could be signalled almost at once to Constantinople by a series of beacon fires.[5] At the warm springs of Dorylæum there was a huge military bathing plant capable of accommodating 7000 soldiers at once.[6]

The high ability and careful attention to detail evident throughout the Byzantine army system is particularly found in their intelligence studies of their enemies. In the "Tactica" of the Emperor Leo the Wise, written about 900, it is most interesting to see how the strong and weak points of each opponent are appreciated and measures recommended to neutralize the first and strike at the second.

The proof of the pudding is in the eating; and the excellence of the Byzantine army is shown by its success in defending for centuries the richest and therefore the most attacked state of the known world. In particular the success of the East-Romans in turning back the fanatical Mohammedan, and holding against him not only Constantinople but also all Anatolia west of the Taurus, has been insufficiently admitted. Their temporary checks have been dwelt upon by Western historians, and their victories have been ignored, such as that of the year 863 when a great Saracen army

---

[5] Bury: Eastern Roman Empire, 247.
[6] Bury: Eastern Roman Empire, 229.

was surrounded and completely destroyed by the well-timed concentration of the forces of ten separate "Themes." Any practical soldier can testify to the high degree of skill required for so elaborate a concentration in the face of the enemy. In Italy they held Apulia and Calabria, the toe and long heel of the boot, against all comers until late in the eleventh century.

That the East-Roman military system was superior to its rivals is additionally proved by the tenth- and eleventh-century expansion of the Empire.

Towards the end of the ninth century, political disintegration began to split up the enormous Saracen State. Now it was Saracen pressure that for two hundred years had been the greatest military liability of the East-Romans. Once this pressure was removed, they began to advance on all fronts and their advance went on from about 950 to after 1050 A. D.

In the Mediterranean they recovered Crete, Cyprus, and part of Sicily. On the Eastern frontier, advancing by little steps in the immemorial Roman fashion, they took first Cilicia, then Antioch (the great metropolis of northern Syria). The Emirs of Aleppo and Tripoli were made vassals. Farther to the north, Edessa beyond the Euphrates, together with all of Armenia, was added to the Empire. In Europe the entire Balkan peninsula was conquered and held up to the line of the Danube.

However, about the year 1000, although the East Roman military expansion was still going on, the economic position of the Empire began to change for the worse. The enormous wealth of Constantinople had been derived in part from the superiority of her arts and handicrafts to those of Western Christendom, and in part from her seaborne carrying trade. Now the West, where the level of civilization had been sinking lower and lower ever since the beginning of the Dark Ages, suddenly began a rapid recovery. Improved local arts and manufactures began to lessen the demand for Byzantine goods. The commercial Republics of the Italian coast began to compete with Byzantine shipping. The decline was gradual. Her vast accumulations made Constantinople still the richest city in the world. Nevertheless a professional army is always expensive in money and therefore the shrinking of Byzantine profits was a serious thing for the Imperial army. At the same time it seems that the civilian element in the Imperial bureaucracy was jealous of the army and correspondingly anxious to cut down military expenditure. Furthermore, without the backing of a warlike population, a professional army is necessarily brittle.

In such a state of things, a single great disaster in battle at Manzikert in 1071, followed by ten years of civil war, was enough to lose Asia Minor and thereby to break the immemorial tradition of the Roman service.

About the middle of the eleventh century a new enemy, the Seljuk Turks, began to press the Roman eastern frontier. They were formidable from their numbers, their savagery, and their fanaticism, for they were recent converts to Islam. On the other hand, they were horse archers pure and simple, and the tactical method worked out by the Romans for dealing with such troops had always been particularly successful. Briefly, that method consisted: first, in supporting the cavalry by infantry and especially foot archers who could always gain a superiority of fire over the horse archers; second, in never going all out in pursuit of the elusive swarms of the enemy unless there was an obstacle against which he could be pinned; and third, in taking pains with the service of security at all times, including security on the flanks and rear during combat. The rash Emperor Romanus neglected the first two rules and the treachery of one of his chief subordinates laid open the Roman rear and brought disaster.

The action took place far to the east at Manzikert near Lake Van. Romanus had concentrated all available mounted troops in a single great field army of over sixty thousand. He seems to have had no infantry with him except perhaps a campguard. Having established contact with the Turks in an open plain, he drove them before him, but could do them no serious harm because of their greater mobility. When fatigue and the approach of night compelled a retreat towards camp, the Romans had suffered less than the enemy. During the retreat, the encircling Turkish tactics were favoured by the treachery of the commander of the reserve. When Romanus ordered a halt to beat off the pursuing Turks, the reserve kept on towards the camp. Thereupon, the higher units still in action were beset on all sides by the Turkish skirmishers and drifted further and further apart in the twilight, until at last disorganization set in. The Emperor was captured and the Roman army virtually destroyed.[7]

Given the brittleness of a professional army based upon an unwarlike population, such a terrific smash as that of Manzikert jeopardized the whole military position of the Empire. When to such a peril there was added ten years of constant civil war it is no wonder that 1081 saw the Turks established on the eastern shore of the Marmora. Antioch held out behind her great walls until 1084, but of Asia Minor the Romans retained nothing except a few scraps of coast. The districts which had been the heart of the Empire were permanently turned into deserts by the savage and barbarous Seljuks.

A bit of military statistics shows how sudden and appalling was the collapse. The contingents of the standing army formerly recruited from Asia Minor have been estimated at 120,000 men. In 1078, only seven years after Manzikert, their survivors who could be mustered for service numbered only 10,000.[8]

The corporate tradition of the Roman service was broken. The Emperors and their generals might still show flashes of the old tactical skill. For a century after Manzikert, they might even win brilliant victories. But they won them at the head of an army that was little more than a hodge-podge of ill-assorted bodies of foreign mercenaries.

In 1071 the Roman service had been chiefly a cavalry army ever since Theodosius—about seven hundred years. It had been a professional force ever since Augustus—eleven hundred years. Since there is no reason for rejecting the date of the foundation of Rome itself in 753 B. C., we may say that the army that marched to Manzikert was heir to a continuous military tradition of over eighteen centuries.

I now turn from Eastern to Western Europe, from the armies which took orders from the Emperor, to those forces maintained (from the fifth century on) in the autonomous provinces of the West. The reader must not imagine that the appearance in the West of local governments practically independent of Constantinople implied a break in the tradition of Roman civilization by which those provinces lived. Indeed the tradition of Europe

---

[7] Oman, Vol. 1, 219–221.

[8] Oman, Vol. 1, 223, quoting Nicephorus Bryennius, Bk. 4, sec. 4.

(of which we in America are a part) remains Roman to this day. The new local governors were, for the most part, Roman in education. The tiny auxiliary units which followed them were of mixed recruitment despite their far-off tribal names which had been fossilized as mere labels in the Roman army list.

Nevertheless, the assumption of local power in the West by barbarian-born men, who necessarily suffered from the mental limitations of the barbarian, was an important step in the decline of the fatigued Roman society. Whereas Constantinople remained the capital of a highly civilized State, in the West the level of civilization sank lower and lower.

On the military side, the mark of the decline in Western civilization is that armies ceased to be professional and became feudal. In other words, the soldier, instead of serving a government which paid him, followed into battle an overlord who had guaranteed his land titles in return for his promise of military service. This capital change, appearing in the ninth century, determined the composition of armies until the sixteenth.

However, before discussing feudalism it is necessary first to appreciate the long survival of heavy infantry as the chief arm in Gaul. In the last chapter we saw that as early as the battle of Mursa in 315 A. D. the Roman troops stationed in that province were better infantry, although worse cavalry, than those from the eastern part of the Empire. Even after Theodosius' reorganization of the Roman army in 380 the infantry seems to have retained a greater importance relative to cavalry in Gaul than elsewhere in the Roman world.

Britain may be left out of account as military conditions there at this time are hopelessly obscure.

In the last chapter we also saw that among the local governments set up in the West by Roman commanders of barbaric descent, the Frankish state in Northern Gaul was exceptional because the Frankish dynasty was not Arian but Catholic in religion. It was therefore in sympathy with the mass of the provincials; whereas the other local governments of the West were disliked by the provincials because their dynasties and privileged classes were Arian heretics. The Frankish dynasty had another advantage, in that its territory included a large section of the frontier between civilization and barbarism, to wit, the Rhine. Since the Imperial

Roman armies had been stationed chiefly along the frontiers, the Franks inherited, as it were, a far larger number of the old localized Roman units than did the barbarian local governors of Spain, Africa and even of Italy. Accordingly the armies of the Arian chieftains of Spain and Italy were organized as cavalry and light infantry just as they had been when they served as auxiliary units in the armies of the centralized Empire. In Gaul, on the other hand, the army commanded by the Frankish chieftain was organized on the traditional Roman plan stiffened by the presence of heavy legionary infantry. We are distinctly told by Procopius that the Roman frontier troops of the Rhine command took service under Clovis (481-507) and that in the middle of the sixth century they were still equipped in the traditional Roman fashion, including the heavy nailed military boots, and still carried the Roman standards.[9] Modern historians who consider the Frankish chroniclers mere pedants because they continue to write of "legions" and "cohorts" may be entirely mistaken. The terms may still have been entirely applicable, for we cannot tell how long true legions were still organized. Indeed our general knowledge of the Frankish state tells in favour of the idea of continuity. No Frankish king before Dagobert (629-639 A. D.) put his name on the coinage. The Roman road system was systematically kept up and may even have been enlarged up to the eighth century.

Unfortunately we know practically nothing of the details of all this; tactics, for instance, are a blank. We cannot exactly fix the site even of the most important actions, such as the defeat of Attila in 451, the victory of Clovis over the Visigoths in 507, and that of Charles Martel over the Mohammedans in 732. Only the chance phrase of a chronicler informs us that heavy infantry was present against Attila, who makes a speech to his troops telling them to despise the Roman "testudines," i. e., their legionary infantry formed in solid masses.[10] All the knowledge we have of Charles Martel's tactics is a chronicler's metaphor that at Tours, Poitiers, or wherever the battle was actually fought, the Christians "stood motionless as a wall; they were like a belt of ice frozen together and not to be dissolved as they slew the Arabs with the sword." [11]

---

[9] Procopius: De Bello Gothico, Bk. 1, sec. 12, quoted Oman, Vol. 1, 53.
[10] Jordanes Gothicus, quoted Hodgkin, Vol. 2, 130.
[11] Isidorus Pacensis, quoted Oman, Vol. 1, 58.

This unmistakably suggests an infantry engagement, although it is so vague as to permit the supposition that the Frankish nobles were already accustomed to fight on horseback and dismounted merely to stiffen their infantry.

The strategics of the turning back of the Saracen tide in the West are simple enough. Compared with the great armaments which had attacked Constantinople, the considerable Mohammedan forces operating in Gaul must have been mere detachments. Their first check was experienced when Toulouse successfully stood a siege in 720. In 732 a considerable force crossed the western Pyrenees and again attacked Toulouse, just as Wellington did in 1814. Unlike Wellington, the Moslems were beaten off. Instead of retreating they started off on a huge plundering raid, sacked Bordeaux, and made for Tours, attracted by the riches of the Shrine of St. Martin there. With such an important centre of population and communication as Toulouse untaken in their rear, it is impossible to think of the move north as a regular campaign. It was no more than a raid in spite of its large scale. Somewhere between Tours and Poitiers they were met and defeated by Charles Martel. The battle, fought just a century after Mohammed's death, marks the turning of the tide in the West. Thenceforward the Saracen was no longer a mortal danger but rather a constant irritant.

After 732 the Saracens' ability to irritate sprang from sea power. They held all the Mediterranean islands, and, although they could generally be kept out of the Ægean and Ionian Seas, they were always harrying the Provençal and Italian coasts. They even fortified and held headlands in the western Riviera and the Latian coast, and bedevilled the Campagna up to the gates of Rome.

In the ninth century appeared the Viking pirate, who was even more dangerous than the Saracen. He was a bolder and better fighting man. He was particularly formidable in dealing with islands, like Ireland and Britain, or with a coast deeply cut by navigable rivers such as that of Gaul from the Rhine to the Garonne. Sometimes he would sail around Spain and raid up the Rhone. His seamanship was admirable, and when he temporarily cut loose from his ships he was always careful to leave them beached under the protection of a stockade and a garrison. On such occasions he would secure mobility by stealing horses from the countryside although he would always fight on foot. Although his object was plunder he had no objection to fighting when attacked, and he soon learned all the siegecraft of the time.

Success encouraged the Vikings until piracy became the chief Scandinavian industry. They became so bold that they would winter on islands or defensible promontories in hostile territory, and push their mounted raids deep into the country. They ruined Ireland. They came within an ace of ruining England in Alfred's time, and they besieged Paris. Towards the end of the ninth century they brought Christendom lower than we have ever been brought before or since. Such an achievement on the part of men who were, after all, only bandits on a large scale indicates exceptional military weakness on the part of the civilized society attacked. What were the conditions of that weakness we shall see in a moment, when we consider the means to correct them.

Besides the Saracens and the Vikings, the third scourge of Christendom during the Dark Ages was the Magyars. These were a tribe of Tartar horsebowmen, originally no doubt from the Steppes of Central Asia or Southern Russia. Late in the ninth century, just after the worst of the Viking raids had passed, they established themselves in what is now Hungary. They had no bases like the Viking ship camps, nor were they skilful besiegers of cities like the later Vikings, but depended altogether upon their extraordinary mobility. This was so great that even when in great force they could often outstrip the unsystematic news-bearing system of the time and surprise peaceful districts before their approach was known. In battle, their method was to avoid hand-to-hand fighting and circle around their enemy, pouring in arrows, to retreat when charged, still firing; and if possible to lure their opponents by feigned flights, into some trap of unfavourable ground. Their horsemanship may be judged by the extent of the last and worst of their great circular raids, that of 954 A. D. Starting from Hungary they devastated Bavaria and what is now Württemberg and Baden, crossed the Rhine near Worms and pillaged as far north as Maestricht and as far west as Laon. From Champagne they moved into Burgundy, where for the first time they met with resistance. Accordingly they crossed the Alps, hurried across Lombardy and Venetia, and got back again to Hungary, a circuit of nearly 2000 miles.

The reason for the extraordinary weakness of civilized Christendom in the face of the Saracens, Vikings and Magyars was the complete paralysis of initiative among populations accustomed for seven hundred years (from Augustus to the dynasty of Charlemagne) to Imperial bureaucratic government, supported by a professional army. Both government and military service had so long ceased to concern the average man that he had become sheeplike. Now that ever-increasing impoverishment and slackness had weakened the central government's power to defend him and every district must beat off the heathen robbers for itself, he put up a poor fight. Even where he was willing, the poverty of the time denied him proper equipment. He utterly lacked mobility and the habit of arms.

The remedy chosen was feudalism. In the high Imperial time there had appeared a very rich class which had administered local government. Wealth had remained highly concentrated although the rich had become countrymen instead of townsmen. In the second half of the ninth century, those local magnates were one by one given, or permitted to assume, hereditary lordship and especially military command over the countrysides which they dominated. The Counts and Dukes who administered whole provinces, each containing many local lords, achieved hereditary powers. All these "feudal" lords were expected to keep always on foot, at their own expense, a band of fully equipped troops who were their personal followers, exactly as the 5th- and 6th-century Roman commanders of auxiliaries had done. Even certain rich Roman landed proprietors in the countrysides of the lower Empire [12] had done the like. Earlier in this chapter we have seen that the Roman conscription ever since the 4th century had been based not upon population but upon the holding of property in land. Of course such localized troops could not be kept long away from home. As early as the reign of Charlemagne, about 800 A. D., we find the Imperial laws establishing limits of time beyond which men could not be forced to keep the field at their own expense outside their own district. [13] The Western world was beginning to return to the principle of short service.

Such a system solved the all-important 9th-century problem

[12] Lecrivain: Soldats privés du Bas Empire; in Mélanges de l'école de Rome, Vol. C, 1890.
[13] Boutaric, 73–80.

of local defence. For campaigns on a large scale it had obvious weaknesses, for even if the contingents of the great vassals were fairly uniform in equipment and training, still the loyalty of these contingents would be to their immediate superior rather than to the king or other commander-in-chief. Furthermore the service was short—usually only 40 days. Accordingly discipline was apt to be bad. Only under exceptional circumstances, to quote Belloc, "upon occasions at long distances from home, and after long companionship in the field, if there were also present a very leading character among the feudal superiors, and especially if that character were clothed with titular rank . . . could the typical feudal army achieve unity of command." [14]

I repeat, the idea of raising an army by summoning various lords each to bring his vassals, could not have arisen except in a time in which the problem of local defence was paramount. It is idle to enlarge upon the shortcomings of the feudal system. The men of the 9th century had to use the social forces ready to their hand. Just so, no statesman of to-day can long persuade our town-bred proletariat to behave like independent self-supporting citizens.

The formula of feudal law was that each great vassal "held his lands of the king," i. e., the king guaranteed his title to them and in return he owed the king so many "knights," i. e., fully armed and armoured cavalrymen, for a certain number of days in the year, exclusive of defence of his own locality for which he was fully liable at all times.

The new magnates were also expected to keep in repair at least one highly fortified point or "castle" for their own domicile and a refuge for their poorer neighbours. Town fortification was encouraged.

Fortification saved invaluable time and feudal cavalry were exactly the troops needed for the emergency. Even in small numbers they could enormously lessen the area subject to loot, by hanging on the flanks of the raiders, especially the Vikings who were the worst raiders of all, and cutting off stragglers. Being mounted, they could concentrate quickly. Being fully equipped and well practiced in arms, they could smash the bandits when they had caught them. Of course the new methods would have

[14] Belloc: Crécy, 84–85.

accomplished little had the morale of society continued to decline, but it did not. Christendom discovered just the necessary degree of vigour within itself to use the new methods successfully against the gravest of all her perils. By the end of the 9th century the tide was turned against Vikings and Saracens, and soon after the middle of the 10th the Magyars were broken. The crucial date is the successful resistance of Paris to a Viking siege in 886 A. D.

This siege of Paris (885–886) merits description not only because of the immense political importance of the successful defence but also because we know its details better than those of any other siege from Justinian's wars in the 6th century to the Crusading sieges in the 12th.[15]

Besides the importance of the place in itself, its position on an island in the longest navigable river in France, the Seine, made it a protection to the country further upstream. The city had a wooden bridge to each bank of the river. The bridge piers had stone foundations, and each bridge had a fortified stone bridge-head although the northern one was unfinished. The Danes sailed up the Seine in great force, carried a fortified bridge at Pontoise, and appeared before Paris, November 25, 885. They promised to leave the city alone if permitted to pass upstream under the bridges, which was refused. They then assaulted the northern bridge-head but failed, and next morning found that the defenders had doubled its height with a wooden superstructure. Until February 26, 886, they vainly attacked it with every device known to ancient siege-work at its best, except catapults. Of these the besieged had a number, and were therefore able to retain fire superiority until late in the siege. On February 5th a flood carried away a section of the northern bridge while the bridge-head was held by only 12 men whom the besiegers were able to smoke out. Curiously enough, since their aim was plunder and since the fall of the bridge opened to them the unprotected interior of the country, the pirates stayed on instead of moving upstream. In March a relieving force appeared. The place was reprovisioned, the northern bridge restored, and the bridge-head built up again.

After this, although the relieving troops retired, communication with the outside world was kept up after a fashion. In May a surprise attack came near success but failed. In June a second attempt at relief was defeated. Soon afterwards the pirates delivered a last assault which proved to be the crisis of the siege. By this time they had built so many catapults that they had fire superiority. With this advantage they attacked the place on all sides but were again, and this time finally, repulsed. Whereupon, having learned that the feeble Emperor, Charles the Fat, had gathered a great army, they were glad to take a bribe from him to quit Paris, and ravaged for a while further to the south. This lame and impotent conclusion did not spoil the moral effect of the successful resistance. Afterwards Viking defeats were more numerous than victories. It was the turning point in the peril of all our civilization.

CHAPTER V

GENERAL DISCUSSION OF FEUDAL WARFARE, TOGETHER
WITH THE CAMPAIGN OF HASTINGS, 1066 A. D.

FEUDALISM, through which ninth-century Christendom had been
able to beat off the Vikings, endured as the framework of society
for over half a thousand years. Its persistence enables us to treat
as a whole the period extending from the ninth to the sixteenth
century. I therefore begin this chapter with the general discussion
of military conditions throughout the period.

It so happens that we have an outside description of the early
feudal type of armies from the critical pen of an enemy, the East-
Roman emperor Leo the Wise, who reigned at Constantinople
about the year 900.

The Franks and Lombards are bold and daring to excess, although the
latter are not all that they once were: they regard the smallest movement
to the rear as a disgrace, and they will fight whenever you offer them battle. When their knights are hard put to it in a cavalry fight, they will turn
their horses loose, dismount, and stand back to back against very superior
numbers rather than fly. So formidable is the charge of the Frankish
chivalry with their broadsword, lance, and shield, that it is best to decline
a pitched battle with them till you have put all the chances on your own
side. You should take advantage of their indiscipline and disorder; whether
fighting on foot or on horseback, they charge in dense, unwieldy masses,
which cannot manœuvre, because they have neither organization nor drill.
Tribes and families stand together, or the sworn war-bands of chiefs, but
there is nothing to compare to our own orderly division into battalions and
brigades. Hence they readily fall into confusion if suddenly attacked in
flank and rear—a thing easy to accomplish, as they are utterly careless
and neglect the use of pickets and vedettes and the proper surveying of the
countryside. They encamp, too, confusedly and without fortifying themselves, so that they can be easily cut up by a night attack. Nothing suc-
ceeds better against them than a feigned flight, which draws them into an
ambush; for they follow hastily and invariably fall into the snare. But
perhaps the best tactics of all are to protract the campaign, and lead them
into hills and desolate tracts, for they take no care about their commissariat, and when their stores run low their vigour melts away. They are
impatient of hunger and thirst, and after a few days of privation desert·

100

their standards and steal away home as best they can. For they are destitute of all respect for their commanders—one noble thinks himself as good as another—and they will deliberately disobey orders when they grow discontented. Nor are their chiefs above the temptation of taking bribes; a moderate sum of money will frustrate one of their expeditions. On the whole, therefore, it is easier and less costly to wear out a Frankish army by skirmishes, protracted operations in desolate districts, and the cutting off of its supplies, than to attempt to destroy it at a single blow.[1]

This passage is of the utmost interest. From it we see at once that we are dealing with a level of civilization lower than that of ancient Rome or mediæval Constantinople. The Romanized provinces of the West no longer maintain highly organized, professional armies. For want of regular echelons of command, their troops manœuvre with difficulty. They are undisciplined. They have no service of security and no staff departments. On the other hand, they are full of fight, and of a sense of military honour.

Of course Leo's interest was the purely practical one of how best to oppose the Westerners. His account of them must therefore be supplemented by some consideration of the social conditions underlying the simple organization of feudal troops.

Throughout western Christendom in the early Middle Ages agriculture, rather than industry or commerce, was the chief source of wealth. Indeed this is true of all simple times. Feudalism was based upon a combination between agriculture and military service. The cultivator, who was in practice almost a free peasant, was not in legal theory the owner of his land. Theoretically his land was owned by a local lord to whom he must pay certain fixed dues in amounts fixed by custom. In return the lord with his household of armed retainers was bound to protect his dependents. The local lord in turn owed military service to some great lord who on his side guaranteed the local lord's land titles. Thus all vassals were required to fight in defence of the territory of their feudal superiors, and in return were entitled to protection.

Feudalism was not essentially an oppression. The fixed dues paid by the cultivator were but a small part of his total produce. They were more of a tax (payable to those who governed and fought) than a rent. These small dues once paid, no man could be dispossessed of his holding. He was secure in his tenure. Men were proud of being good lords and loyal vassals. In the Song of Roland when a fighter has performed some conspicuously distinguished service the poet says of him that he has "done great vassalage." [2] There seems to have been no higher term of praise. To any disparagement of feudalism it is answer enough to ask whether the modern proletarian is cheerfully willing to die for his capitalist employer.

On the other hand, feudalism, which had solved the all-important problem of local defence, was weak and chaotic at the top. In a time without strong central governments it was one of the simplest and most natural ways of protecting a district, but for more extensive operations it was deficient. Indeed a lover of peace might call it an admirable device for minimizing aggressive war on a large scale at any distance from home.

The limitation of feudal troops was that they were at the disposal of their commanders only within severe limitations of place and time. Although the upper class spent much of their time in individual military exercises, there was no chance for drill and manœuvre of large bodies except on the rare occasion of an actual campaign. Not only was the time within which a man was bound to follow his lord in offensive operations, outside of the territory of that lord, strictly limited in time, generally to forty days, but also it was difficult for a king or great lord to get his vassals to serve for any great length of time in distant parts of his own territory. Finally, before a combination of local lords the overlord would be powerless. It is notable that between the fifth and the sixteenth centuries we hear nothing of disciplinary executions. Accordingly, a feudal superior planning large-scale operations had first of all to get around the limitations of the feudal obligation.

He might try to pay his vassals to keep the field beyond their stipulated obligatory term of service. The difficulty there was that it would usually be hard to pay them enough to offset their natural desire to go home. He might hire soldiers of fortune, cosmopolitan mercenaries: such troops would at least stay with the colours as long as they were paid. They would serve against anyone, except perhaps their own individual feudal superiors, and therefore they were the natural resource of an overlord who wished to subdue rebellious vassals. The trouble with them was that they

[2] A good verse translation, by C. Scott Moncrieff, publ. Dutton, 1920.

were indiscriminate plunderers and could rarely be expected to endure operations involving strain for the sake of a cause which interested them only financially. An even more important limitation on the paying of vassals and the hiring of mercenaries was that no mediæval state could raise money on any considerable scale. Taxation and credit were equally undeveloped. It was the shortage of cash which enfeebled all attempts to hire men.

The greatest mediæval operations were conducted by volunteer armies, willing for some exceptional reason to disregard the limitations of feudal service. Thus the army of 50,000 men which followed William the Conqueror to England were moved by his promise of lands when that country should be conquered. The most important volunteer armies of the Middle Ages were the Crusaders to the East. Local Crusades against the Moors in Spain or the heretics of Languedoc were partial exceptions; like that of the Crusades to Palestine, their motive was religious enthusiasm, but the shorter distance to be traversed was a temptation to shorten the term of service. It was no use starting for Jerusalem unless you were willing to stay out a long time.[3]

Furthermore, it should be noticed that even these exceptional volunteer expeditions were composed of men whose whole notion of the conduct of war was derived from the short local mobilizations characteristic of the time. All mediæval campaigns and battles were the work of men accustomed only to short-service, highly localized, troops. Even the germ of regularly paid national armies is not found before the fourteenth century.

The obvious strong point of short-service troops, at their best, is the enthusiasm common to amateurs in any occupation. Their obvious weak point is that, as compared with professional armies, the mechanism of operations is deficient. Thus the tactics of short-term troops always tend to approach those of a horde or mob, although under civilized conditions they seldom fall quite as low as that.

Now although the level of civilization had fallen low during the Dark Ages, nevertheless civilization of a sort was always maintained. Indeed the primary fact about the Dark Ages is the tenacity with which Christendom, impoverished and degraded though she was, clung to the forms which had been handed down to her

[3] Boutaric, Bk. 3.

from the high Imperial time. Her titles, Emperor, King, Duke and Count, were those of the later Empire. She inherited and preserved intact the organization of the Church. Her learning was repetitive, her arts simple and sometimes even crude copies of traditional Roman forms.

So it was with the Art of War. One of the tests by which civilized man is known is his power to learn not only through observation and analysis of the present but also through records of the past. The soldiers of the Middle Ages meet this test by their study of Vegetius' book "De Re Militari." Vegetius came down from the fourth century to the Mediævals as a representative of the great past from which they had received their religion, the Latin language spoken by all their educated men, and, in general, the full tradition of their society.[4]

A more developed historic sense applied to the ancient documents (such as Cæsar) in the possession of the Mediævals, might have discovered that the Imperial Army of Vegetius' day was inferior to that of earlier times. On the other hand, we have seen that feudal social conditions tended to perpetuate a manner of conducting war which resembled Vegetius' practice and differed from Cæsar's, particularly in giving most of the offensive work to the cavalry. In many ways Cæsar's army, four hundred years before Vegetius, differed from the fourth-century Roman army far more than that army differed from those of a thousand years later, in the time of Edward III.

The direct influence of Vegetius upon mediæval warfare is proved not only by testimony that his book was the habitual reading of the educated soldiers of the time, but also by the many striking resemblances between his precepts and what they actually did.

Around 1000 A. D., he was the favourite author of Fulk the Black, the able and ferocious Count of Anjou. Two hundred years later, the "De Re Militari" was carried everywhere in the campaigns of the Plantagenets, especially Fulk's great-great-great-grandson, Henry II of England, and Henry's son, Richard Cœur de Lion. The book was popularized for court and camp by a French translation made about 1300, under the title of "The Art of Knighthood," for the word "miles," a soldier, had come to mean "knight," i. e., the soldier par excellence. Towards the end of the 15th cen-

[4] For the influence of Vegetius see Delpech, especially Vol. 2, 125-146.

tury a half dozen editions of Vegetius were among the first books printed, one of them an English translation from the Caxton press. The main point in which mediæval practice resembled Vegetian precept was in considering cavalry as the chief, infantry as the auxiliary arm. The foot are to assist charges of horse by means of missiles. When armed with spear and shield they may play the chief part in an immobile, defensive action, but Vegetius recommends that they should not attempt to advance, as this tended to break up their ranks. Being immobile they could almost never achieve a decision. Mediæval heavy infantry who disregarded this advice were invariably beaten, as were the English detachments at Hastings (1066), the Flemish and German townsmen at Bouvines (1214), and the Londoners at Lewes (1264).

In comparing ancient with mediæval war, I venture once more to remind the reader that ancient infantry never had to resist heavy cavalry equipped with stirrups. It is possible that the Greek and Macedonian phalanx could not have advanced against mediæval cavalry for fear of opening its ranks. How difficult it is to advance without breaking ranks can easily be proved by watching a contemporary war strength company trying to advance in close order under peace-time conditions across a parade ground or even on an armory floor. Even with everything in its favour it requires the highest discipline and training, and it is not surprising that in action the job was too much for all mediæval infantry except Swiss.

The European reputation achieved by the 15th-century Swiss is one of the chief indications that mediæval war was about to become modern war.

Even the Roman legions of the great time, armed with the pilum (a sort of heavy javelin) and the short stabbing sword, never had to face cavalry who could not be pulled off their horses at close quarters for want of stirrups.

But besides the main point as to cavalry vs. infantry there are a number of other striking points of likeness between Vegetius and the soldiers of the Middle Ages. They agree in considering the right as the post of honour—perhaps because of the desire to get at the enemy's weaponless left-hand side. In the mind of the Latin author, the circle, with pikes sloped forward, butts resting on the ground, is the strongest defensive formation for infantry;

we find it adopted over and over again in mediæval defensive battles. Vegetius considers a wedge-shaped formation useful for the rare occasion of an infantry offensive. We shall see it adopted by the infantry of the Flemish and Rhenish cities at Bouvines in 1214 and recommended in the manual, known as the "Siete Partidas," of Alfonso the Wise of Castile in 1260. As to equipment, Vegetius criticizes severely the abandonment of defensive armour by his contemporaries; it was among the strongest desires of the mediæval fighting man to make his armour as invulnerable as he could. Vegetius recommends the usual mediæval practice of carrying two swords of unequal length. There are other points of correspondence such as getting the sun at your back, the use of the dragon as a common emblem for the designation flags of units, and the name dragon-bearers for the men who carried them. There is the same method of firing the wooden props used to shore up mines in siegework. Finally there is the striking fact that Vegetius speaks of the crossbow, calling it a manubalista or arcubalista. Thereafter we have no mention of such a weapon earlier than that of William's crossbowmen at Hastings in 1066.[5]

Of course we cannot be certain how much of all this was due to a general survival of Roman tradition, irrespective of any particular manual such as that of Vegetius, or how much to the mother wit of the mediævals themselves acting independently of all tradition. In general we know that the Middle Ages were strongly traditional; they preferred to develop what they had rather than to innovate. Thus it is common knowledge that their marvellous creation of Gothic architecture crowned a regular process of development. It had roots in the recent past. On the other hand, what we know of the educated men of the early Middle Ages, with their revival of the Roman law and their enthusiasm for antique philosophy, would lead us to believe that in military things there may possibly have been a certain amount of deliberate revival due to the study of documents—in this case Vegetius. In the matter of the crossbow, those direct heirs of Rome, the Byzantines, certainly knew nothing of such a weapon. The Byzantine Princess-Historian Anna Comnena has recorded her surprise at seeing the crossbowmen of the First Crusade.[6]

[5] Delpech, Vol. 2, 266, quoting "Ex Gestis Guillelmi."
[6] Oman, Vol. I, 139.

The reader must not take the men of the Middle Ages for pedants. On the contrary, all that we know of the 11th, 12th and 13th centuries—considering not only their equipment and military architecture but also their arts and crafts together with their economic, social and political arrangements—shows their temper to have been exceptionally practical. However much such men might enlarge their knowledge by study, they were not likely to lose their simplicity of aim and directness of method. I have dwelt upon the matter of Vegetius because it was for a long time the fashion to regard the men of the Middle Ages as far more crude and limited than they really were.

At all events, the popularity of Vegetius in the Middle Ages emphasizes the continuity of ancient and mediæval military thought. It is astonishing to note how these short-service troops, with all their headlong lust for fighting and their simple tactics, imitated in every way they could the permanent professional army of the later Empire.

On the economic and social side, another important survival was open-field agriculture as opposed to fields enclosed by fences. This must have existed in the fourth century or cavalry could not have become dominant over infantry at that time. We know that it existed in the Middle Ages. Indeed had it not continued, we may be sure that cavalry could not have survived as the chief arm, for obviously any system of fences would have emboldened infantry to resist a mounted charge. The Bayeux tapestry represents a mediæval plough with a forward truck resting on two wheels and a man sitting upon it exactly as men sit on the forward carriage of ploughs in the large fields of the American West.[7] In smaller enclosed fields there would more often be the necessity to turn the furrow and under such conditions a single ploughman walking behind is better able to make the frequent adjustments required.

The men of the Middle Ages, although united as to the desirability of complete armour, were limited in their power of realizing this ideal by want of money. A complete armour cost the price of a small farm. Therefore in any large force only a minority would be fully armoured and many would not be armoured at all. Besides being expensive, complete armour was heavy. Even in the chain-mail period previous to the fourteenth-century introduction

[7] Belloc: Book of the Bayeux Tapestry, Fig. 12.

of plate armour, a complete suit weighed over thirty pounds.[8] Furthermore, the chain mail had to be backed with heavy quilting or wadding to cushion the shock of a heavy blow. To fight in complete armour, and even to march in it when near contact with the enemy, was so fatiguing that it seemed desirable to spare the armoured man all possible strain. Accordingly he was normally accompanied by one or more unarmoured or half-armoured attendants who helped him put on, take off and adjust his armour, cared for his horse and performed general fatigue duties. Such attendants would themselves be mounted in order to accompany their master. Below them again were the feudal infantry, the lees or residue of the army—men too poor to afford either armour or a horse.

The reader inclined to disparage the mediæval knight because of the crowd of attendants he dragged about with him should remember that the same line of reasoning would compel him to condemn the contemporary tank, aeroplane, railroad artillery and other specialized services because of their numerous mechanics and other non-combatant personnel. Obviously, any specialized category of troops is cumbrous compared to an all-around personnel. This accusation has some force against the mediæval knight, and against the late-Roman mailed cavalryman, who also required attendants, as we have seen. On the other hand, it is equally obvious that the lower categories of all specialized services have some combatant value in themselves. Indeed we shall see in a moment that this was even truer of mediæval conditions than it is to-day. Finally, it is clear that specialized troops, with all their defects, have corresponding virtues.

The different categories of mediæval troops roughly corresponded with differences of social rank, especially at the beginning of the Middle Ages. The mediæval chroniclers used the Latin word "miles"—a soldier—in the sense of the soldier par excellence, that is the fully armoured cavalryman. This word "miles" came to have our modern meaning of "knight" with the connotations of social rank and highly developed sense of honour which our word knight implies. As time went on, however, its social significance became more important and its military significance correspondingly less so, and by the fourteenth century the number of

[8] Dean, 45–50.

"knights" in an army bore no relation to the number of fully equipped men at arms.

Finally, in connection with the different categories of mediæval troops it should be remembered that the numerical proportion of unarmoured and ill-armoured men would be large in a force raised for local defence, smaller in one which was to operate at a distance from its base, and smaller still in one which was to go overseas, inasmuch as it would not pay to arrange for the transportation and subsistence of a greater number of low-grade troops than would suffice to attend the well armed and fully armoured men.

Having considered the social conditions underlying the feudal armies and the different categories into which their recruitment was divided, the reader is now able to appreciate their tactics.

Mediæval battles divide into two classes according to the presence or absence of solid heavy infantry or dismounted cavalry on the field.

If neither side possessed solid infantry or chose to dismount a part or all of its cavalry, then the action took the form of a rapid and shifting cavalry fight. Such actions were decided by dash and by the judicious handling of reserves. Of this sort were Muret (1213), Charles of Anjou's battles (1266–1271), the Marchfield (1278), and Patay (1429).

When one side had solid infantry (or dismounted cavalry) steady enough to serve as a core or pivot for the action, then the fight developed into a sort of siege of this body. Such an action may be considered as the typical mediæval battle for it was natural for the side which felt itself the weaker to dismount all or part of its armoured men, so as to be able to stand on the defensive, which cavalry cannot do. Such a policy enabled a commander to get some work out of the low-grade components of the force under him. Obviously low-grade troops would be of little use in an attack upon the enemy's armoured men. Therefore in an attack they would play little or no part. But in a defensive they could be formed up in solid masses behind a front rank or so of armoured comrades. Man for man their part in the fighting would be far less than that of the front ranks. Still it would not be negligible, for numerically they would form by far the greater part of the mass against which the attacking cavalry would surge. Examples of this typical kind of mediæval battle are numerous. Our one scrap of information as to Charles Martel's battle near Tours in 732 seems to put it in this class. Thereafter we have cavalry attacks against infantry or dismounted cavalry at Hastings (1066), Bremûle (1119), Legnano (1176), Steppes (1213), Falkirk (1298), Courtrai (1302), Crécy (1346), and most of the Spanish battles.

As long as the dismounted troops stood fast, sheltering themselves behind a solid hedge of pikes, they were hard to break. The butt of the pike would often be rested on the ground and steadied by the right foot as recommended by Vegetius. Such a pure defensive might win by itself as at Crécy, in case the enemy persisted in attacking until the cohesion of his own force was broken. Or the dismounted men might win by a short offensive return following the repulse of repeated attacks as at Courtrai and Bannockburn.

Since true infantry as the chief reliance of mediæval armies is to be found only in impoverished districts like Scotland, Ireland, Wales, Scandinavia and Switzerland, it is not surprising to find few cases in which troops on foot assume the offensive—as distinguished from the counter-offensives of Courtrai or Bannockburn. Moreover, infantry attacks always fail, as at Bouvines (1214), Majorca (1229),[9] and Lewes (1264)[10] and as did the dismounted cavalry attack at Poitiers (1356).

Poitiers and Tinchebrai (1106), if we except lesser fights like Cocherel and Auray (1364), are the only examples before the fifteenth century of battles fought between cavalry armies in which both sides dismounted all, or by far the greater part of their horsemen. It should be noted that at Tinchebrai the side won which kept some troops mounted against its entirely dismounted enemy. And at Poitiers the Black Prince's decisive counter-attack was a mounted charge.

In a purely cavalry action the fire of dismounted archers or crossbowmen was of little effect. They were easily brushed out of the way. On the other hand, when the action centred about an immobile mass of foot, then the question of fire superiority became important. The tactical principle here is the same as that which increases the importance of artillery in position warfare. Of course the mediæval cult of armour tended to reduce the importance of archery, but we have seen that complete armour was so expensive that it could never become universal. Furthermore

<hr>

[9] Delpech, Vol. 1, 318.   [10] Oman, Vol. 1, 421–431.

the armour of the horse was seldom as complete as that of his rider. Accordingly in typical mediæval cases of a mounted attack against dismounted pikemen, fire superiority was usually decisive. Indeed it was almost invariably so.

Outside of Spain, Hungary and the East, we find no use made of fire delivered mounted. This device, so important in later Roman times, was not entirely unknown. In the pursuit scene of the Bayeux tapestry a horse archer is represented. It probably went out of general use because the fierce combative spirit and the convention of knightly honour made men want to charge straight for their enemy and decide the issue by hard knocks.

When mounted fire is used we never find it delivered by mailed cavalry equally able to charge as in late Roman times. Mediæval fire power cavalry were invariably Hungarian or Turkish light horse, armed with the bow, or Spanish javelin men. In any case they were not expected to charge home.

Incidentally the persistence of the javelin from Hannibal's Numidians to the African Moors who invaded Spain, from them to the Spanish Christians of the Middle Ages, and from them to the Portuguese (not the Spanish) bullfighter of to-day, is a curious example of continuity over nearly two thousand five hundred years. To this day the Portuguese bullfighter avoids the shock of a charging bull by dexterously wheeling his horse, and at the same time tries to knock a coloured rosette from the bull's withers by means of a light javelin much like those which helped win Cannæ and put Cæsar in peril at the Ruspina.

Mediæval strategy was always simple and direct. Immediate battle was almost always its first consideration, especially on the part of the aggressor who had to get a decision quickly before his army melted away from him. If the defender were decidedly the weaker, and if he wished to spin out the campaign, he would usually stand behind walls. Once surrounded there, his troops could not get away from him except to the enemy. Usually he would fight, for it was a point of knightly honour to protect one's vassals from ravage, and the same sense of honour made it a questionable proceeding to refuse battle on anything like equal terms, On the other hand, this simple strategy was often very good. especially in the early Middle Ages. In the fourteenth century it fell off.

So much for the general discussion of mediæval military conditions.

We have seen that, from the third century on, civilization was steadily going downhill on its material side, and that its lowest point was reached during the ninth-century Viking raids. After the repulse, conversion and incorporation of the Vikings and Magyars, Western Christendom sank into a sort of lethargy until about the year 1000. Then matters began to improve. The long dormant energies of Europe began to revive in a sort of sudden springtime. The improvement was many-sided; a general historian of the period would chiefly consider it in the new strength of the Papacy, which I mention here only to remind the reader that the politics of the time tended to turn chiefly on points of religion. The seafaring Italian cities began to drive Saracen shipping from the Western Mediterranean. Volunteers streamed out to join the men of the Pyrenean valleys in their slow, constant, southward drives against the Moslems of Spain. But in military matters, and indeed in all secular affairs, the leaders in the springtime of Europe were the Normans.

Northmen or Normans was an alternative name for the Scandinavian Vikings. In Gaul, Christendom had incorporated a number of them into its body by assigning to their chiefs the government of a considerable district, still called Normandy, about the mouth of the Seine. The move was quite in the spirit of the fifth century. Unlike the fifth-century settlements, however, the slight infusion of Scandinavian blood into the governing class of this Gallic district produced a new thing, to wit, a breed of men of greater energy and precision of mind than had been seen in the West for centuries.

The Normans made armies worthy of the name once more possible because they introduced accuracy into the surveying of land, and method into the collection of taxes. Since mediæval taxation was based on land value, a fairly accurate survey was requisite to an efficient system of collection. The tax-gatherer is the ultimate foundation of an army, as our own Regulars have been reminded since the Armistice. The Norman forces remained feudal, but the occasional employment of mercenaries became possible; larger numbers of feudal troops could be mobilized and when mobilized could be maintained for a longer time. Mailed cavalry, as everywhere else in Europe, remained the chief arm, but its tactics were improved and made regular and it could be intelligently supported by infantry armed with the bow. Furthermore, the Normans were great fortifiers. Wherever they conquered, they closely dotted the country with works so solidly built of stone that they remain to this day. The details of their fortifications and siege-work we shall discuss presently. For the moment it will be enough to remind you that in a country so covered, operations tended to become either a war of raids or a war of sieges.

At this point it is convenient to consider briefly the chief articles of eleventh-century equipment. In hardly any particular did it materially differ from that of Vegetius' time. The sword was long, straight, and two-edged, exactly as the "spatha" of the auxiliaries had been ever since the first century. Even the word "spatha " has come down to our own time as the name for a sword in the Latin languages, "épée " in French and "espada" in Spanish. The lance was light enough to be held at arm's length or even used to thrust overhand.[11] Even in the eleventh century it was sometimes "laid in rest" by holding the hinder part of the shaft under the armpit so as to counterbalance the weight of the head.

As in ancient times, the chief missile weapon was the bow, in the immemorial short form drawn to the breast. The crossbow, which was at least as old as Vegetius, was also known, for William the Conquerer had crossbowmen with him at Hastings.[12] Arguing from what we know of the time in general, we are probably safe in believing that it had remained in use, at least in Gaul, throughout the Dark Ages. The effective point-blank range of archery fire is not certain. In Roman times it must have been over 70 yards, for that was the regulation Roman interval between towers on a wall. Of course, using high-angle fire against large targets such as a massed body of men, it would be much further—over 150 yards at least.

In the matter of defensive armour, the shield was sometimes narrow and kite-shaped with a rounded top, sometimes rounded or oval with a raised boss in the centre. The helmet was usually a conical steel cap; sometimes it had a nose guard hinged at the top so that it could be raised if desired. The mail shirt usually

[11] Belloc: Book of the Bayeux Tapestry, Figs. 22, 61, 63, 65, etc.
[12] Delpech, Vol. 2, 266, quoting "Ex Gestis Guillelmi."

took the form of metal rings sewed closely on a leather jerkin with elbow sleeves. This leather base of the mail shirt might take the form of a union suit with knee-length drawers.

The cavalryman used stirrups, as his Roman predecessors had done at least since Maurice's time. He sat upon a saddle with high pommel and cantle like a cowboy saddle to-day.

A curious fact is that the mace was often used by clergymen serving as soldiers. With this weapon these holy men escaped the text "he that taketh the sword shall perish by the sword," and also the maxim that the Church abhors bloodshed.

As a specimen of eleventh-century war, we cannot do better than take the Norman Conquest of England.

We have seen that Normandy differed from the rest of Latin Christendom in degree but by no means in kind. Her administration and military science were feudal but she applied them better than was done elsewhere. So England was feudal, although her feudal system seems to have been looser than that of the Continent. The one anomaly about her military methods was that, in a defensive, English armies made great play with a huge long-handled, two-handed pole-axe known as a "Danish axe." She was rich. In the generation before the conquest many Normans had emigrated to her, and individuals among them had obtained high position. No national feeling hindered this penetration, for the time had no such feeling, and lacked clear-cut national divisions. Its politics turned either upon points of religion or upon individual loyalty to an individual feudal superior.

William, Duke of Normandy, having a claim upon the English crown, declared war against Harold, who had gotten himself crowned. He built a numerous fleet and mobilized a great army, about fifty thousand strong, including volunteers from Italy and Spain. Some of his troops were serving for pay, others in the hope of securing English lands. I repeat that we shall misinterpret entirely the moral background of these wars if we imagine that there was any such thing as national patriotism involved, for there was not. Men were proud to serve as the sworn vassals of their "lord," or else (as in William's army) they would serve voluntarily as members of a sort of military stock company for the conquest and partition of certain territories in which the commander had been denied his rights. Nor must this moral claim be likened to the purely formal claims so often put forward as justification for modern wars of dynastic or national aggression. In such a time of united Christendom no mere marauding expedition directed against Christian men could have attracted so much support. It was the whole basis of William's action that he had been designated by Edward the Confessor, the last King of England, as next heir to the throne. Furthermore, Harold had been rescued from captivity by William, had become his brother in arms and received the honor of knighthood from his hands, and had solemnly sworn upon holy relics to support William's claim. Harold's conduct therefore involved gross personal ingratitude as well as perjury.

Harold, with the feudal forces of most of his kingdom, concentrated in the south of England. A strong detachment consisting of the vassals of the two northern earldoms remained near York to oppose an expected Scandinavian invasion in aid of Harold's exiled brother Tostig.

The early stages of the campaign are notable for two extraordinary pieces of marching by Harold and for the calculated self-restraint of William. The latter, after embarking from the Norman coast, was weather-bound by northerly winds in the Somme estuary. The same winds brought Tostig and the army of his Scandinavian friends to the mouth of the Humber. They must have been in considerable force, for they had 300 ships. In an action fought just south of York, on September 20th, they destroyed the forces of the two northern English earldoms and occupied the northern capital. Note carefully the time and distances involved in what followed. Harold had marched forth, leaving London on the 16th. On the 24th—nine days—he and his army had put nearly 200 miles of road behind them and reached Tadcaster, on the great North road of the Romans, ten miles southwest of York, a splendid piece of marching even if we assume that all his troops were mounted. They can hardly have been on foot, for they were in condition for a general action on the following day, the 25th.

Harold met the Norwegians at Stamford Bridge. They were on foot, and arrayed in solid masses. He attacked them with his mailed cavalry, delivering charge after charge until at last he broke and destroyed them.

He then moved to York and there rested his sorely tried troops.

Meanwhile, far to the south, William at last succeeded in crossing the Channel. He landed at Pevensey on the 28th, the third day after Harold's victory at Stamford Bridge. It is hard to imagine how Harold, at York, could have heard of that landing before the 1st. Nevertheless, he reached London in person on the 5th or 6th. More astonishing still, the greater part of his army duplicated its nine days' march and moved south out of London on the 11th. Most astonishing of all, Harold's troops did over 56 miles in the next 48 hours and established contact with the enemy late on the 13th. Such an achievement would have been possible only to troops in high training and possessed of the finest kind of march-discipline. There must have been a well-organized commissariat and the great Roman road between York and London must not only have been well kept up as a military highway but also efficiently cleared of civilian traffic.

On the other hand, Harold's impetuosity had caused him to run unnecessary risks. The northern levies, most of them certainly on foot and even their horse inferior in quality to his own striking force, could not keep up, and the local troops from the west had not had time to join. A few days' delay would have greatly increased his numbers. As it was, his strength was about equal to that of the Normans, i. e., around fifty thousand men. But in average quality Harold's force was inferior. His own large military household, the best of his troops, had just been through a severe strain fighting and marching at top speed steadily for nearly a month with only five days' rest. The greater part of his army was unarmoured, ill-armed levies hastily swept up from the country-sides.

William's conduct contrasts with Harold's inasmuch as the Norman's action was calculated and evidently followed a predetermined plan. He had not permitted Harold's absence in the north to tempt him into a dash at London less than 50 miles away, but had kept near the south coast, throwing up entrenchments at Hastings and Pevensey to protect his ships and stores and to cover a possible embarkation should he be defeated in the coming battle. William's chances of winning that battle would be bettered should Harold seek him out, because of the long distance separating Hastings from the north and west from which reinforcement for Harold might come. Meanwhile the Normans systematically

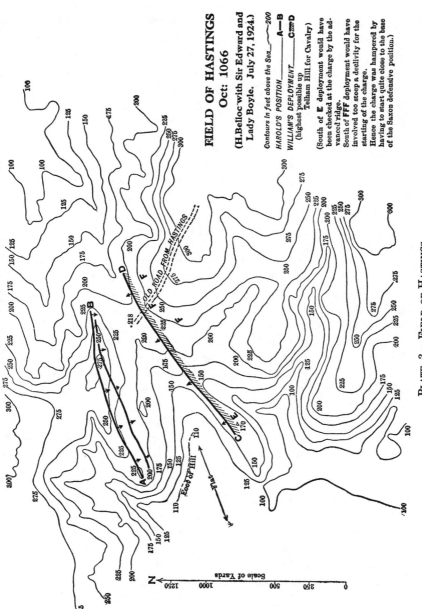

PLATE 3.—FIELD OF HASTINGS.

FIELD OF HASTINGS
Oct: 1066

(H. Belloc with Sir Edward and
Lady Boyle. July 27, 1924.)

Contours in feet above the Sea ——— 200
HAROLD'S POSITION ——— A—B
WILLIAM'S DEPLOYMENT ——— C⟹D
    (highest possible up
        Telham Hill for Cavalry)

(South of **E** deployment would have
been checked at the charge by the advanced ridge.
South of **FFF** deployment would have
involved too steep a declivity for the
starting of the charge.
Hence the charge was hampered by
having to start quite close to the base
of the Saxon defensive position.)

Scale of Yards
0   250   500   1000   1250

ravaged Kent and Sussex far and wide. William knew his man
and judged—correctly as the event proved—that this might bring
Harold to accept battle before all the northern and western contingents had joined. Over and above the strong feudal obligation
to protect one's vassals, the Englishman had the additional motive
that he himself was an usurper. The slightest sign of weakness on
his part might bring his shaky political position down about his
ears.[13]

Harold therefore advanced to the ridge which has ever since
been known as Battle Hill, about five miles from William's entrenched camp at Hastings, and there waited to be attacked. His
position was very strong. In his rear he had the great forest of the
Weald, through which he could retreat in case of a check.

Seen from the north, a little east of south, the position itself
was shaped like a "T" with a short upright which connected with
the higher ground in rear and a long cross-bar nearly a mile from
end to end. The front of the cross-bar was a long slope so steep
that cavalrymen in armour must have had difficulty in charging
up it. On the defenders' left, where it is gentlest, it is 1 in 15. Over
most of the front it is 1 in 10, and on the right it is almost 1 in 8.
Either end of the cross-bar is rounded, and between it and the
higher ground to the north are gullies not so deep as the front
slope but even steeper so as to be quite impracticable for charging
cavalry. The summit of the cross-bar itself is not quite level; it is
highest at the left centre.

There Harold posted himself with his large military household,
the flower of his army. The rest, including his masses of hastily
raised levies, stood on either side.

Incidentally, the length of the position enables us to estimate
the depth of Harold's formation. I have said that the sharply de-
fined ridge is just under a mile long, say 1500 yards. If Harold had
50,000 men his formation must have been just over 30 deep. In
itself there is nothing surprising about such a depth, for Maurice
dealing with the highly organized Roman army of the 6th century
recommends a depth of thirty-two men when light troops inter-
calate themselves between the sixteen ranks of the heavy foot.

Despite the great natural strength of the position, William was
bound to attack. The passage of time would increase Harold's

[13] For the strategy of 1066 see Belloc: "Warfare in England," 92–101.

numbers. Meanwhile the presence of the English army would limit foraging. Therefore, when contact was established late on the thirteenth of October the Duke prepared for an advance on the following day.

The Normans moved at dawn. After a march of about five miles they saw from Telham Hill the English army drawn up on the Hill of Battle opposite to them. They thereupon deployed for action in three lines; first, the lightly armed archers, then the pikemen (some if not all of whom wore armour), and last the armoured cavalry.

Like most engagements, the battle began with a fire fight. In spite of the steep slope of the hill against them, the Norman archers obtained an immediate fire superiority over the few bowmen in Harold's army. But when the Norman pikemen in their turn moved up and charged, the English received them with javelins, and with stones tied to the ends of sticks like the old-fashioned throwing-hammer familiar to athletes of a recent generation. The invaders were able to reach the English line but could make no impression whatsoever. The archers, although they had caused the English considerable loss, had not been able to shake them.

The Norman cavalry who were next to charge fared no better. Everywhere they were beaten back. Opposite the English right where the slope is steepest the repulse was so bloody that William's left fell into a panic. Now, however, came the turning-point of the action. It was vital to English success that they should stand fast on the summit of their ridge; in no other way could they meet the better armed and better disciplined Normans. Instead of standing fast, the ill-armed yokels of the English right lost their heads at the sight of the confusion among their recent assailants and rushed down the slope in pursuit. This gave William his opportunity. For a moment, indeed, the panic among his troops threatened to become general. A rumour ran down the line that he had been killed. In order to disprove it he had to raise the nose guard of his helmet and ride to and fro, showing his face to his men. But once the morale of his centre had been re-established it was easy to charge in on the left flank of the disorderly swarm of English who had tried to pursue the routed Norman left. In their disorder they were cut to pieces in a few moments. From this point on, Harold must have known that his chance was slim.

Nevertheless the next charge against the ridge, after some local and temporary success, was repulsed like the first. Thereupon part of the Norman horse either deliberately executed a feigned flight or else broke up in a second real panic. However their headlong retreat came about, it was enough to draw down another great body of the defenders, who were in their turn cut to pieces in the valley below.

This second piece of folly on the part of his own men made Harold's cause hopeless. Nevertheless his military household and the rest of his centre stood firm and rallied about them the remnants of the wings. By this time the battle had continued for several hours. Probably it was already afternoon. If by a miracle they could hold out until darkness came, they might get away.

The last stage of the action was a sort of siege of what was left of Harold's army, closely grouped upon the highest part of the ridge. Beset on all sides, the remnant of the English stood firm for hours and beat off every attack. For a time the Norman archers would shoot into the immovable target presented to them. Then their cavalry would charge, fail to break the ring, and draw off to allow the archers to shoot again. Finally, William ordered the archers to try high-angle fire. This proved effective. An arrow so shot wounded Harold in the eye. Not long afterwards a last charge got home, Harold was killed, and the English—what was left of them—broke and fled.

Even at this stage there was still some fight in the defeated army. In the twilight a number of Norman horse, plunging forward incautiously in pursuit, fell into one of the steep gullies between the cross-bar of the "T" and the higher ground farther to the north; whereupon some of the fleeing English turned upon them and inflicted considerable loss.

It is eloquent testimony to the "fog of war" and the severe strain of a day-long battle that at this point one of William's chief subordinates advised a retreat. Fortunately for the Duke, he himself was made of better stuff; he ordered the advance continued, or rather the pursuit of the beaten enemy.[14]

Completely victorious, William continued to act with method and restraint. Instead of dashing forward to London, he moved by

[14] Delpech, Vol. 2, 264–273. Oman, Vol. 1, 152–165, is still troubled by Wace's impossible palisades.

the right flank and secured Dover, the chief port of entry into the island. Then only did he march against the capital. When it was not surrendered to him at his approach, he wisely forbore to attack it. It should be noted that a first-class city was always, from its mere extent, too great to be contained by a mediæval army. The governmental finance of the time, even at its best, had not kept pace with the rapid growth of population and especially of towns. Simon de Montfort before Toulouse in 1218 and Joan of Arc's English opponents before Orleans in 1429 were unable, even with the aid of elaborate entrenchments, so much as to block-ade the circumference of the place attacked. Against London in 1066 the Conqueror contented himself with burning the southern suburb south of the Thames. He then circled westward, devastating the country systematically, crossed the Thames at Wallingford, fifty miles up river, and moved northeast. By this time those in London saw that when he reached the coast northeast of the town they would be starved out, so wide and thorough had his devastation been. They therefore sent out a delegation which met him at Berkhampstead, some 30 miles northwest of London, and surrendered to him the city and the crown. This practically completed the conquest. Since the men of the time had no such thing as national patriotism, only isolated factional risings in distant districts remained to be suppressed; and in their suppression native levies willingly assisted William, now the legitimate king.[15]

William's rapid consolidation of his conquest was possible because England was then without any highly organized system of fortification. No sooner was he possesssed of his new kingdom than he began to secure himself therein by thickly studding it with permanent works of stone. The spirit of this enormous undertaking was altogether in the Roman tradition and the individual works were known as "castles" from the Latin "castellum," i. e., a fort. The complete difference between mediæval campaigns in theatres of war without castles and those conducted in theatres closely dotted with such works is obvious. To the strategic effect of the system, and to the strategic location of individual castles, I shall return in connexion with John Plantagenet's brilliant campaign of 1216, a campaign entirely dictated by the castle system. Meanwhile I will describe the principle upon which they were sited, not

[15] Belloc: Warfare in England, 102–104.

with reference to the countryside as a whole but with regard to the actual location of their walls.

Unlike the Romans, the Normans (and with them all the other men of the Middle Ages) preferred inaccessible sites. The Romans of the high Imperial time, with their disciplined infantry, expected to hold their works easily and were always considering an active defence. Therefore, while they might prefer to build upon an elevation whose slopes would hinder assaults and give the defender's missile weapons a range greater than those of the besiegers, at the same time they would not site works upon a cliff or unduly steep hill or behind a river or marsh because such obstacles would prevent the garrison from sallying out. On the other hand, the mediævals preferred such sites to all others because, as we have seen, they normally lacked disciplined infantry altogether, and were concerned chiefly with passive defence. Therefore they were always trying to increase the number of obstacles opposed to a besieger, in order to make him win the fortress stone by stone—even if the accumulated obstacles hindered sorties. Up to 1300, they were even willing to hamper their own lateral communications in order to lengthen the besiegers' task although, as we shall see, this last policy was found to be mistaken and therefore given up.

Throughout Western Europe, no stone fortifications have come down to us from the Dark Ages. Apparently the men of those weak and troubled times used masonry chiefly in repairing some of the numerous and splendid ancient works about them. When they built on a new site, lack of money seems to have compelled them to content themselves with digging a ditch, heaping up the earth from the ditch into a mound, and crowning that mound with a palisade. Most of the forts that rendered such service against Vikings, Magyars and heathen Slavs must have been of this sort. The argument against the frequent use of stone-work in the Dark Ages is chiefly a negative one. No such stone-work has survived. However, many documents, even when not explicit, nevertheless imply that wood was the material normally used. We know that there was some stone construction—for instance in the two Paris bridge-heads which resisted the Vikings so well in 886. The analogy of contemporary church building would lead us to think that such works were exceedingly simple, heavy and squat.

The use of wood in fortification persisted into the 11th century in Western Europe, even into the early part of the 12th century. In one of the early scenes of the Bayeux tapestry, William the Conqueror's men are shown attacking with burning torches the defences of Dinant in Brittany [16]—which would of course, have been useless against masonry. Many of the Conqueror's own works with which he studded England seem to have been of wood. In Flanders, up to 1130, the local nobles were accustomed to build stockaded mound fortresses, with some sort of towers or turrets in the stockade and a citadel or keep to dominate the whole.[17] It is strange to find Flanders still so poor in the 12th century as not to be able to afford stone.

The Norman castle can easily be studied from the abundant remains still standing from Scotland to Sicily. Almost all its strength was concentrated in a single enormous tower known as a donjon or keep. There was an outer wall which enclosed a courtyard but the flankments upon it were only little turrets, not much more than sentry-boxes, and it was only a subordinate feature.[18]

The reason why the Norman military engineers preferred to put most of their money into a single tower was that it combined height and a maximum of space inside with only a narrow perimeter to be defended. Only men enough were needed to man the battlements and drop things down on anyone trying to sap the base of the wall. Increased height made it harder for the sappers to resist the fall of whatever was dropped. It also gave a more extensive view.

Sometimes the Norman keep was of the type known as a shell-keep—round with an open space in the centre. Such a work was more or less a natural development from the palisaded ring of the Dark Ages and might be used to replace it—especially as the artificial mounds might not be firm enough to stand the weight of a solid tower. The typical Norman keep was solid and square, with a square turret at each corner and often a flat strip buttress up the middle of each side. The entrance was usually one story above ground, up a stairway inside an oblong lower building resting against one side of the main structure. The masonry was rude, the stones small and separated by broad mortar joints. In the

[16] Belloc: Book of the Bayeux Tapestry, Fig. 25.
[17] Oman, Vol. 2, 12–13.
[18] Dieulafoy: Château Gaillard, 15–18, 22.

Conqueror's keep, the "White Tower" in the Tower of London, the joints are so broad that the wall contains more mortar than stone. The walls are no less than 15 feet thick at the ground level and 10 feet even at the top.[19]

In mediæval sieges we never hear of the Roman "agger," a huge mound high enough to command the defences which was established out of effective range and gradually extended towards the walls. Once it was complete the defenders had to resist storming columns advancing with a fairly broad front on a level, or even on a downward slope. No mediæval army could command the labor necessary to make such a thing.

But with the exception of the "agger," all the ancient siege devices were used throughout the Dark Ages and the 11th century. There seem to have been no new discoveries, except Greek fire, and undoubtedly the old machines were copied crudely and on a much smaller scale. Nevertheless it is surprising to find practically every one of the individual devices of ancient siege-work so continually in use.

Position warfare, as everybody realizes since the Great War, enormously increases the part played by the artillery. Up to 1100, the only known kinds of artillery were catapults worked by torsion and tension. A torsion catapult was made of a heavy timber frame with a mass of twisted rope strung across near the front. In this twisted rope was secured one end of a movable beam having a spoon-shaped hollow in its other end. This free end was pulled backwards and down by a sort of capstan or large winch at the rear of the frame, against the resistance of the twisted ropes, and the stone to be thrown was placed in the spoon-shaped cavity. The free end of the movable beam was then liberated by releasing a catch. The force of the twisted ropes then made the beam describe an upward and forward curve, moving fast enough to flip off the stone at a high angle of elevation. Such a catapult was known as a mangon, mangonel, or sling. Of course the projectiles would seldom be uniform in weight. Furthermore a wet or dry day would affect the ropes. Accordingly the shot group of such a machine was so large that it was generally used for bombarding large objectives.

A tension catapult, usually known as a ballista, was simply an

[19] Dict. de l'Arch., Articles "Donjon" and "Château."

exaggerated crossbow wound up by winches. It shot bolts or enormous arrows with great force, flat trajectory and considerable accuracy. Of course it could not penetrate walls; it was useful against small fairly distant objectives—such as men exposing themselves out of range of infantry weapons.

In making good their approach the besiegers would protect themselves against the plunging fire of the defenders behind mantlets, i. e., screens—strong but light enough to be moved as desired.

Unfortunately there is nothing to guide us in estimating the range of catapult artillery. To a man, the chroniclers are clergymen with the vaguest possible notions of military technique. Indeed their vagueness is such that they do not even name them uniformly but use all sorts of names interchangeably for the tension and torsion types.

Movable towers, as high as or higher than the defences, might be rolled up until drawbridges near their tops could be dropped upon the battlements. An assault might then be delivered up the towers and across the drawbridges. Meanwhile archers or crossbowmen posted on the tower tops would try to pick off the defenders who were resisting the storming party. It was by means of movable towers that the crusaders took Jerusalem in 1099.

The defects of the movable tower are obvious enough. It was not only heavy but top-heavy. Accordingly it could be moved forward only over ground that was smooth, level and particularly firm. Besides it needed protection against combustibles, generally by means of rawhides in front and to some extent upon its sides also. The defenders, like Red Indians besieging a frontier blockhouse, would shoot at it with arrows carrying balls of burning tow. Most effective of all would be the huge arrows from the tension type of catapult.

It was a little easier to move forward some sort of low shelter which would serve to protect an attack against the base of the defenders' walls. Such shelters were known as "cats," perhaps because their occupants were to claw their way into the wall. The Roman name for them had been "musculus," a rat, apparently because they gnawed their way in. They were fairly long, so that their occupants might come and go by the rear end (which must not be too close under the wall), and narrow and steep-roofed in proportion to their length so that they might be strong enough to resist stones and heavy weights dropped by the besieged from above. For greater strength, the roof would be steeply pointed, and protected against fire by means of rawhides.

Either the cat might be brought up within a few feet of the wall, which could then be attacked with ram or borer, or its head might be pushed up against a wall to give cover for pioneers attacking the masonry with pickaxe, hammer and crowbar. The ram and borer were both great beams, the largest that could be found, swung by chains from the ridgepole of the cat that sheltered them. They differed in that the ram had a broad solid head (like the forehead and horns of a true ram) with which it butted against the wall, whereas the borer had a pointed head intended to break down the opposing masonry stone by stone. If the wall were not too thick or too well built, the ram would crack and finally break it by repeated blows in the same spot. The action of the borer would, of course, be slower and more localized.

It is hard to see what any ram could have accomplished against a wall fifteen feet thick like those of the Conqueror's Tower of London. Nor can we estimate the time necessary for a borer (which was used less often than the ram) to make any sort of impression on such walls. Meanwhile the defenders, even if they failed to smash or burn the cat from above, might grip the head of the ram or borer with large pincers to prevent it from being pulled back for its forward stroke, or might try to deaden its blows by means of rope pads or sacks thickly stuffed with soft material with which they would cover the face of the wall at the point where the blows were falling. If pincers or padding succeeded, there was nothing for it but to advance the cat and sap the base of the wall with the pickaxe or with hammer and crowbar. As the mine gallery was driven into the wall, it was shored up with lumber. When it was judged that enough had been done, the lumber shoring would be burnt away and (if the hole had been made large enough) a section of the wall would come down, leaving a breach. This method of mining had been familiar to the ancients, like the ram and the movable tower, and is described by Vegetius.[20]

During this period, the defenders of a first-class stone fortress

[20] For mediæval siege machinery see Dict. de l'Arch., Article "Engin," and also Oman, Vol. 1, 131–138.

could usually content themselves with a passive defence of the most absolute kind, trusting in the height and thickness of the walls rather than in any effort of theirs to hinder the besiegers' operations. Of course such fortresses were costly to build. Once built, their enormous solidity enabled a handful of men inside one to resist an army for a long time. You will often see the statement that, under the military conditions of the time, such a fortress could not be taken except by famine. That is untrue, unless we enlarge the term military conditions to include political and economic conditions as well. It was because no one had the resources to keep a numerous army on foot and hard at work against such fortresses, that throughout the eleventh century they were almost never taken by regular siege. On the merits of the case in military engineering alone, they must have fallen in the end, even if provisions and water had held out. The military axiom still held good which makes the resistance of any fortress, however strong, calculable within limits of time, if besieged by numbers sufficient to blockade it and carry on an active regular siege at the same time. A garrison persistently attacked must decline in strength through casualties and through fatigue. Not even the Dark Ages and the eleventh century are exceptions to this invariable rule, although it must be admitted that they come near being the proverbial exception which proves it.

Such was the eleventh-century Art of War in Western Europe before the Crusades, those great campaigns which are a landmark in every department of mediæval civilization. I conclude this chapter with a discussion of their strategy.

The problem was the transport and subsistence of great and heterogeneous armies, based upon Latin Christendom centring about northern France, to the theatre of war in Palestine. Obviously the difficulties of such a problem, measured in terms of what we call staff work, were so great that it is hard to overstate them. It is true that the Magyars had been converted about the year 1000, so that the Danube Valley was now open to Christian armies as it had not been since the fifth century. Constantinople and part of the coasts of Anatolia, together with Cilicia, were also in friendly hands, although political difficulties with the Byzantines limited their co-operation with the Crusaders. To pay for passage by the sea at the hands of the Italian maritime republics was to avoid the risk of starvation by taking a heavy risk of being drowned. Moreover, the cost of such a passage was ruinous.

In the many books on the Crusades, none has yet attempted to study their staff work, with its financial and administrative ramifications. How well equipped and provisioned crusading armies sometimes were, can be judged from the achievement of the Provençals in 1096 bound for the First Crusade. Under Count Raymond IV of Toulouse, they most unwisely and unnecessarily tried to march down the rugged and inhospitable east coast of the Adriatic. The ignorance of geography which would permit such an attempt contrasts with the surprising measure of success. Instead of losing his entire command through starvation and exposure, Raymond actually came out at Durazzo with half his effective.

In Anatolia, the Byzantines had elaborate information of their lost provinces, including roads and distances, but this information was out of date because the Turks who had held the country for upwards of fifteen years had allowed many bridges and cisterns to become unserviceable and had ruined the country generally. In particular they had protected themselves by deliberately and minutely devastating a broad belt of country on their borders. As if this was not enough, the Turks, with admirable self-sacrifice, would devastate their own land about the line of march of a crusading army, as it approached. Furthermore, there was between the Byzantines and the Crusaders a divergence of political aim, the Byzantines desiring the recovery of Anatolia and the Crusaders the conquest of Palestine. Accordingly the Byzantines were always tempted to use the geographical ignorance of the Crusaders to make of them the unintentional servants of Constantinople.

The strategic successes and failures of the Crusades were as follows.

The penniless advance guard of the First Crusade (1096–99) reached Anatolia only to be promptly massacred by the Turks. The main body cleared the western coast of Asia Minor and captured Nicæa in return for refitment at Byzantine hands. They then took the southern of the two great routes across the interior, by way of Dorylæum (now Eski-Sher) and Iconium, and so to the chief pass over the Taurus, known as the Cilician Gates. They defeated the Turks at Dorylæum and again just before reaching the Taurus. Accordingly they won through safely although they suffered severely and lost many men from starvation.

Various detachments marched in 1102. One was destroyed by a mixture of folly and geographical ignorance which caused its leaders to entangle it in the mountains near Amasia east of Angora, contrary to advice given them in Constantinople. The other two, although their line of march was sensible enough, were ruined through lack of water and inability to cope with the perpetual skirmishing of the Turks.

The Second Crusade of 1148–49 marched in two detachments. The Germans moved from Nicæa via Dorylæum but ran out of food 70 or 80 miles short of Iconium and had to turn back, losing most of their effective by starvation and the Turkish arrows. The French, under their King Louis VII, kept within Byzantine territory by marching down the west coast as far as the mouth of the Mæander and then ascending the valley of that stream. Checked by the Turks east of Laodicea, they turned southeast to Adalia. This place they reached safely, although beginning to suffer from short rations. There the king, knights, and nobles embarked for Palestine, leaving the infantry to be destroyed in the impossible attempt to march along the impracticable sea-coast east of Adalia.

The Third Crusade of 1190 was led by three great soldiers, Richard Cœur de Lion, Philip Augustus, and the Emperor Frederic Barbarossa. Richard and Philip went by sea. Frederic and his Germans followed the route of Louis VII as far as Laodicea; thence they moved east on Iconium, which they took by assault. On the way they lost many horses by the Turkish arrows, but thanks to their crossbowmen they inflicted more harm than they received. As usual, they were beginning to suffer from starvation before reaching Iconium. After the capture of that place, the Sultan proposed a truce, so that they finished their march in peace.

After the successes of the First Crusade and of Barbarossa in crossing Asia Minor, it is surprising to read Oman's statement that they had "little or no organization." [21] Of course no large disorderly mass of men without discipline or organized transport could possibly have fought and marched successfully for six weeks through devastated country.

[21] Oman, Vol. 1, 251.

Once established in the Holy Land, the Crusaders failed because their Army of Occupation, aside from temporary reinforcements, was never sufficiently numerous to extend their holdings eastward to the desert. At the height of their power they were able to annoy but never wholly to interrupt communication between Egypt and Damascus. When the Mohammedans of Mesopotamia, Syria and Egypt became united under an able man like Saladin, the position of the Christians became one of deadly peril.

In their two invasions of Egypt, the Crusaders failed through ignorance, or insufficient appreciation, of geography. They should have landed at Alexandria, or better still at Pelusium near the modern Port Said, and then marched on Cairo along one side of the Nile Delta. Instead, they twice made the mistake of being tempted by the town of Damietta, on the coast of the Delta itself. Inasmuch as the Delta was a network of branches and canals, impassable under military conditions, both invasions failed completely.

CHAPTER VI

CRUSADING TACTICS AND MURET

1099–1213 A. D.

IN every department of civilization and in every phase of the military art, the returning Crusaders were the schoolmasters of Latin Christendom. The mind of the West, already alert and vigorous, was enlarged enormously by travel and by the energy generated through participation in a vast common effort.

First of all, the economic side of crusading warfare was altogether different from that of the sporadic struggles in Western Europe. In one form or another the Christians of Palestine were able to count on heavy subsidies from their home lands. This made possible not only the construction of complicated fortresses on a scale hitherto unknown; it also resulted in gains as to the permanence and specialization of personnel.

Let us consider for a moment some of the ways in which this increase in the permanency and specialization of personnel came about. The military orders of the Temple and the Hospital were able to give their number a continuous military education, often enough to fit them to act as chiefs of staffs to kings. Thus we see Gilbert the Templar successfully extricating the army of Louis VII of France from the Anatolian mountains east of Laodicea in 1147, and we shall see Garin the Hospitaller acting as an efficient chief of staff under Philip Augustus at Bouvines. On several occasions we seem to see an organized pioneer corps at work, in the army of Louis VII and again in that of Cœur de Lion in 1190. In each case this corps was recruited from the unarmed pilgrims to the Holy Land. Finally, something like an Intelligence Department was created in the shape of a highly paid espionage service. Even regular written studies of the forces of prospective opponents together with the topography of prospective theatres of war were made. Two of these reports dealing with the forces of the Sultan of Egypt and the topography of that country have been preserved. They include a description of the roads and a schedule of road distances from Gaza to Cairo and Alexandria.[1]

In equipment, after 1100 the rapid progress of Christendom is reflected by a series of improvements in armour. Ring-mail sewed to a base becomes true chain-mail with each link engaged to the links adjoining. Mail breeches become common and the sleeves of the mail shirt are extended to the wrist. The helmet becomes the pot-helm furnished with slits through which to see and breathe. Anyone who has never tried it will be surprised to find how much he can see through even tiny slits when they are properly placed, as in some aviators' goggles, and in Eskimo wooden snow goggles. The trouble with the great pot-helm was first its weight, which might amount to 18 pounds. This produced fatigue and made it necessary to support it upon a great roll or lining of padding. Second, there was the fact that on account of its weight it consequently could not be made to fit the head closely and therefore its wearer risked his nose if his helmet were thrust violently back against his face. About the year 1200 this last defect was remedied by making the helmet pointed in front. With the improvement in chain-mail the shield became smaller and less pointed. The chain-mail, being flexible, hindered the wearer's movements very little. A full suit might weigh as little as 31 pounds; the shirt alone ranged from 14 to 32 lbs. Nevertheless chain-mail had one defect; however impenetrable, it could not protect its wearer from a bruise or even from having his bones broken. It offered no resistance to shock. Accordingly it had to be backed with a coat of leather or heavy padding called a gambeson or hacqueton. These gambesons were so strongly made that even by themselves they could keep out the arrows of the short bow. Sometimes they alone were worn by mounted men-at-arms engaged in some mission requiring even more than the usual high mobility of 12th- and 13th-century cavalry. Usually they were the sole armour of foot soldiers. One Moslem chronicler speaks of Cœur de Lion's crossbowmen at Arsouf (1191) with their gambesons stuck so full of Turkish arrows that they looked like hedgehogs, and still marching along quite unhurt.[2]

---

[1] For the military orders, see Delpech, Vol. 2, 222–223; for pioneers, Vol. 2, 225–226; for the intelligence service, Vol. 2, 226–237.

[2] Oman, Vol. 1, 309, quoting Boha-ed-din.

After 1200 helmets gradually began to be furnished with movable visors. At the same time appear the partial beginnings of plate armour. Even with a good gambeson no chain-mail could protect against the shock of the heaviest sort of blows—especially downward blows in which the weight of the weapons was added to the force of the striker. When cavalry was fighting cavalry, and infantry, infantry, a downward blow which missed the helmet was apt to strike the shoulder. Cavalry fighting infantry were apt to receive cuts on the knee or thigh. Accordingly during the 13th century we see first shoulder plates and then knee and thigh plates gradually coming into fashion. Such plates were worn over the usual chain-mail so that they added to the net weight to be carried. Commanders of the time were sensitive about the loss of mobility caused by this extra weight. One of many examples is Simon de Montfort at the siege of Toulouse in 1218, five years after his great victory at Muret. Since the besieged were more numerous than his own men, the striking force under his own hand intended to reinforce any point in the partial besieging lines needed the greatest possible mobility. De Montfort therefore was careful to have his men strip off their thigh pieces. Horse armour, in the form of housings or "bardings" of loose hanging cloth or felt is found in the 13th century. Occasionally toward the end of the century it is even reinforced with mail.[3]

In the matter of tactics, the crusading fights show a marked and fairly regular progress, divided into three definite phases.

The first phase of six years, from 1097 to 1102, may be called the phase of encounter. During this time neither side made any effort to adapt its tactics to those of the enemy, and the actions were decided chiefly through the chances of war and the errors of individual commanders. The Christians were usually, but not invariably, successful through their superiority in shock tactics and close combat.

In the second phase of fifty-four years, from 1102 to 1156, the Christians had learned their lesson, which was that their mailed horsemen must be supported by solid infantry armed both with pikes and with missile weapons. The Moslems were unable to work out any counter-move, so the Christians were successful in every

[3] For 12th-century armor and equipment see Dict. du Mob., Vols. 5 and 6. Also Oman, Vol. 2, 3–9; Delpech, Vol. 1, 423–426, and Dean.

action. That the victories won did not bring greater results was due to no circumstance connected with tactics, but solely to the want of permanent Christian numbers.

In the third phase of over a century, from 1156 to the end of the Crusades in 1271, the Mohammedans had come to see that their chance lay in attempting to separate the Christian cavalry from their infantry. When the attempt succeeded the Crusaders were usually beaten; when cavalry and infantry stuck together they usually won. Even so, the victories of the Christians outnumbered their defeats. It was unfortunate political circumstances, together with the old chronic shortage of permanent numbers, which finally resulted in their expulsion from Syria and Palestine.

At this point the reader should note that there were two distinct tactical methods among the Moslems. The Turks of Asia Minor, northern Syria, and northern Mesopotamia were skirmishing horse archers of the immemorial Eastern sort, such as the Parthians and the Magyars had been. Their immediate ancestors had been Nomads. The Egyptians, and in general the Moslems of the old Arabic tradition, resembled their own ancestors in that their armies were composed of cavalry acting by shock supported by hordes of rabble infantry of whom the least worthless element consisted of negroes. In other words, they were the same Saracens against whom the Byzantines had fought.

The first general action was against the Turks. It was fought at Dorylæum, recently prominent in communiqués of the Greco-Kemalist war under its modern name of Eski-Sher. For greater ease in foraging, the huge army of the Crusaders was marching in two parallel columns only about five miles apart but not in continuous close touch with one another. The Turkish horse archers, also in great force, attacked the left column, but committed the serious error of not keeping the Christian right under proper observation. The left column formed in the usual western order of battle which we have seen at Hastings, with the infantry in front. Although the crusading command had organized their whole army in companies of 100 and platoons of 50 under designated leaders,[4] this organization had not succeeded in solidifying the infantry enough to enable them to resist the novel Turkish skirmishing

[4] Delpech, Vol. 2, 150, quoting William of Tyre.

tactics. When the knights charged, their blow was spent in air. The Turks nimbly avoided the shock and then lapped around their flank units as these became exposed so that they were continually forced back on their infantry. These last attempted a defensive on true Vegetian lines but lacked the cohesion to make it good. Demoralization threatened, and fatigue on the part of the knights, who could neither close with the nimble enemy nor obtain repose because of the weakness of the Christian foot, would have brought disaster had it not been for the appearance of the cavalry of the right-hand column, which came suddenly over a ridge upon the Turkish left and rear. The Turks were thus trapped not by design on the part of the Crusaders but merely because the distance gained by the right (while the left was fighting) naturally brought it against the Turkish left rear. In such a position the heavier Western men and horses easily smashed their opponents.

At Antioch, where the next general action was fought, the crusading foot was stiffened by the presence of many knights who had by this time lost their horses during the long campaign. Secondly, the Turks foolishly engaged in a narrow plain only two miles wide, between an unfordable river and a range of hills too steep for cavalry. The Crusaders had only to extend from river to hills, meanwhile protecting their rear by a suitable detachment, in order to win.

Even when Jerusalem had been taken and the mass of the Crusaders had gone home, the handful who remained, as at the first battle of Ramleh in September, 1101, were still able to win victories by virtue of their superior military qualities—provided that horse and foot kept together. A great army of Egyptians was dispersed by less than 300 Christian knights supported by 900 infantry.

A few months later another action on the same field showed the lesson had not been thoroughly learned. In passing, it should be said that the importance of Ramleh was that it was a great road centre. In infidel hands it cut off Jerusalem from Jaffa and the coast.

Finding an Egyptian force in possession of this important crossroad, the King of Jerusalem, Baldwin I, correctly decided to attack, but committed the folly of doing so with only about 700 mailed cavalry and no infantry. It is true that he had beaten a similar force on the same field with even fewer armoured horse-men, but on that occasion he had been supported by foot who had borne themselves well. Now his knights were swallowed up and massacred, Baldwin himself barely escaping. This time the lesson was learned, for thereafter no crusading army marched without infantry.

Shortly after his defeat Baldwin sallied out from Jaffa, where he had taken refuge. This time his cavalry numbered less than two hundred, but with the aid of a solid body of infantry (com-posed of the crews of a fleet newly come from the West) he beat off great numbers of Egyptians and finally occupied their camp. In square or, more probably, circular formation, the Christian pike-men and crossbowmen stood firm against the Mohammedans, furnishing an asylum for the knights within which they could rest safely between charges.

For half a century, the Christians were never beaten. After Jaffa, Hab, Hazarth and Marj-es-Safar were equally glorious victories against heavy odds. In the campaign of Bosra in 1146, they marched for over a hundred miles through the desert east of the Jordan and back again, always in the presence of a numerous enemy whom they defeated in every combat. In this operation they lost so few men that they were able to bring back all their dead and so permit the infidels to believe that not one Christian had fallen.

Not until after 1156 did the Moslem hit upon the idea of attack-ing the Christians only when their horse was separated from their foot. The first break in the long series of Christian victories was in this year at the Ford of Jacob over the Jordan. The infidels, who had retreated before the crusading cavalry and infantry combined, successfully attacked the cavalry when separated from its infantry support. Sometimes they would bring this about by simulating flight. When the Christian horse and foot could be attacked separately Islam usually won. When the two arms kept together the infidels were usually beaten.

The one conspicuous exception to this rule seems to prove not the self-sufficiency of mailed cavalry, but under favourable cir-cumstances, that of infantry. In 1124 the militia infantry of the Commune of Jerusalem, acting absolutely without cavalry, showed so bold a front against an Egyptian raiding force that these last

retired without daring to attack. We shall meet with municipal
militia infantry again.

The endless war hung level with varying fortunes until 1183.
Then the political situation shifted against the Christians because
of the consolidation of Egypt, Mesopotamia and the Moslem parts
of Syria under the rule of Saladin who virtually destroyed the
Kingdom of Jerusalem at the great and disastrous battle of Hattin
in 1187. His army on that occasion was, as usual, very large.
It included 10,000 mailed cavalry intended for shock action
together with numbers of horse archers. To relieve the town of
Tiberias on the Sea of Galilee, which was besieged by Saladin,
the Christians reduced the garrisons of all their fortresses danger-
ously low and took the field with practically their entire force.
This amounted to five or six thousand mailed cavalry, 18,000 foot,
and many light horse archers armed in the Turkish fashion and
called Turcopoles. They concentrated at Saffaria, only 16 miles
west of Tiberias, but separated from that town by waterless
desert which was particularly hard to cross in the height of summer,
for the month was July. Furthermore, Saladin had ravaged the
country well. After much discussion, pro and con, the Christians
resolved to advance, confident in their unusual numerical strength
and tempted by Saladin's dangerous position with the lake at
his back. On the first day they advanced ten miles. Meanwhile
Saladin had refused to show his hand. He had contented himself
with skirmishing and setting fire to the parched grass. In the
afternoon the Christians were so fatigued that it was, most unwisely, decided to make a waterless camp. All night the Turks
kept up a harassing fire of arrows. In the morning the march was
resumed under distressing conditions. All were suffering so from
thirst that when a stream of water was reached the infantry broke
ranks to drink. Hitherto the watchful Saladin had seen no chance
to attack as the two arms had covered one another admirably.
Now when charged, the foot became demoralized. Refusing to obey
orders to rally on the cavalry, they tried to make a separate stand
by themselves on the hill of Hattin where they were soon destroyed.
Saladin now surrounded the Christian cavalry. So many horses
had been shot that the main body lost all momentum and huddled
stupidly together at a standstill. Seeing this, the advance guard
saved themselves by a sudden charge which broke through the

Saracens in their front. The main body finally surrendered from thirst and fatigue, for the armoured men had suffered little from the arrows, which had been effective only against their horses.

It is significant of the atmosphere of these wars that Saladin treated the captured King of Jerusalem with honour, but instantly massacred two hundred and thirty knights of the Military Orders. Reginald of Châtillon, a baron who had greatly harassed the Moslems, being offered the alternatives of Islam or death, proudly chose death. Saladin himself struck the first blow at him as he stood there defenceless, and he was then cut to pieces by the guards. Hattin is an example of bad leadership. Even at the last, the successful charge of the advance guard proves that more could have been done. It should be noted that the crisis of the action was the moment when the tired infantry misconducted themselves and became separated. It is interesting to learn that Saladin had organized his ammunition supply of arrows with particular care.[5]

Although Hattin ruined the Kingdom of Jerusalem, nevertheless that great soldier Cœur de Lion four years later at Arsouf (1191) was able to beat Saladin handsomely in a general action. Richard's force was very strong, perhaps as high as 100,000. The staff and medical services were carefully organized. Inasmuch as clean clothing reduced the danger from Oriental epidemics, there was even a corps of laundresses, strong enough to keep up with the column on foot and carefully recruited so as not to be a cause of scandal and disorder in the Christian army![6] Cœur de Lion was particularly famous for his success in espionage work, in which he spent money lavishly.

The line of operations lay along the coast southward from Acre in order to prepare a base for a subsequent advance eastward to Jerusalem. On the march the column was closely beset by Saladin, whose plan was especially to harass the rear so that it would have to halt and face about, thus making a gap into which the Moslems might be able to charge. So high was the Christian discipline and so great Richard's prudence that the opportunity never came. Richard's tactics were for the infantry to cover the marching column with their missiles. Only if the Moslems should so thoroughly commit themselves to the action as to have difficulty in

---

[5] Delpech, Vol. 1, 372, quoting Roudatain.
[6] Delpech, Vol. 1, 377, quoting the Itinerarium.

breaking it off, were the cavalry to charge. Just before reaching Arsouf the opportunity came and the charge was delivered. Saladin's army was so thoroughly defeated that only political dissension prevented an advance against Jerusalem.

Want of space prevents consideration of Mansourah, the last of the great crusading actions, where St. Louis was nearly destroyed through the indiscipline of his brother the Count of Artois, and through his own necessity of separating from his infantry in order to cross a deep ford. The position was finally saved by the arrival of the footmen.

The ultimate failure of the Crusades was due to no inferiority in fighting power. Man for man the Christians were better fighters and, for the most part, better generals. They solved their tactical problem in five years (1097–1102) whereas it took the Moslems fifty years even to begin to match them. It was geographical difficulties, the want of permanent numbers, and (after 1150) an unfavourable political situation which brought about the ruin of the Kingdom of Jerusalem by the single disaster of Hattin, and prevented the success of later efforts to re-establish the position.

In Spain, the chief theatre of war against Islam and one in which conditions were more equal than in Palestine, the Christians won.

In the Spanish wars we can trace only one distinctive tactical development, that of the light cavalry known as "Genetours." Mounted on the light Spanish horses known as "Jennets" and armed with long light lances or javelins, the Genetours were intended for skirmishing. The survival of their method of combat among the Portuguese bullfighters of to-day was noted in the last chapter.

With the exception of the Genetours, tactical developments in Spain seem to have resembled contemporary developments in Palestine. Our scanty knowledge of the 11th century and earlier battles, indicates that they were cavalry fights pure and simple. After 1150 we find solid infantry, pikemen and crossbowmen, on both sides; indeed they seem to have been more prominent among the infidels than among the Christians.[7] Such infantry, however, were no more fit for the offensive than any other mediæval infantry. A striking demonstration is the combat of Majorca in 1229. There the young king Jaime of Aragon, although he had only four

[7] Mangin: La Force Noire, 126–127 and 133–139.

hundred mailed cavalry with him, overruled his timid councillors and decided to attack some 2000 Moslem pikemen advancing against him. Noting that the advance had disordered their ranks and made gaps in the hedge of spear-points, he very truly remarked that under such conditions any troops could be beaten. He charged and destroyed them.[8]

After 1100 the increase of Christendom in energy, wealth and knowledge brought about rapid improvement in fortification. Much larger and more complicated works could now be built. On the other hand, siege machinery was improved and sieges grew more methodical, so that a more active defence became necessary. The result was that the typical first-class fortress completely changed its character. The Donjon became only the last refuge of the garrison. The outer walled enclosure now became the main line of resistance and was accordingly strengthened with towers whose size made them little fortresses in themselves, while their bold profile enabled their defenders to flank the adjoining towers together with the intervening curtain walls. Overhanging wooden galleries known as hoardings were provided at the crest of walls and towers so as to give the besieged a better command of the base of the defences—the point which the besiegers must attack. In deforested Syria these hoardings were replaced by permanent stone machicolations which served the same purpose and served it better.

The castle of Kerak-in-Moab, in Palestine east of the Dead Sea, may serve as an example of the new type of fortress with its accumulation of obstacles. It was probably built about 1140. In plan it is an irregular parallelogram, protected on three sides by natural escarpments. In front there is a dry ditch cut in the rock. Immediately behind this rises the front curtain wall, flanked by good-sized square towers at the corners. The gate is close to one of these towers. On entering one finds oneself not in the castle court but in a long narrow passage between the outer wall and an inner wall close to and parallel with it. This passage is closed by two portcullises which with that of the gate itself makes three in all. The main gate of Tientsin, familiar to the Chinese Expeditionary Force of 1900, had a somewhat similar arrangement. Inside, another inner wall divides the total enclosed space into an inner and an outer court or "ward." At the rear end of the inner ward

[8] Delpech, Vol. 1, 318–319, quoting Jaime of Aragon.

is the Donjon Keep. The entire rear end of the castle surmounts a steep escarpment running down to a large cistern.

This castle is a fine specimen of the mid-12th-century fortification. It was often attacked but never with success and it was taken by Saladin in 1188, the year after Hattin, only by starvation after months of close blockade. Obviously such a fortress marks a great advance over the isolated Norman keep with its outer ward of mere palisading, or at most of light stone-work with a plain flat trace and no powerful flankments.[9]

The finest fortress of the 12th century, at least in the West, is the Saucy Castle, "Château Gaillard" on a cliff over the Seine between Paris and Rouen. It was built in a single year, 1195, by Richard Cœur de Lion (whose talents as an organizer and tactician we have touched upon in considering the campaign of Arsouf) to be the citadel of a vast entrenched camp intended to cover Normandy against Philip Augustus of France. Unfortunately our space does not permit consideration of Richard's entrenched camp as a whole. The castle itself is too good to be typical of even the first-class fortresses of its time. It is a supreme example of what an exceptional genius could do about the year 1200 when that genius ruled from Scotland to the Pyrenees and controlled the finest treasury in Europe.

Château Gaillard is built upon a typical mediæval fortress site—backed up against sheer precipices, with a single narrow approach on the level, only about twenty yards wide at its narrowest point.

A besieger attacking by this single approach was confronted by the apex of a triangular outer ward flanked by five towers. At the base of the triangle was a ditch crossed by a movable bridge with a zigzag approach ⌐ᆗ so that a storming party would not be able to rush it at speed.[9] Behind the ditch was the second ward, also flanked by towers, and within the second ward is the third or inner ward—the most powerful of all. This inner ward was unique in mediæval fortification inasmuch as it had no towers but had its entire wall scalloped as if towers had been cut in slices and placed alongside one another. In the inner ward rose the Donjon, the culminating point of the entire scheme. Experience

[9] Oman, Vol. 2, 31.

had shown that the corners of the old square Donjons were weak
points. Accordingly this huge tower (60 feet high and 50 feet
broad at the base) was round with a pointed spur of solid masonry
toward the side from which attack must come.

The ditches were cut in the solid rock upon which the walls
rested. The walls themselves sloped forward at their bases to
give the sapper a more difficult task and to make stones bound
outward when dropped from the battlements against the base-
slope. In his anxiety to avoid dead space, the designer increased
the height of the slope in the re-entrants between the scallops of
the inner walls so that the scalloped trace was far more pronounced
at the top and flatter at the bottom. The Donjon was furnished
with stone machicolation widely spaced and carried on pointed
arches resting on projecting buttresses. The battlements of all the
other works were provided with holes at the base of the crenela-
tion just above the top of the curtain for the insertion of beams to
carry projecting hoards.

A fortress like Château Gaillard was designed primarily to resist
mining. Its masonry was too good to have been vulnerable to
rams and borers. Movable towers for escalade could rarely be
used in 12th-century sieges because of the improvement in combustibles. In 1190, just six years before building Château Gaillard,
Cœur de Lion himself, at the siege of Acre, had found himself
obliged to coat his movable towers with iron sheeting—a ruin-
ously expensive business.

Besides the improvement in combustibles, there had been an
improvement in artillery. To the tension and torsion types of
catapult a third and still more powerful type was added, worked
by a counterpoise. The counterpoise catapult was generally
known as a trebuchet—although the chronic mediæval confusion
in all military terms continued to complicate artillery nomencla-
ture. Such a catapult had a high timber frame for base. To the
upper part of this frame was pivoted a movable beam, with the
pivot much nearer one end than the other. To the short end was
attached a huge hanging timber bucket which was filled with
stones to serve as a counterpoise. The long end had either a spoon-
shaped rest for the projectiles (as in the mangonel) or else a sort of
sling. It was drawn down and released like the mangonel and like
the mangonel was generally used for high-angle bombardment of

large objectives. During the siege of Acre a projectile probably from such a catapult surprised all who saw it by a carry of well over 800 yards.[10] What the ordinary maximum was we do not know. Thirteenth-century artillery had the same fascination for its users as has the artillery of to-day. In 1210, at the siege of Termes during the Albigensian War, de Montfort's chief of artillery was a priest, the Archdeacon William of Paris, who during the Crusades in Palestine had conceived such a passion for his catapults that he refused the fat bishopric of Beziers—"loving better to follow the wars and handle the artillery." [11]

How the sieges of the time were conducted we can see by following step by step Philip Augustus' great siege of the unrivalled fortress of Château Gaillard in 1203–04. The fortress was particularly strong and only seven years old and Philip was one of the richest and most formidable rulers of his time.

The King of France sat down before Château Gaillard in August, 1203, beating off an attempt at relief. He easily took the extensive defences of the great entrenched camp of which the castle was the citadel, for the garrison which held the place against him numbered only 200. He spent the autumn in building lines of circumvallation and contravallation to hold off relieving forces and shut in the place. In February the regular siege was begun. The first step was to widen the high neck of land leading to the apex of the outer ward. The besiegers then built shelters like early modern parallels of approach and set up a number of catapults. They built movable towers which were still useful in obtaining fire superiority on account of their great height, although it was no longer thought safe to risk them right up against the walls. Apparently fire superiority was obtained, for when the ditch had been partly filled an escalade of the tower at the apex of the triangular advanced work by means of ladders was tried. The attempt failed because the ladders were too short, but the assailants were able to maintain their position at the base of the tower. Here they began to sap the defences. A mine-chamber was made, shored up with wood, and fired in the traditional Vegetian way. So large a breach then appeared that the small garrison did not try to defend it but

[10] Belloc in "Land and Water" for April 3, 1919.
[11] Rev. J. Astruc: "Conquête de la Vicompté de Carcassonne" (pamphlet, Carcassonne, 1912).

retreated to the second ward, setting fire to whatever would burn
in the outer ward and raising the drawbridge behind them.

Surprisingly enough, the second ward was taken by surprise.
One of its forward corners was occupied by the castle chapel whose
basement was used for latrines. This basement had a window
looking out over the cliff which was large enough to admit a man.
One night a handful of daring Frenchmen managed to get into
it. Apparently the besiegers had not thought it worth while to
watch closely a side so difficult to approach. When the few French
in the latrines set up a ferocious din to simulate the presence
of a large force, the garrison became panic-stricken. Instead of
destroying the gallant handful as they could easily have done,
they took refuge in the inner ward. The assailants then were able
to lower the drawbridge leading to the outer ward already in
French possession. In defence of this timid decision it should be
said that the defenders were now only 180 strong. Therefore they
had reason to fear being cut off from the inner ward in case the
French had been more numerous than they actually were.

The attack upon the scalloped inner ward was now begun.
A particularly large catapult (which seems to have hurled stones
pointblank or nearly so) was set to work. At the same time a
mine gallery was driven under the base of the walls. The defenders
succeeded in getting possession of the gallery by means of a counter-
mine. However, all this digging had so weakened the foundations
that a considerable part of the tottering wall was finally brought
down by the catapult. By this time the garrison was reduced to
twenty knights and 120 other ranks—140 in all. Although they
concentrated to defend the breach they failed to hold it. They
could not even make good their retreat to the Donjon which could
be entered only by a steep and narrow flight of steps leading to
a tiny door fifty feet above the inner court. The surrender took
place on March 6th—only five weeks after the regular attack on
the outer ward had been begun. It would be interesting to know
the effective of the garrison on February 1st and also how many
of the casualties which finally reduced it to 140 were due to famine
and how many to the activities of the besiegers.[12]

[12] For the construction and siege of Château Gaillard see Dieulafoy: Château Gaillard et l'Architecture Militaire au XIIème Siècle; also Dict. de
l'Arch., various articles, especially Vol. 3, 93–102.

Before we pass to the description of western campaigns, certain changed conditions of recruitment and strategy must be mentioned. By 1200 A. D. the knights were only a small part of a normal force of heavy cavalry. The majority of such troops were "sergeants"— a name originally given to feudal tenants whose incomes were too small to be considered a "knight's fee" and afterwards used of mounted men-at-arms not of noble blood serving for a fixed rate of pay. Usually in a 13th-century army there would be four or five sergeants per knight, although the proportion might fall as low as two to one, or rise as high as ten (or even twelve) to one in exceptional cases. Thus the numbers of a force can never be accurately established from the figures for knights alone.

Besides sergeants, a 13th-century knight would normally have with him a mounted and fully armed personal attendant known as a "squire," and at least one imperfectly armed mounted groom.

Besides sergeants, another new sort of troops was municipal troops—townsmen independently organized as such and serving as infantry. Mediæval towns were rapidly growing in numbers and prosperity. Moreover, the Guild system gave to the town populace a far greater measure of economic liberty and a correspondingly higher spirit than that of the town proletariat of to-day. It is therefore not surprising to learn that their militia were apt to be solid troops.

We have seen the brave stand of the Jerusalem municipal militia in 1126, and at Legnano in 1178 it was the obstinate resistance of the Lombard pikemen to the Emperor's knights which permitted the routed men-at-arms of their own side to rally unmolested, charge, and win the day.

At this point it is necessary to say a word as to the effect of fortification and in particular the castle system upon mediæval strategy. On the one hand, the enormous number of strong castles dotted thickly all over Christendom required an invader intending permanent occupation of a district to settle down to a long series of sieges. When the castles were strongly garrisoned it was dangerous to thrust an army deep into hostile territory. On the other hand, the low economic development of the time, which made it exceedingly difficult to keep on foot large permanent garrisons, tended to make the garrisons too weak numerically to cut the communications in rear of an invader. Not military incapacity but the smallness of the garrisons of the time caused so many mediæval armies to astonish modern students by leaving untaken fortresses in their rear. Philip Augustus could have marched past the 200 men in Château Gaillard with impunity had he so desired.

The campaign of Muret, which we shall now consider, is an example of just such marching past fortresses and also of the unequal morale of warfare within Christendom. It is not an example of raiding because Pedro of Aragon was marching toward a secondary base in Toulouse.

The Albigensian Crusade was almost entirely a war of positions; its twenty years of fighting can show only two general actions, Castelnaudary and Muret. The Crusade had been undertaken in 1209 against Raymond of Toulouse and certain other southern lords, notably the Counts of Foix and Comminges, who had been protecting the Manichean heretics known as Albigenses. A huge army took the field and captured Béziers and Carcassonne. After which almost all of them went home in the typical crusading fashion, leaving Simon de Montfort (the father of the Magna Charta Simon de Montfort) to carry on with very slender resources. This he did by means of his own genius, by the high strategical value of Carcassonne, and by the high morale of his troops. This high morale was kept up by the fact that the Albigensian heresy was of a nasty repulsive sort. Even the southern lords favoured it not from belief but because it was, in a sense, their ally in their perpetual attempt to get hold of church property.

The cowardly and slothful Count of Toulouse did not dare meet the Crusaders in the field. On the other hand, de Montfort was unable to do anything against Toulouse, because of its size. William the Conqueror had been equally unable to attack London. Furthermore, he was in a theatre amply covered by fortified towns and by the castle system. Since his army was much smaller than William's had been, it was his game to encircle Toulouse as closely as possible by holding strong points round about. The morale and fighting power of his numerous enemies was so low that by 1213 Raymond's large holdings were reduced to little more than Toulouse and Montauban. Pujols, only eight miles east of Toulouse, and Muret, twelve miles south of Raymond's capital, were held by Montfortist garrisons. The summer of 1213 saw the war transformed by the intervention against de Montfort of the King of Aragon.

So unmilitary are mediæval chroniclers that we are not certain of Pedro's route across the Pyrenees. He may have used the Somport pass, but his concentration point, Lerida, makes it probable that he moved by the Spanish part of the Cerdagne and then by the Puymorens pass. If he did so he would have found Foix friendly but would have been forced to circle around de Montfort's garrisons in Pamiers and Muret. That in Muret was weak, that in Pamiers probably so. Pedro was politically compelled to win quickly, before the Pope in distant Rome could take diplomatic action against him.

Even before his arrival the Toulousans had been so encouraged that they had taken Pujols and massacred its garrison. Their junction once made, Pedro and Raymond moved upon Muret together. Their strategy was as simple and logical as de Montfort's had been. The first stage of their task was evidently to disengage Toulouse from the neighbourhood of crusading garrisons. Pujols gone, Muret was their obvious next objective.

The position of Muret was strong—a narrow triangle with the unfordable Garonne on one side and the Louge (a brook with banks so high and steep as to make it a first-class military obstacle) on another. The castle, which stood at the apex of the triangle, was strong but the defences of the town were weak. The garrison numbered only thirty knights and seven hundred poorly armed infantry. The place, being ill provisioned, must soon have fallen if not relieved.

When de Montfort heard of the move against Muret he was even weaker than usual in numbers for he could muster only 870 mailed cavalry. On the other hand, this little force was of excellent quality and included the high proportion of 270 knights. With even more than his usual boldness, de Montfort threw himself into Muret. Starting from Fanjeaux he made the intervening 75 miles in two and a half days' marching—a creditable performance considering that some of his detachments had done an extra 17 miles between Carcassonne and Fanjeaux which made over 90 miles in all.

In spite of the great disparity in numbers (for Raymond's and Pedro's combined armies were probably at least as high as 4000 cavalry and thirty or forty thousand infantry) de Montfort was compelled to take the offensive because of political necessity. He and the Crusade were by this time so unpopular in the South, where his name is still hated to-day after 700 years, that he feared that the slightest sign of weakness (or even of caution) on his part would start a general insurrection in which his scattered garrisons would be nowhere. He must at all costs keep up the terror of his name which was his chief asset.

So thoroughly afraid of de Montfort were the southern lords that Raymond actually proposed to Pedro to strengthen the entrenchments of the camp and behind them to await the microscopic crusading army. Pedro merely laughed at the idea that de Montfort might attack.

The crusading leader's first move was a ruse intended to commit the besiegers to an assault on the town. This he did by throwing open the Toulouse Gate, at the northwest corner of the place, which opened upon a bridge over the Louge ravine. The first of the three "battles" of hostile cavalry, together with many of their infantry, promptly attacked. Most foolishly, the southerners charged through the gate, naturally found themselves helpless in narrow and crooked streets typical of a mediæval town, and were easily driven out by the crusading infantry. Nothing daunted, the attacking troops fell out of ranks not far from the town and began to eat and drink.

De Montfort now executed a second ruse by simulating flight with his cavalry. Between the walls and the Garonne was a roadway on a lower level than the town itself. Near its centre it communicated with the bridge over the river by which the Crusaders had come. At its northeast end it led to the narrow bridge over the mouth of the Louge by which the castle communicated with the open country. Its southwest approach was through a low outwork which covered the southern corner of the town and communicated with the "Sales Gate"—the one opening in the wall between the Garonne and the Louge.

Over the low walls of the outwork the besiegers saw the crusading cavalry file out of the Sales Gate and turn the corner. Very naturally under the circumstances, they assumed that de Montfort meant to retreat by the bridge over the Garonne and were thrown still further off their guard. Instead of retreating, the crusading

column continued on, crossed the castle bridge out of sight of the
southerners who had been attacking the Toulouse Gate, and
(still unobserved) gained the north bank of the Louge.[13]

What must have been the southerners' consternation when the
first of the "battles" of the Crusaders appeared on their flank,

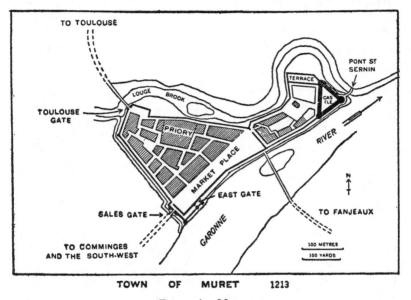

TOWN   OF   MURET   1213

PLATE 4.—MURET.

formed line to its left, and charged them. They were scattered in
an instant; some of their knights had even taken off their mail
shirts.

This operation, together with Simon's whole performance at
Muret deserves to be dwelt upon as a perfect example of the rapidity and precision of manœuvre possible to 13th-century cavalry
at their best. The time element can be computed with some
accuracy as follows.

The full distance from the Sales Gate, past the town, over the
bridge, and up the abrupt ramp leading to the plain is nearly
seven hundred yards. From the numerous mediæval gates extant,

[13] For de Montfort's whole manœuvre see Dieulafoy, Muret. See Plates
14–17.

together with the extant brick remains of the northern abutment of the bridge in question, we may be certain that the formation was a column of twos. We may be almost equally certain that the gait was a walk, for (in the first place) it would have been nearly impossible to trot up the final steep ramp, (secondly) silence was desired, and (thirdly) to trot through such a long narrow space would

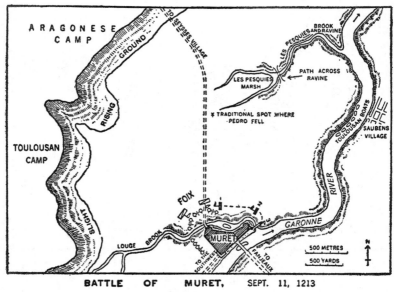

BATTLE OF MURET, SEPT. 11, 1213

1 ST PHASE: DE MONTFORT'S SORTIE AND SURPRISE OF FOIX

⛴ ALLIED CAVALRY ◊◊◊ ALLIED INFANTRY ⚓ CRUSADING CAVALRY (SQUADRONS 1, 2, & 3)
÷ CATAPULTS

PLATE 5.—BATTLE OF MURET: 1ST PHASE.

have exposed the cavalry to the risk of a serious snarl in case a single horse fell or behaved badly—in which case the whole operation would have been compromised. Assuming the gait to have been a walk, we are entitled to reduce the distance occupied by each horse to three yards, allowing a bare one foot between nose and crupper. The length of the entire column must therefore have been at least 450 × 3 = 1350 yards, nearly double the distance to be traversed, and the minimum length of each squadron must have been 450 yards. Before falling out to eat and drink, we may be sure that the Toulousans and Catalans must have retreated at least a hundred and fifty yards north of the Toulouse Gate in order that so large a target as they would present might be out of long bowshot. Therefore the head of the crusading column would come into plain sight practically as soon as it topped the ramp and gained the plain. Historians who assume that the deployment could have been made out of sight of the Toulousans and Catalans have simply never troubled to walk over the battlefield. Assuming a walking gait to be four miles per hour, i. e., 117 yards per minute, the rear of the first crusading squadron would be in the plain almost exactly four minutes after the van had come in sight of the enemy in front of the Toulouse Gate. The greater part of the 600 yards separating the Crusaders from the enemy would almost certainly be covered at a trot of, say, eight miles an hour, before breaking to a gallop for the final shock. Two minutes plus the time necessary for deployment, must therefore be added to the original four. In all, at least seven minutes must have elapsed between the first observation of the Crusaders by Foix's command and the delivery of the crusading charge.

Meanwhile the main body of the besiegers was getting to horse, crying "Aragon," "Foix," or "Comminges," according to their allegiance. The Spaniards formed, but the formation was ragged. In part this may have been due to haste, although they must have had over fifteen minutes in which to get in line, assuming a minimum of eight minutes from the disclosure of the operation to the deployment of the second crusading squadron plus an additional minimum of eight minutes for the second squadron to catch up with the first and for the two together to do the mile which separated them from Pedro's people. In part it certainly resulted from the folly and indiscipline of the Spanish knights; every important man among them (so Pedro's son, King Jaime, tells us) wanted to fight his own battle with the enemy, making strict alignment and combined action impossible. Furthermore, as we learn from other chroniclers, Pedro himself exercised no effective command but yielded to his chivalric enthusiasm by exchanging armour with one of his knights and posting himself in the front ranks—a piece of generous but unmilitary folly surprising in a soldier of his considerable experience since it lost him all control over his forces in reserve. The Aragonese were facing south astride the Seysses road about a mile out of Muret, with the Pesquies marsh covering their left.

Having broken Foix's command, the first crusading squadron had to wheel half right in order to strike Pedro. By spurring hard, the second, with a straighter course to follow, was able to catch up. Both together went at the Aragonese, sweeping before them some of Foix's routed horsemen. Count Simon's orders on no

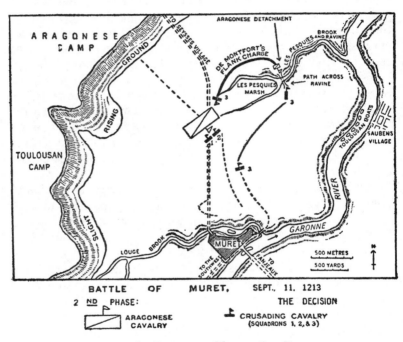

PLATE 6.—BATTLE OF MURET: 2ND PHASE.

account to engage in individual jousting but to charge boot to boot were so well obeyed that the shock was simultaneous all along their line. It was so violent that the Crusaders plunged into the horsemen opposed to them "like a stone into a pool." Pedro's people stood firm and closed around them, hiding them from the third "battle," and the mêlée swayed back and forth with a din "as of countless axemen hewing down a forest."

De Montfort, with the idea of charging in on Pedro's left,

worked rapidly north and east around the marsh until he found himself blocked by Pesquies ravine, which the chroniclers describe as a "fossatum" (i. e., a ditch or trench). Cut in the steep banks of this obstacle was a narrow path, blocked at the further end by a strong Aragonese combat patrol or covering detachment. Such covering detachments were familiar enough, as we learn from the "Siete Partidas" of Alfonso the Wise of Castile, written about 1260, in which they are called "Alas" or "Citaras."[14] If it be objected that Pedro was in no mood to think of such details as posting this detachment, we may fairly imagine some grizzled knight of Aragon who knew enough to take on the job by himself with his own immediate followers.

To go from line to column and try to force the narrow path in the face of opposition was a bad business, but de Montfort had no choice. Time was passing, he had the marsh on his left and the ravine stretching away at his right. At the head of his men he crossed the ravine and set his horse to scramble up the further bank. In this unfavourable position, as he struggled to protect himself from the blows he could not yet hope to return, he broke his left stirrup leather—the third time one part or other of his equipment had played him false that day—but with great dexterity he kept his seat. Reaching the summit of the bank, he unhorsed the nearest enemy with a blow of the fist to the jaw—the Spaniard must have been wearing not a closed pot-helm but an open-faced steel cap. This man seems to have been the detachment commander, for when his followers saw him fall they broke up and fled on the instant. The flight exposed to Count Simon the left flank of the Aragonese main body. He got his three hundred across, deployed them and charged.

All this time the first two crusading squadrons had been fighting hard. Although their close formation and the fury of their charge had carried them deep into the ranks of their enemies, still these last had not broken but closed in around them. Strict order and alignment had gone and the fighting was man to man. The knight who had taken the part of Pedro could not equal his master's prowess, and Pedro himself forgot caution and cried out "I am the King," whereupon those who had sworn to have his life closed around him and killed him despite his valour and his skill in arms.

[14] Quoted by Delpech, Vol. 1, 275.

Whether the king fell after or before de Montfort's charge is uncertain; those who killed him were with the second squadron. In either case, his fall and the flank charge decided the day and a general rout ensued. The five hundred knights of his household fell almost to a man around his body, unsupported by the rest of the leaderless mass of horsemen. The southerners paid a bitter price for Pedro's chivalrous folly in jamming himself into the fight-

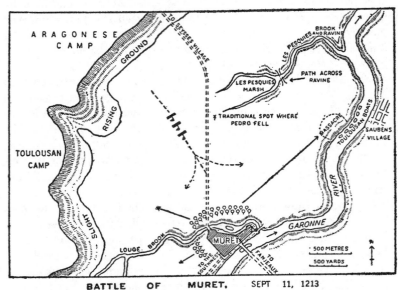

BATTLE OF MURET, SEPT 11, 1213

3 ᴿᴰ PHASE: DE MONTFORT, RETURNING FROM PURSUIT ROUTS
THE TOULOUSAN MILITIA INFANTRY ATTACKING THE TOWN
⬡⬡⬡⬡⬡⬡ TOULOUSAN INFANTRY ⚓ CRUSADING CAVALRY

PLATE 7.—BATTLE OF MURET: 3RD PHASE.

ing and thereby giving up all attempt to direct operations. Raymond and the Count of Comminges seem never to have been engaged at all. We hear of them only as fleeing from the field.

Count Simon, on the other hand, was as wise in victory as he had been furious in attack. While directing, or (more probably) permitting the pursuit of the fugitives by his first two squadrons, he kept the third squadron (his own immediate command) well under his hand and followed the pursuit at a distance so as to intervene in case of a rally. After a short pursuit, he judged that

the fleeing horsemen were making for Toulouse, incapable of
renewing the battle. Recalling the pursuers, at the head of his
three squadrons he returned towards Muret.

Meanwhile the Toulousan communal militia had altogether
misconceived the result of the cavalry action. Only a part of these
troops had taken part in Foix's unsuccessful attack and subsequent rout at the hands of the first crusading squadron. And of
that part only those north of the Louge had actually endured the
crusading charge and the rout, those between the Louge and the
Garonne had merely retreated (hastily enough no doubt) in order
to conform to the flight of those to the north. By far the greater
part of them therefore were quite fresh. At first they barricaded
themselves in their camp, fearing they would be attacked. But
townsmen in mediæval warfare were apt to suffer from rashness;
one of many examples is the behaviour of the Londoners at Lewes
in 1264. It has been supposed that dust may have hidden the
cavalry flight from the Toulousans or there may have been clumps
of trees to block their view. Knowing de Montfort to be heavily
outnumbered, they believed a rumour of his defeat, sallied out from
their camp, and beset the town from all sides.

In Muret, Count Simon's victory was already known by messenger. Bishop Fulk of Toulouse, who was of Simon's party and
had remained in the town, sent to tell his obstreperous flock of
this and offered them mercy but they would not believe and
wounded his parlementaire. Startled at the sight of the Crusaders
returning victorious and about to fall upon the rear of their
extended formation, they broke up in a panic and were slaughtered
far and wide. Some fled to camp and were killed there, others
made for the boats which had brought up their siege material and
were now anchored about a mile north of the town. A few
escaped so, but most were butchered on the high banks by de
Montfort's people.

In 1875 a flood of the Garonne undercut and brought down
much of the bank, revealing an immense mass of their bones,
opposite Saubens and about seven hundred yards upstream from
that village. Other skeletons are scattered about to the north of
this spot; to this day they are turned up sometimes by the spade
and the plough.

The total losses of the vanquished were enormous while the

victors lost only one knight and, at most, eight "sergeants"—a fully armed man in a position to defend himself was already in 1213 so completely protected by his chain-mail armour. Infantry normally accounted for most mediæval battle casualties. Furthermore the dismounted and wounded knights of the losing side could be massacred at leisure if the victors so chose, as they emphatically did on this occasion.

De Montfort's rashness in attacking with only a narrow bridge for retreat in case of a check is explained as Napoleon's putting in the guard at Waterloo is explained, by the political necessity for victory. The tower of the castle commanding the bridge could perhaps, by a plunging fire of missiles from its great height, have kept a little space clear should the Crusaders be driven back.

The rout of Pedro's infantry, most of whom were communal militia from Toulouse, may seem like an exception to the general conduct of such troops. However, it should be remembered that the men of southern France were richer and less warlike than most Christians of the time, that on this occasion they were completely surprised by the sudden arrival of the terrible de Montfort whom they had thought destroyed, and finally that flexibility and speed at getting into formation to stand off cavalry was never a strong point with mediæval foot.

It should be noted further that the victory of Muret did not cause the surrender of Toulouse, which continued impregnable to de Montfort and finally yielded through political action, not to capture.[15]

[15] For a fuller account of the Albigensian War, including Muret, see Chs. 4 and 5 of "The Inquisition: A Military and Political Study of Its Establishment," Hoffman Nickerson.

Anglade's "Muret" reprints in full all the original authorities.

CHAPTER VII

CULMINATION OF MEDIÆVAL WARFARE

1214–1302 A. D.

In this chapter I shall consider first the campaign and battle of Bouvines, second, John Plantagenet's campaign of 1216, and, third, the culmination of mediæval cavalry tactics in the battles delivered by Charles of Anjou. I shall end the chapter with a discussion of the causes which, in the following century, were to bring about the decreasing efficiency and consequent decline of the mounted man at arms.

In regard to the number of troops engaged, the greatest battle of the European Middle Ages is Bouvines. Fought in 1214, the year after Muret, it was an action of a very different sort. Here it is the infantry of the communes who form the pivot upon which everything turns. Before taking up the battle itself, let us consider the strategy leading up to it and the political circumstances which determined its morale.

Again, as at Muret, we find religious enthusiasm on the part of the French as the cause of their high morale; their King Philip Augustus could truthfully represent himself as the Champion of the Church against the Coalition which menaced both the Papacy and himself. The soul of that coalition was John Plantagenet, King of England in succession to his brother Cœur de Lion. Like all the men of his family, John was a highly educated man and a great soldier. He had for allies his nephew Otto IV, Holy Roman Emperor, and also the Count of Flanders, one of Philip's chief vassals.

Although prevented by political circumstances from putting forth their full strength, both sides made great efforts to raise troops. The Pope had put up a candidate for Emperor against Otto and that candidate was alienating South Germany. Furthermore, John could not trust the English baronage. Philip Augustus, on his side, was somewhat weakened inasmuch as a number of

157

his barons would go off from time to time to fight under de Mont-fort against the Albigenses, but this drain on his resources dimin-ished them less in proportion than did the difficulties of Otto and John. On the other hand, John had the finest Treasury Depart-ment in Europe and hired mercenaries lavishly. His father, Henry II of England, had been the first sovereign in Europe to commute feudal military service by a system of money payments known as "scutage"—an important step in the transition from personal ser-vices and dues in kind to so-called "money economics." Flan-ders, the most populous district in Latin Christendom, turned out in great force.

John now conceived an extensive strategic scheme. Although he had lost Normandy in 1204 after the fall of Château Gaillard, he still held southwestern France. He himself, with part of his mercenaries, would land at La Rochelle and advance into the Loire districts taken from him by Philip ten years before, refusing battle when the French attacked him and so manœuvring as to draw them as far as possible to the south and west. Meanwhile Otto was to march westward on the familiar line—Cologne—Aix-la-Chapelle—Liége. In what is now Belgium the Germans would be joined by the Count of Flanders, the contingents of the minor allies, and the remainder of John's mercenaries. They would then march unopposed on Paris.

This very reasonable plan failed through inaccurate timing and through Philip's combination of good judgment and good luck. John did his part admirably. Braving winter storms, he crossed to La Rochelle in mid-February and began consoli-dating his political and military position in the counties of Poitou, La Marche and Angoulême. When Philip hastened to meet him he continued to move to and fro erratically so as not to be brought to battle. Early in April he turned south through Limoges and Périgueux to the county of Agenais on the Garonne. Wisely refus-ing to follow, Philip returned to Paris leaving a detachment in John's front to contain him. Against this detachment John showed great activity. In May he advanced northward, won an engage-ment under the walls of Nantes, and occupied Angers. He would probably have destroyed Philip's detachment, which he out-numbered, had it not been for the last-minute defection of a number of French barons serving in his ranks, which forced him to refuse battle and retreat south of the Loire. It was now June.[1]

Meanwhile after beginning well by reaching Aix-la-Chapelle on March 23rd, Otto had lingered inexcusably there until July, getting himself married and consolidating his political position. At last he reached Nivelles on July 12th and was in Valenciennes on July 20th. By this time Philip, without too greatly weakening his detachment against John, had had time to raise a considerable army and concentrate it at Péronne.

In mailed cavalry both sides had about eleven thousand. The poorly armed feudal infantry may be disregarded. In solid municipal militia infantry the French had from twenty to thirty thousand whereas Otto had a huge multitude of perhaps seventy-odd thousand. Of course the French were a homogeneous force acting against a coalition.

Even yet, although his inexcusable slowness had prevented his marching unopposed upon Paris, Otto's game was a winning one. The theatre of war was more wooded and the river valleys far more marshy than to-day. As long as Otto stayed behind the marshes of the Scheldt his overwhelming numerical superiority in infantry made it impossible for the French to attack. At the same time they could not prevent him, in Valenciennes, from raiding far and wide—so many roads converged upon that town. Meanwhile, reinforcements for his army kept coming in.

In this difficult position Philip moved from Péronne on Tournai, by Douai, Seclin and Bouvines bridge. The semi-independent municipalities of Douai and Tournai (although in Flemish territory) sympathized with the French. The march took five days, beginning with a forced march of 45 miles and ending July 26th with an easy stage of 9. Between Bouvines and Tournai the country was open and suitable for cavalry. Philip therefore hoped to draw out Otto by devastating the countrysides of the German's Flemish allies.

The move failed; Otto merely moved some ten miles up the Scheldt to Mortagne. Here, being only about six miles from Tournai, he was able to observe Philip closely, while still well covered by terrain difficult for cavalry because of woods and inundations. Also he was almost due south of the French army and between it

[1] Norgate, 196–202. See Plates 18–19.

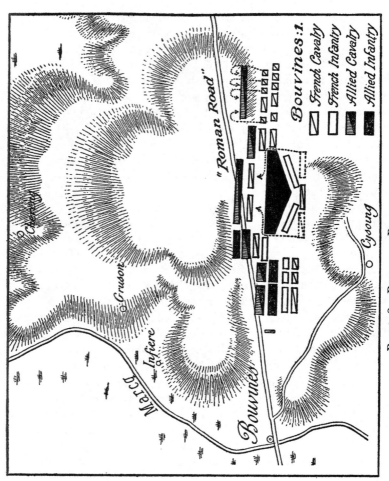

Bouvines:1.

▨ French Cavalry
▢ French Infantry
▨ Allied Cavalry
■ Allied Infantry

PLATE 8.—BATTLE OF BOUVINES.

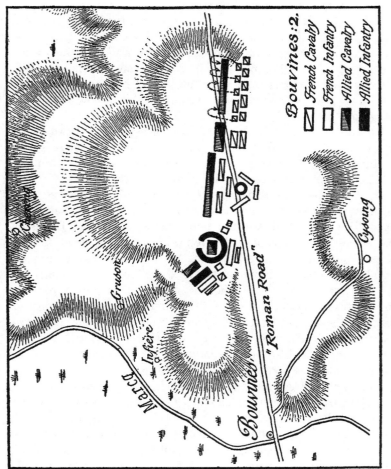

PLATE 9.—BATTLE OF BOUVINES.

and Paris. The intelligence service of both armies was working well. Disaffected nobles on both sides systematically reported to each of the hostile commanders the proceedings even of the secret councils of war held in the other camp.

Philip saw that he must retreat. So far, in the earlier leisurely stages of the campaign in which there had been plenty of time to consider each decision, the French had had somewhat the worst of it. Philip's aim in moving on Tournai, that is his hope of tempting Otto into attacking him in open country, had not been realized, and the French position was dangerous.

On July 26th decision followed upon decision in the two headquarters with a rapidity which reminds us of the Campaign of Waterloo. First Otto called a council and showed complete intelligence returns of the inferior numbers of the French. Thereupon it was decided that some vigorous move should soon be made in order to take advantage of the rashness of the French advance upon Tournai. A disaffected noble hastily informed Philip of the entire discussion, and also reported on the difficult terrain about Mortagne over which it would be impossible for the French cavalry to attack. Philip instantly called his inner council, in the greatest secrecy. It was now afternoon. The French decided to retreat on Bouvines, slowly and well in hand but with simulated panic, in the hope of tempting Otto to attack them while they were crossing the bridge and causeway over the rivulets and marshes of the Marque. News of the intended retreat was given out in the afternoon and was promptly carried to Otto, magnified by the genuine panic of the citizens of Tournai at the prospect of being abandoned. On receiving this news, Otto called a second council in the evening, at which it was decided to attack the French next day at the bridge of Bouvines. A minority held that it would be imprudent to attack in such open country but the majority believed the reports of panic in the French camp and were unwilling to miss the chance of attacking their enemy strung out while crossing the obstacle.

In the morning the French slowly retreated, moving first their transport, next their foot, and finally their cavalry. All combat troops were kept well closed up and prepared to form front to the rear. The bridge had been widened, in order to hasten a possible retreat. Otto followed so hastily that he could have been attacked as his advance guard cleared the marshes and this course was advised by Garin the Hospitaller whom we find acting as a sort of chief of staff to Philip. However, it was finally decided to draw him further out.

The stand was made about three miles east of the bridge. Otto lost a possible advantage by drawing up his front northwest to southeast instead of north to south. A north-south front would have backed the French up against the bridge, and assured his own retreat. The front he chose gave him only the advantage of a slight slope down which his centre could charge. The order of battle was the same on both sides—the municipal militia infantry of the communes in the centre, cavalry on each wing, and a cavalry reserve in rear of the centre under the commander-in-chief.

The numerous Rhenish and Flemish pikemen, apparently in a wedge-shaped formation, succeeded in splitting the centre of the French communal infantry. When Philip charged them he was unhorsed and for some moments in great personal danger. On the other hand, we have seen that the ranks of mediæval pikemen were always disordered by a forward movement, even when that movement (as in the present case) had been successful or even (as in the case of Moorish pikemen of Majorca in 1129) when it had been absolutely unopposed. Presently some units of French horse either cut through the mass or worked around its flanks, checked the Emperor and his cavalry reserve, and then charged the Imperial infantry in the rear. The Rhinelanders and Flemings were the best municipal infantry in Europe. Nevertheless, when struck on two fronts by the French knights and sergeants they were broken and massacred. Meanwhile the French right wing commanded by Garin the Hospitaller had broken the Imperial left. Otto fled.

The last act of the battle was to overcome the desperate resistance of part of the Imperial right. Here certain units of infantry and cavalry were closely combined, quite as in Palestine, the pikemen forming a circle and affording a refuge for their horsemen between charges. It should be remarked that to open the necessary gaps in the circle for the passage of retreating horsemen and then close them against pursuit implies cool, well-drilled troops. Only

by an overwhelming concentration against them were these determined men finally beaten.[2]

The battle destroyed the anti-Papal coalition and ended John's
hope of re-establishing his position on the continent.

In 1216, two years after Bouvines, we find John driven to bay
in England by wealthy rebels aided by French troops. Against
this combination he preserved the English Crown to the Plantagenets by winning a masterly campaign which shows us mediæval
strategy at its best. It shows us also the strategic effect of the
system of castles.

We have already seen how strong castles were under mediæval
conditions. The point I now wish to emphasize is their great
numbers. In England every port on the south coast was held
by a castle. From Dover to Southampton—not much over a
hundred miles—there were eleven and these eleven were backed by
a double line further inland. The line of the Thames was held as
in a vise by the Tower of London, Windsor, Reading, Wallingford
and Oxford, five first-class fortresses within less than sixty miles
as the crow flies. And so it was everywhere.

We are accustomed to think of castles as the private possession
of rich men. But in all the good time of the early Middle Ages,
including the thirteenth century, they were crown property and
their commanders the revocable appointees of the King.

In part the castles which were to play so large a part in 1216
were of earlier construction. Many of them dated back to the
generation after the conquest. Nevertheless before considering
1216 it will be convenient to consider thirteenth-century fortification and siege-work in general even if the order of time be
somewhat violated thereby.

In the thirteenth-century castles, we find that the mistake
made in putting the entrance to the Donjon of Château Gaillard
so high, is never repeated. Thenceforward, Donjons were entered
from the inner court level. The Donjon itself begins to lose in
importance relative to the inner ward with its flanking towers.
Instead of being the core of the defence (as it was before 1200),
it is now often placed, as at Coucy, directly in the assailants'

[2] For the campaign and battle, see Delpech, Vol. 1, 4–175 and 456–457.
Oman, Vol. 1, 467–490 is not so good, especially on the preliminaries of the
action. Dieulafoy, "Muret," 5–6, has a note on tactics.

path in attacking the inner ward. Sometimes there is no Donjon at all, as at Krak-des-Chevaliers, Athlit, and Caerphilly.

The reason for the decreased importance of the Donjon in the general scheme of defence was that the military engineers of the time were so impressed with the importance of the flanking fire to be obtained from towers mutually supporting one another that when building new fortresses they did not care to spend money on a single great tower which, by itself, did not develop any flanking fire at all. They preferred to increase the size of the towers set in the curtain wall. They were concerned to rid themselves of dead space, for at Provins and in the addition made to Carcassonne about 1280 we find the towers no longer rounded in front but pointed like a Vauban bastion.

Besides the attention paid to flanking fire by the thirteenth-century builders, we find them providing for a more active defence. This was done by means of barbacans, a word supposedly derived from the Arabic Bab-Khaneh, meaning a gatehouse. A barbacan, as its name implies, was often placed just outside a gate. They were comparatively low works of considerable extent, built with a rounded trace, their purpose being to shelter bodies of men assembled for sorties.

It is surprising that stone machicolation gained ground so slowly, for wooden hoardings could be burned and were far more vulnerable to stones thrown by catapults. But although we have seen stone machicolation at Château Gaillard (1196), and although it was common in thirteenth-century crusading castles built in deforested Syria, it is not found again in the West before 1300. The Donjon of Coucy (1230) had masonry corbels or brackets for its hoardings, but the hoardings themselves seem to have been of wood. It is equally surprising to find the excessive subdivision and difficulty of communication between the various parts of the defence continued in the thirteenth-century work after they had proved disastrous at Château Gaillard. It is true that Coucy had only one main line of defence outside of its Donjon; the designer preferred to put his money in increased height and thickness of walls rather than into an accumulation of obstacles. But even Coucy was so cut up that Viollet le Duc estimated that at least 500 men would be needed to guard its circuit of 475 yards, of which only about 150 are approachable on level ground.

In siege-work, the twelfth century had refined upon the counterpoise catapult by making the counterpoise movable. This ensured greater ease in the adjustment of fire, for the range could be controlled by regulating the distance from counterpoise to pivot. An even more satisfactory arrangement was to have the main counterpoise fixed and to supplement it by a smaller secondary counterpoise which was movable. Unfortunately even with the movable counterpoise there was another variable which must have been next to impossible to control, i. e., the weight of the projectile. Before an accurate fire of any intensity could be directed against a given point, say the roof and battlements of a particular tower, a besieger had to have so strong a corps of artificers chipping stones down to a uniform weight that the game was not worth the candle.

Not improved catapults but improved mining was the chief study of thirteenth-century engineers. When the fortresses to be attacked were not founded upon bare rocks, they preferred to dig an underground tunnel or gallery. A "cat" could be attacked from above and had the further disadvantage of showing the besieged the precise point where the mine-chamber was to be dug.

In 1285, when the Mameluke Sultan of Egypt besieged Markab, a Syrian castle of the Knights of the Hospital, he first took the outer defences and then attacked the inner ward. By mining he then brought down part of a tower of the neighbouring curtain wall, making a breach from which he was repulsed with heavy casualties. He then mined again and in eight days established a mine chamber under the great tower. Preferring to capture the place intact for his own use, he forbore to fire the mine and instead he sent a flag of truce to the besieged, offering safe conduct to engineers whom they might send out to inspect his mine. The Christian engineers on their return reported that the great tower must fall when the mine was fired. Whereupon the knights—professional enemies of Islam though they were—surrendered on terms and retired unmolested with their horses, baggage and treasure.[3]

At John's siege of Rochester Castle in 1215 interesting details of the working of what we should call his ordnance department have been preserved. On the second day of the siege, we find him

[3] Oman, Vol. 2, 51–52.

ordering all the smiths of Canterbury, 30 miles away, to make as many pickaxes as they could and send them to him as fast as they could be made.   A little later he writes to the Justiciar—as we should say, the Chief Justice of the Kingdom—to send him 40 bacon pigs of the fattest and least good for eating, the grease to be used in firing the timbers of the mine chamber by which he brought down one of the square angle turrets of the rectangular Norman keep.   Even then the garrison defended the breach until weakened by famine, when they surrendered.   The siege began Oct. 13 and lasted until November 30—48 days in all.[4]

John's campaign of 1216 is an example of a campaign won by strategy alone without a battle in the field—like Napoleon's campaign of Ulm in 1805.   It differs from Ulm in that its success was less crushing, although quite as definite, and was achieved not by marching alone but by a combination of marching and siege-work.

In June, 1215, John had yielded to his gang of wealthy rebels and signed Magna Charta.   Immediately after that surrender he began preparing to renew the struggle.   As usual in the Middle Ages, we find the mass of the nation (including all the towns except London) in sympathy with the King, whose power was a sort of shield for them against the oligarchy of the nobles.   On the other hand, London, the centre of wealth and (as in 1066) a military factor of the utmost importance, was for the rebels because London was controlled by the influence of rich merchants who sympathized with the feudal oligarchy.   John hired mercenaries right and left on the continent and used many of them in garrisoning the castles.   Although the sympathy of the nation with him was at first only passive, nevertheless his own skill as a soldier and diplomat was so high that by the end of 1215 he had reduced his opponents almost to despair.   In their despair they proposed revolution and offered the crown of England to the son of Philip Augustus—Louis, afterwards Louis VII of France.   French aid to the rebels began to come in during the winter of 1215–16.

The decisive summer campaign of 1216 opened with a series of reverses for John.   He tried to prevent Louis's landing but late in May the French prince made good his crossing to the eastern

<hr>

[4] Norgate, 249–251.   For 13th-century fortification and siege-work see Dict. de l'Arch.   See also Oman, Vol. 2, 38–53.

tip of Kent. John's next decision was to attack the French before the English rebels could join them. But when the moment came he dared not deliver battle for most of his mercenaries were vassals to the house of Capet. An action in the field against the son of their own overlord might strain their loyalty. Leaving a strong and trusty garrison in Dover Castle, John retreated on Winchester.

Considering only the military aspect of affairs, Louis should have laid siege to Dover at once. However, in a civil war political factors are even more important than in foreign wars. Either from political motives or from folly, Louis preferred to enter London in triumph and be fêted there. Even then he made no move against the untaken fortress in his rear but moved on Winchester, taking the castles of Reigate, Guilford, and Farnham, as he came. Again John dared not risk an action, and on June 14, Louis entered Winchester unopposed. Here he received homage from the chiefs of the minority of English nobles who had up to that time supported the legitimate king. Meanwhile detachments of rebels had swept the eastern counties and taken the town (although not the castle) of Lincoln.

From about the end of June to the middle of July there was a pause. John had retreated into the southwest, apparently lost. It was true that he still held a number of strong points throughout the kingdom. In particular there were the four great strongholds of Windsor, Reading, Wallingford, and Oxford which commanded the line of the Thames and split almost in two the rebel holdings north and south of that river. Dover Castle had not even been attacked. Moreover, the English municipalities (except London, the greatest of them all) were loyal throughout. On the other hand, London's support of the rebels, together with John's inability to deliver battle, made the position seem hopeless.

Now when the Plantagenet cause was lowest the nation began to move. For the first time in English history there appears a true national resistance to the foreigner and to the oligarchic revolutionaries allied to the foreigner. Of course the movement was not on the scale of similar modern movements. National patriotism was in its infancy. Still it was real enough to change the whole situation. In the districts held by the rebels the farmers began banding together much like American minute-men—except that the thirteenth-century minute-men took arms for the King instead of against him. Although such troops can effect nothing decisive, they have an infinite capacity for worrying an invader.

The national movement might not have enabled John to resist had it not been for Louis' error in failing to secure Dover. From Paris, Philip Augustus taunted his son for trying to conquer England without first seizing its key. Nevertheless soon after taking Winchester Louis went back to London—to be again feasted and to do his best to reconcile the quarrels and jealousies between his French and English supporters. Not until July 25th did he move from London on Dover. It was too late. John was now strong enough to begin the operation which was to assure the continuance of his dynasty.

About July 27th a considerable body of French and rebels besieged Windsor to free London of its nearest hostile garrison, very much as Pedro and Raymond three years before had tried to disengage Toulouse.

Dover resisted so gallantly as to immobilize Louis himself and an important part of his force far from the decisive theatre of operations. The garrison of Windsor did so well that the siege there dwindled to a blockade. The garrison of Lincoln Castle likewise held out against a detachment of rebels.

In the worst of his defeat John had consolidated the southwest, strengthening and provisioning the royal castles there. Now, about the middle of July, before Louis and the rebels had started from London to besiege his garrisons in Dover and Windsor, he felt himself strong enough to move. From Dorset he marched north and recovered Worcester. Thereafter until the end of August he went up and down establishing the line of the Severn as a western limit to the rebellion.

As late as August 19th one of his letters shows that he still expected or pretended to expect an attack by Louis upon the west. In reality the forces of the invader and the rebels were fully occupied before Dover and Windsor. Neither siege was making rapid progress and Louis's Frenchmen, as was the exasperating custom of feudal armies serving far afield, were beginning to melt away homewards. At Dover where the rebels and the invaders were making their main effort the resistance was particularly stout. Louis himself in front of the place was entirely out of the game about to begin elsewhere. Thus the resistance of Dover had already made possible the recovery of Worcester and was to be the foundation of all that followed.

When informed of the true position of his enemies, John formed a plan which in conception and execution shows his high ability as a strategist. No first-class city of the Middle Ages could be directly attacked with success. They were too big and too populous for the armies of the time. Therefore he could not move on London. Weakened as he was by his numerous garrisons he did not yet desire battle. He had already established a westward limit for the rebellion by his chain of garrisoned strong points in Dorset and along the Severn. He would now establish a northward limit by throwing another chain of strong points eastward to the North Sea. His enemies would then be penned in the extreme southeast. With the national resistance already afoot, their surrender or destruction would be only a question of time. In an age without maps or any other of the mechanical aids to modern staff work, such a plan stamps its author as a great soldier.

John's execution was as clever as his conception was broad and sound. On September 2nd he moved east from Cirencester to Burford, then to Oxford, Wallingford, and Reading. His advance appeared to be aimed at Windsor, and in order to convince the besiegers of that point that he was about to attack them he sent a contingent of Welsh archers to shoot into their camp at night. The French and the rebels stood to arms to receive him and thus he achieved his object, which was to gain a start on them for his northward march. Instead he slipped away by Anglesbury and Bedford, making for Cambridge. As soon as this was known to the besiegers of Windsor they saw at once the strength of his move. The movements of their party had been cramped all along by the Thames castles. They were now limited on the west. To be limited on the north would bring them to the brink of defeat. They therefore raised the siege, burnt their siege machinery and hurried towards Cambridge. If they could reach that place ahead of John they could prevent him from getting control of the northern roads.

The situation was now the familiar one of two armies converging on the same point, in this case Cambridge. Perhaps the best known parallel is Moore's and Napoleon's race for Benavente in

1808, although Moore was not out to garrison road centres (as John undoubtedly was) but was merely trying to get away. John won the race with his well-trained mercenary army and in so doing won the campaign and saved his dynasty. He now had the opportunity of planting a garrison across every road north from London. With his army in being near by, the rebels were trapped unless they could achieve the difficult task of breaking his ring.

PLATE 10.—THE CAMPAIGN OF JOHN PLANTAGENET IN 1216.

After John's arrival in Cambridge on September 15th, the rest of the campaign followed by itself. As the enemy approached he refused battle and continued his eastward movement by Clare and Hedingham. Baffled, the recent besiegers of Windsor turned south to help Louis besiege Dover. The rebel siege of Lincoln Castle was easily raised. The Scotch king who had marched past John's northern garrisons right down to London now scuttled home again. Indeed he was almost caught by John as he did so. From Lincoln John moved to the east coast so that the ring about London was complete. It was just after mid-September, and in the countrysides of the southern counties the national resistance to the foreigners was continually growing.

The final surrender of Dover, and even John's death late in October, came too late to affect the result. Now that he had enclosed the rebellion, the loss of his splendid generalship was balanced by the political gain to the royal cause through the softening of the enmities his strong personality had aroused. As Belloc truly says "John was in his grave, but he had won. And he had won as a strategist." [5]

If the campaigns of John Plantagenet may be considered typical of mediæval strategy at its best, the culmination of mediæval tactics is found in the operations of Charles of Anjou. That wicked but able brother of St. Louis could handle mailed cavalry with a varied skill never before or afterwards attained.

His first major action was fought at Benevento in 1266 under the following circumstances. Between the Papacy and the Hohenstaufen family who were kings of Naples and Sicily there had been a long and bitter feud. The Pope of the day offered their Crown to Charles and gave him money to hire mercenaries. Like William the Conqueror, Charles also promised lands in his new kingdom to such nobles as would bring a contingent to help him win it. He himself arrived in Rome in May, 1265, but the greater part of the adventurers joined him only in January, 1266. By this time money was running low so that he had to advance at once despite the bad season, in order to reach hostile territory where his army could live off the country. Charles therefore allowed the late comers only eight days' rest in Rome and then led them forward by the Latin Way.

King Manfred posted himself at Capua in great force, fortified the bridge over the Volturno and prepared to hold the line of that river. The weakness of his position was political, for many of his subjects were disloyal. When an advanced detachment of his was beaten on the Garigliano, the whole country between that river and the Volturno went over to Charles. The Volturno position looked so strong that Charles was willing to risk the Apennines in February in order to turn it. The invading army suffered severely from

---

[5] Belloc: Warfare in England, 129–138. Norgate is useful for details here and there but makes no pretence to analyze and understand military affairs. See Plate 20.

cold and snow. All wheeled transport had to be abandoned;
many horses died. Provisions began to run short. Finally, when
approaching Benevento, Manfred and his army were found oc-
cupying that town. The Hohenstaufen had received prompt
intelligence of Charles' move and with a good high road to march
on had easily gained his front.[6]

Charles' position was now as bad as before Capua, plus a grave
peril in the matter of supplies. The Calore was as impassable
as the Volturno. Had Manfred merely refused battle the French
must have dispersed or starved. On the other hand, Manfred's
position was unsuitable for an advance as he had only a single
bridge by which to cross.

Charles was inferior in numbers. Severe march casualties had
reduced him to four thousand six hundred mailed cavalry. To
support them he had a few good mercenary crossbowmen but most
of his foot were mere feudal infantry. Manfred's army was larger
but less homogeneous and in part disloyal. It included ten thousand Saracens, most of them foot archers with some light cavalry,
all devoted to their protectors the Hohenstaufens. In mailed
cavalry there were three thousand six hundred—fourteen hundred
traitorous feudal men-at-arms from Manfred's subjects, nine
hundred Italian mercenaries and twelve hundred German mercenaries equipped not with the usual chain-mail and gambeson
but with a newfangled sort of armour of iron plates. These last
were the most formidable of Manfred's troops.

On the morning of February 26th Manfred sent his Saracens
across the Calore to skirmish. They easily drove in Charles'
infantry who came out to oppose them, but were sent flying by
a charge of a thousand mounted sergeants. Whereupon Manfred's
German mercenaries, in their plate armour, advanced across the
bridge and charged to prevent the massacre of the fleeing
Saracens.

It is not clear whether the decision to advance the Germans was
Manfred's or that of the unit commander carried away by seeing
the defeat of the Saracens. If the king deliberately committed the
folly of engaging, then he must have thought the French to be
in even worse condition than they actually were, or else he must
have feared that his own bad political position might grow still

[6] Oman, Vol. 1, 496–499.

more unfavourable should he temporize. At all events, the Germans charged and battle was seriously joined.

The mailed horsemen of both armies were arranged in three "battles," one behind the other. Advancing at a slow trot with ranks well closed up, at first the Germans swept everything before them. Against chain-mail, even when backed by a heavy reinforcement of wadding, a blow might bruise even when it did not penetrate. But all strokes rebounded from the solid German plate. Seeing his first battle giving way, Charles put in his second. Against these too the Germans still held out, so that a charge by Manfred's rear battles would probably have won the day. Unfortunately for him, they were kept out of action until too late by the slow business of defiling over Benevento bridge. The day was saved for Charles by the discovery that the plate armour—not yet as perfect as it later became—left the Germans' armpits unprotected as they raised their swords to strike. The cry to thrust under the armpits was passed down the French line and by this device the Germans were broken.

The rest of the action was soon over. When the Italian mercenaries of Manfred's second battle finally arrived on the scene, Charles charged them at once in front and in flank and rear as well so that they were dispersed in a few moments. As the second battle had come up too late to support the Germans, so Manfred and his third battle were too late to support them. The numerous traitors in his ranks swerved off just before the shock, and Manfred himself was killed.

The victory was won by Charles' quickness and address in supporting one battle by another, together with the timely discovery of the way to beat the Germans.[7]

Having possessed the Kingdom of Naples for two years after Benevento, in 1268 Charles had to resist the invasion of Conradin, the fifteen-year-old nephew of Manfred and last of the Hohenstaufen.

Naturally, because of his extreme youth, Conradin was in the hands of advisers. He received some support from Alfonso the Wise of Castile, whose mother had been a Hohenstaufen princess, and he himself mortgaged his German duchy of Suabia to raise money, but in spite of all efforts his cause was weak on the

[7] Delpech, Vol. 2, 99–106.

financial side. His strength lay in the zeal with which the numerous imperialists throughout Italy supported him. Charles, on the other hand, had made himself hated, so that the Kingdom of Naples was as full of traitors as it had been under Manfred. Conradin crossed the Alps in October, 1267, and was gladly received in Verona. Meanwhile his party gained control of Rome. Hoping to hold the line of the Apennines, Charles thrust himself forward past Rome into Tuscany. But hardly had he done so when widespread insurrections against him began in Sicily and among the Saracens of the mainland. When a detachment of his was repulsed from Rome he went back to besiege the Saracen stronghold of Lucera in Apulia. Conradin marched unopposed on Rome and in July, 1268, was enthusiastically welcomed to that city. Hurrying back from Apulia Charles concentrated on the Garigliano.

The situation was now much what it had been two years before with Charles as the defending instead of the attacking party. Again the invaders determined to turn the defenders' left. Here, however, the resemblance ends, for Conradin's advisers wanted to join hands with their friends the Saracens of Lucera. Accordingly they marched up the Anio valley by the Valerian Way, intending to cross the Apennines and then march down the eastern side of the peninsula until they could join hands with the Lucerans.

The season was favourable, the plan was sound, and its execution was vigorous. Conradin's troops were all mounted. Leaving Rome on the 18th, they did over sixty miles in four days, passed the town of Tagliacozzo, and came out in the upland plains east of that town. They undoubtedly knew that Charles had many secret partisans in Rome who would send him intelligence of their move. Nevertheless, granted their own speed over the steep passes, the chances of a successful turning movement were in their favour, for the news of their eastward march would have to travel sixty miles south to Charles at, say, Ceprano before that Prince could begin to move to intercept them. That Charles was able to do so was due to no fault in their plan but to his own rapid decision and extraordinary energy. Within twenty-four hours of Conradin's move from Rome, Charles knew it. Whereupon he dashed northward from Ceprano (moving undoubtedly by Sora) at top speed, sometimes even marching into the night. In three days, with a slightly shorter distance to cover, he managed to reach Conradin's front. Despite his terrific march, when Charles' vanguard met Conradin's just east of the upper Salto River, it was the invaders who gave ground, abandoning the obstacle of the Salto and its ravine to the tired French. Had Conradin's advisers known their enemy's extreme fatigue, they might have won by an immediate attack. It is reasonable to suppose that they did not know it, and that the reason why they made no move for the rest of the day was that they were so surprised to find Charles in their front.[8]

On the morning of August 23rd, the two armies drew up facing one another across the Salto ravine which was spanned by a single bridge. Conradin had about five thousand armoured horsemen, several hundred of whom were Spaniards and the rest about equally divided between Germans and Italians. The Spaniards and Germans wore plate armour but (unlike the Germans at Benevento) they wore it over their chain-mail.

Charles had only three thousand mailed cavalry, including a few Italians of his party. The rest were about half French mercenaries, half French knights and squires who had received feudal grants of land in his new kingdom and were consequently devoted to his cause. The rest of his force was foot—apparently not of first quality. In view of this grave numerical inferiority in horse, Charles determined upon a defensive action. On the previous day, the superior dash of his advance guard had given him an obstacle to cover his front—the Salto with its ravine. This he was firmly resolved not to cross. On the other hand, his infantry were not good enough to take up the usual immobile mediæval defensive. Even after their day of rest they must have been badly fatigued by the forced marches.

Charles had, as his chief military adviser, Alard of St. Valery, a veteran of the wars of Syria and a most skilful soldier. Between them they devised a solution of the difficulty not altogether unlike one of the stock tactical methods of Napoleon. Like the Revolutionary Emperor, they proposed to gain time and tire out the enemy by opposing to him a part of their force. Not until after this fraction was completely fought out was the remainder to enter the combat and attempt a decision.

[8] Oman, Vol. 1, 505–508.

Of course, the details of the tactics employed bore no relation to those later used by Napoleon. The reserve, which included eight hundred North-French knights, was kept out of sight just behind a crest. With it were Charles and Alard, who concealed themselves on the crest itself. As to the line of resistance and its supports, the difficulty was the weakness of the infantry. It was accordingly reinforced by the grooms and servants, and placed in close individual support to the cavalry of the forward divisions. These last were formed in successive open lines "as foragers," i. e., with wide intervals. Each horsemen was followed by two dismounted men with instructions to strike at the hostile horses. The necessity for sticking to the infantry would obviously prevent the cavalry from charging more then a few yards. On the other hand, their open order left them free to skirmish by fencing actively with their opponents from the saddle, while the pikes of the infantry would give them some protection against the shock of their enemies.

The device was risky, inasmuch as the skirmishing tactics of mixed forces of cavalry and infantry could not possibly defeat good hostile cavalry. Evidently Charles' infantry was not considered good enough to stand alone. Nevertheless the scheme worked. The mixed force put up so good a fight that Conradin's people took them for Charles' entire army. When at last it was brushed aside, the invaders thought the battle was over. This misunderstanding was aided by the general belief in their army that Charles had fallen early in the action because the commander of his delaying units, dressed in the royal armour, had been killed. Some of the enemy scattered to plunder. Those still with the colours were tired out by the weight and rigidity of their plate armour and the skirmishing tactics of Charles' delaying troops.

Charles now engaged his reserve in two sections. The first section simulated fear by swerving aside just before the shock, then wheeling off to the rear. Charles now charged with his second section, while the first section again wheeled and struck the hostile flank. The hostile ranks had, of course, been loosened by their first charge. Nevertheless the plate armour seemed impenetrable. Charles now hit upon another of his expedients. He passed the word down the line for his horsemen to close with the tired and overweighted enemy, wrestle with them, and throw them down from their saddles. By so doing they broke the enemy's last resistance.[9]

Charles' versatility is still further proved by his conduct of operations against the mobile Mohammedans in Tunisia. At the battle of Carthage in 1280, two years after Tagliacozzo, he executed successfully a movement which superlatively proved the manœuvring power of thirteenth-century cavalry. Charles was anxious to bring his nimble Moorish enemies to close action. He was facing east, they west. Both he and they rested their northern flank on the sea. Charles first advanced eastward, then wheeled about and simulated flight toward the west, followed by the Moors. He then made a left turn through three-quarters of a circle and drove his lighter opponents northward into the sea. To make such an evolution successfully implies the greatest possible suppleness and speed of manœuvre.[10]

I have already called the campaigns of Charles of Anjou the culmination of mediæval cavalry tactics. Their versatility results from a long development beginning in the ninth century and continuing unchecked until the second half of the thirteenth. I have now to describe the way in which mediæval cavalry declined. In its outline the affair is very simple. The plate armour worn by the defeated side at Benevento and Tagliacozzo was adopted throughout Christendom and its great weight destroyed the ability of its wearers to manœuvre.

The reader must distinguish clearly between the absolute decline of cavalry, compared to its own standard of achievement, and the relative decline of cavalry as compared with infantry. Had mediæval cavalry maintained its tactical standard, or had it developed it even further, nevertheless it seems as certain as any historical guesswork can be, that the general rise in civilization would have resulted in better disciplined armies. This, in turn, would almost inevitably have restored infantry to its normal place as the chief arm. At the same time, the fact is that the loss of tactical flexibility on the part of cavalry came about before there was any marked improvement in infantry. When the infantry improvements did come they found cavalry tactics already in decay. For the present we are concerned not

---

[9] Delpech, Vol. 2, 107–119.
[10] Delpech, Vol. 1, 440–441, and Vol. 2, 88–89.

with the later improvement in infantry but with the decline of cavalry.

The reader may well ask why the plate armour which implied such tactical degeneration was not discouraged by the abler commanders of the time, especially in view of the defeat of its wearers at Tagliacozzo and Benevento. A most varied combination of causes converged to bring about its adoption everywhere. First, despite the beginning of English and French nationalism, the framework of society remained feudal. A king or great lord could summon his vassals to take the field but could not prescribe the armour which they were to wear. Only the strongest disciplinary authority could have compelled men to put away so efficient a means of increasing their individual safety at the expense of the collective efficiency of the army as a whole. Now feudalism, while encouraging military honour, was almost the negation of strict discipline. Second, military men continued to learn military theory from Vegetius, who is never tired of recommending invulnerability and of cursing the soldiers of his day for laying aside their armour. At the same time missile weapons were being improved; the crossbow was now so strong that it had to be bent by means of a lever or even by a winch, and the power of the English longbow was to astonish fourteenth-century Europe. Finally the Crusades had ceased, and with them the importation of Arabian blooded stock which had made the European horses faster and more agile. It became necessary to cover the horse as well as his rider with the heavy iron plating, for a man weighted with the new armour could not rise to his feet unaided if his horse were killed under him. All these causes combined to make men forget the lesson of Benevento and Tagliacozzo.

Accordingly, in the course of the fourteenth century, all the heavy cavalry in Christendom adopted plate armour and went so far as to extend its use to their horses. To cope with such armour the cavalry lance was increased from nine to sixteen feet in length and correspondingly thickened. Encumbered with such a weapon and burdened with his horse with over 100 pounds of iron, the men-at-arms of the fourteenth and fifteenth centuries could no longer gallop, wheel, and deliver flank attacks. Charges in open order, like that of Charles' advanced units at Tagliacozzo, were completely beyond them. They became a sort of projectile capable only of charging heavily straight to their front, or at best a one-man tank. By 1410, Monstrelet tells us, the French knights and men-at-arms were amazed at the unheard-of sight of a body of cavalry able to "turn at the gallop."[11]

The decline in cavalry tactics towards the end of the thirteenth century was not an isolated fact. On the contrary it is interesting and curious to note in how many fields the generation of St. Louis saw the zenith of mediævalism. In art it saw the culmination of the Gothic, in philosophy Aquinas. In their political and social life men seem to have been happier than ever before or since. The death of St. Louis in 1271 marked the beginning of a general decline.

Naturally, art and philosophy had no direct influence on soldier-ship. On the other hand, the political and social decline immediately affected military affairs. As in the decline of every society, the heart of the business was moral. There was a tendency to abandon reality for illusion. In the next chapter we shall see even so great a man as Edward III of England making war not with common-sense strategy but in a fashion touched with theatrical unreality.

Another aspect of the political and social decline deeply affected the fourteenth-century armies of the French. That was the sharp new hostility of the feudal nobles towards the lower social strata from which infantry was recruited. The crusading victories, and also Bouvines, had been won by close and cordial co-operation between men-at-arms and footmen. Since then the townsmen serving as infantry had continued to increase both in absolute numbers and in relation to the community. Most of the fire power of the fourteenth-century French army was developed by hired Genoese crossbowmen. The hostility of the men-at-arms toward the infantry had no justification. It was entirely a product of class rivalry and class jealousy from which the earlier Middle Ages had been free.

Just after the turn of the century in 1302, the shocking and unnecessary disaster of Courtrai cast a lurid light upon the weakness of the French armies. A mixed French force comprising both cavalry and infantry was opposed by the infantry of the populous Flemish towns, chiefly Bruges. The Flemings stood in

[11] Monstrelet (Edition d'Arc), Vol. 2, 102, quoted by Delpech, Vol. 1, 443. See also Delpech, Vol. 2, 120–124.

a difficult, boggy terrain cut up by bridges and canals. The French command, very properly, opened the action by advancing its infantry. These last obtained fire superiority and began to inflict severe losses upon the enemy. Victory was in sight, whereupon the French nobles who were of course serving as men-at-arms, instead of rejoicing at the success of their plebeian comrades, flew into a rage for jealousy! A chronicler tells the story:

> Lords, see for yourselves,
> What our footmen are doing:
> The Flemings are all but discomfited.
> Forward great lords and little lords
> Look to it that we have the honour
> And the victory in this battle.
> Let us order the infantry to retreat,
> They have done their duty very well.[12]

To the honour of the French command, the Chancellor opposed the wanton folly of retiring the foot. His opposition, however, was overruled by the Commander-in-Chief, Artois the king's brother, who called him coward and stung him into sacrificing his life by rushing alone among the enemy. Naturally, the successful French foot could not understand the order to retreat. Most of them dispersed in discouragement and disgust. A considerable number were ridden down by their own cavalry. Under such conditions it is not surprising that the charge of the French men-at-arms failed. The heavily weighted horses stuck in the heavy ground and the Flemings massacred their riders.

For the first time since Adrianople nearly a thousand years before, infantry had defeated the proudest cavalry in Christendom. The fact that the defeat was due to special circumstances did not lessen the event, and the behaviour of the French command promised badly for the future.

[12] Rhymed Chronicle of Geoffrey of Paris, quoted in Boutaric, 211:
> "Seignors, regardez à vos elz
> Comment nos gens de pié le font:
> Flamens près de desconfis sont.
> Avant, seignors, grans et menors,
> Gardez que nos aions l'ennor
> Et le pris de ceste bataille.
> Faisons retraire la piétaille,
> Se ont très-bien fait leur devoir.

CHAPTER VIII

THE DECLINE OF MEDIÆVAL CAVALRY AND THE REAPPEARANCE OF INFANTRY

1302–1494 A. D.

IN the last chapter I considered the thirteenth-century culmination of mediæval cavalry tactics and the causes of their decline. In this chapter I shall trace the working out of these causes and the rise of infantry. In spite of the importance of the longbow, together with the habit of dismounting the men-at-arms in battle, I shall consider the Hundred Years War as a step in the decline of cavalry, rather than the reappearance of infantry. True infantry, capable of playing the chief part in an offensive action, reappears with the Swiss pikemen. The account of the rise of the Swiss will be brief, as they will again appear in a later chapter dealing with the sixteenth century. I shall close with a word on late-mediæval fortification and the beginnings of gunpowder artillery.

While the unreasoning contempt of the French nobles for their own footmen (and indeed for all infantrymen) was growing up, the English were developing a new infantry weapon—the longbow—and testing it in their wars against the Scotch.

The longbow was the chief infantry missile weapon of its time. Simple development from the primitive shortbow as it was, it seems nevertheless to have been as powerful as the windlass-crossbow and was far superior to that weapon in range and in rapidity of fire. As to range, modern experiments prove that accurate shooting can be done at a range of 240 yards and a 9-foot target with an 18-inch bull's-eye. With high-angle distance shooting, a good archer ought to be able to carry 300 or even 350 yards. In 1795, a Turkish diplomat in England is reliably reported to have shot 482 yards.[1]

The longbow was the invention of the Welsh. As early as the

[1] E. B., Vol. 2, 365, article "Archery."

siege of Abergavenny in 1182, Welsh arrows penetrated an oak board 4 inches thick. In that campaign a knight was hit by an arrow which went through the skirts of his mail shirt, then through his mail breeches, then through his thigh, and finally into his horse's flank. Nevertheless it was slow to gain in general favour, for as late as 1281 we find crossbowmen in England still receiving double the wages of archers.

I have said that it was against the Scotch that the tactics of the longbow were worked out. The strength of a Scotch army was its pikemen, formed in deep masses. Poverty forbade the Scotch pikemen armour, and also forbade the growth of a numerous Scottish cavalry. What cavalry there was, was good. Scottish archers were few and not particularly efficient.

A series of fights, of which the chief was Falkirk (1298), repeated the lesson of Hastings by showing that (given the achievement of fire superiority by their auxiliary infantry) cavalry could destroy an army composed of infantry alone. The great disaster of Bannockburn (1314) showed that unless fire superiority was maintained, cavalry charges against the steady Scotch pikemen were more than useless.

Bannockburn was on a larger scale than Courtrai twelve years before and the losing command, although bad, was not so abominable as in the earlier fight. Therefore Bannockburn marks a more advanced stage of the rise of infantry and deserves description.

The Scotch were covering the siege of Stirling, the chief strategic point in Scotland. They took up a defensive position with their flanks covered by woods and marshy ground. In front they dug a line of small hidden pot-holes as traps for the English horse. The English cavalry, charging without proper archery preparation, were, of course, bloodily repulsed. Throughout the fight the archers were chiefly used for the risky business of overhead fire—with which they hit a few Scots in the breast and many of their own people in the back. The one try at opening fire from a flank was easily checked by a charge delivered by the few Scotch cavalry present and the entire English army finally broke up and fled.

After Bannockburn, another series of fights, from Dupplin Moor (1332) to Halidon Hill (1333), showed the English that they could successfully stand on the defensive against superior numbers of Scots by dismounting their men-at-arms and supporting them with their archers. As in the cases we have been studying, an infantry force in close formation, pike butts firmly grounded, could generally stand off a much larger force which had to open its ranks by advancing to the actual "push of pike." Meanwhile the archers would be able to inflict heavy casualties upon them. When the unsuccessful Scotch began to fall off to the rear, the men-at-arms could mount and destroy them as their heavy masses could not quickly reform.[2]

It was after a half-century of English experience with the longbow against the Scotch that Edward III in 1345 invaded France and conducted the campaign of Crécy.

In the first place, Edward had a moral claim to the French crown. Throughout the Middle Ages—even in their decay—a barefaced land-grabbing expedition would have been unthinkable among Christian men. Edward's claim was not of the best, nor was it admitted by many Frenchmen except those inhabiting the southwestern corner of France which had been Plantagenet land for two hundred years. Still it had some force.

Edward's military problem was difficult. France was wealthier and more populous than England, so that even under equal conditions of transport the French could have put a larger force in the field. Moreover, the conditions were not equal inasmuch as the English army must be shipped overseas, i. e., across the Channel. There was no question of raising volunteers as in the Conqueror's day; times had changed and the men must be paid. It was financially impossible to transport and maintain an army which should be even approximately equal in numbers to the French forces it would have to face.

In this situation, it was clearly Edward's business to try to make up in quality what he lacked in quantity. Accordingly in 1346 he made use of a new method of recruiting, the indenture system. In the last chapter the reader will have noticed the increasing importance of mercenaries. Edward now sought to combine the advantages of paid volunteer troops with the spontaneous loyalty of feudal forces. This he did by contracting with a number of his subjects to raise troops for him—the contractor to command his

[2] For the development of the longbow and the Scotch wars see Oman, Vol. 2, 57–108.

unit, to keep it in the field for a fixed time, and for so doing to receive a stipulated sum from the royal treasury. In legal theory
all this had no connexion with the feudal obligation. In practice
the contractors would be found chiefly among the king's greater
vassals, and their men (especially at this early stage of the indenture system) would be the more warlike and adventurous of their
own feudal dependents.

By this system of indentures Edward collected a force of between
six and seven thousand men-at-arms, about ten thousand archers,
and between three and four thousand Welsh infantry. Adding to
these numbers the squires and armed attendants of the men-at-
arms, we get something like 35,000 for the grand total. The staff
departments, i. e., smiths, artificers, etc., were carefully organized
and there were five small cannon.

Obviously such a force was insufficient for the conquest of
France. Granted the power of the longbow and the disorganization of the French as shown at Courtrai, still Edward had
only the choice between attempting to consolidate a foothold
on the French coast or making a great raid deep into the
country. With the theatricalism of the mediæval decadence
strong in him, Edward decided to raid. By landing on the
Channel coast he could relieve French pressure on his lands in
the southwest. Strategically that was something. He might
pick up enough plunder and ransom money to make the expedition
pay its way, and at any rate he would have had a chance to do
chivalric deeds.

Even the trivial objective of raiding was neither actively nor
judiciously pursued. Having landed almost unopposed near the tip
of the Cotentin Peninsula on July 12th, Edward drifted eastward
across rich Normandy, until on August 7th he was stopped by
the Seine at Elbœuf about twelve miles up river from Rouen.
It is an eloquent commentary on his claim to the French crown that
as he went he sacked towns and ravaged right and left. Meanwhile the large forces of the French were slowly concentrating on
Paris. In particular the French command desired to await the
arrival of certain contingents which had been operating against
Edward's possessions in the southwest. Accordingly, no field force
opposed his slow eastward march and (by what seems mere sloth
and folly) that march was not even closely observed. This much

was done; the bridge over the Seine at Elbœuf was broken and thus the English were checked.

From the seventh to the twenty-fifth of August, Edward's aim was to escape. He must at all costs avoid battle with superior French numbers until he had a clear line of retreat. No point on the Norman coast would do, for he had sent home his fleet. Accordingly he must cross the Seine and get away, northward.

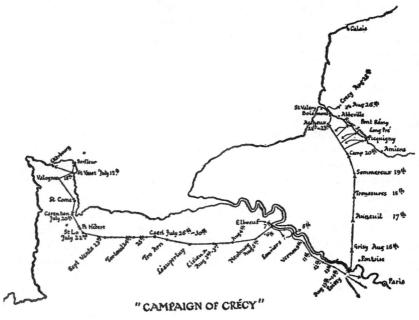

" CAMPAIGN OF CRÉCY "

PLATE 11.—CAMPAIGN OF CRÉCY.

The only bridge downstream from Elbœuf was at Rouen—a first-class city too formidable to be attacked. Therefore he was under the hard necessity of working upstream, looking for a chance to cross, and all the time drawing nearer to the gathering French army in Paris. It was a desperate game which might well have ended in disaster, for the bridges were all broken. Not before reaching Poissy, over 50 miles upstream from Elbœuf and only 13 miles as the crow flies below Paris, was an imperfectly destroyed bridge found which his artificers (his engineers as we should say) were able to repair. On August 15th he crossed.

While the English were crossing, a formal challenge came in from the French king inviting them to battle near Paris. Edward sent back word that he would fight far to the south, then hurried his command northward by forced marches, gaining a day and a half start by the trick.

Even so, the crossing of the Seine gave him no safety, for he would soon be pinned against the Somme with the great French army on his heels. Only a second and still more remarkable piece of luck got his command across near the river mouth on August 24th. At that he lost his train and his booty. Having at last a clear line of retreat toward the Straits of Dover, he turned on the 26th and waited to be attacked.

After such a haphazard campaign, it is a relief to consider the brilliant conduct of the action itself on the English side. In the first place, Edward's position was well chosen. The English front was about 1700 yards long, and therefore tenable by their force now reduced by the losses of the campaign to about 25 or 30 thousand men, of whom 10,000 lay in reserve under the King. The right was covered by the village of Crécy and by the marsh valley of the little river, Maye, the left by the village of Wadicourt and by a park of wagons. In front was a gently sloping valley. The precise formation of the troops, as in practically all mediæval fights, is unknown. The men-at-arms stood in three "battles," one in reserve in rear of centre and the other two separately near the flanks of the front line. On either side of the bodies of dismounted men-at-arms in the first line were 7000 archers in open order, in quincunx like the trees in an orchard, so that any five of them made a figure like a five-spot at cards in order to get the best fire effect. It is possible that archers even stood before the men-at-arms in the front line. They had dug many little holes, like the "pots" at Bannockburn, to make the French horses stumble, and they may have had pointed stakes driven into the ground before them. Edward's entire army was strictly disciplined, largely no doubt by his own forceful character.

The French were more than twice but less than thrice as numerous as the English. For missile infantry they had 6000 Genoese mercenaries armed with the crossbow. In men-at-arms they were very strong and they had a great rabble of ill-armed peasant infantry.

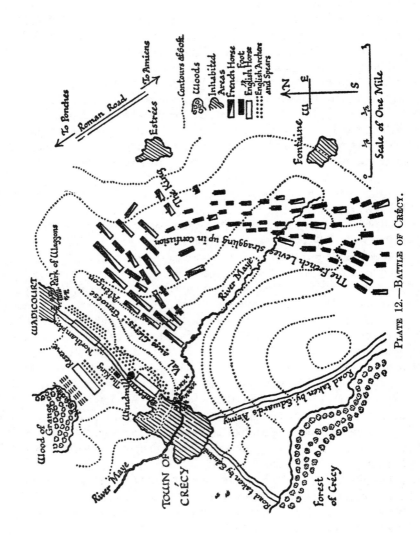

PLATE 12.—BATTLE OF CRÉCY.

Against Edward's disciplined force in their prepared position, the French came struggling up confusedly. The action began about five in the afternoon after a rainstorm which drenched the ground. It opened with a fire fight between the archers of the English front line and the only disciplined body opposed to them—the Genoese mercenary crossbowmen. These troops advanced slowly, pausing twice to rectify their alignment as is necessary for the full effect of short-range weapons. They had been 15,000 strong as the campaign opened but one chronicler reduces their battle effective to 6000. At any rate, they were overwhelmingly defeated in the first few seconds of the fire fight. The English longbow not only outranged them but could shoot three arrows while they were laboriously winding up their machines by means of their little winches.

Disgusted at what he saw, the Duke d'Alençon, who led the men-at-arms of the French van, spurred his command forward upon the Genoese, their own comrades, exactly as had been done at Courtrai forty-four years before and with the same result. The ground, although not marshy or broken by ditches as at Courtrai, was slippery from the severe summer shower. The front of the charge was irregular from the first, and riding over the wretched Genoese tangled it still more. Even at their best, the heavy fourteenth-century chargers burdened with 140 pounds of iron could not rapidly cross a beaten zone. Their twelfth- and thirteenth-century predecessors had been crossed with Arabian racing blood, and had carried men weighted only by wadded coats and light chain-mail. Above all, no army on the Continent had ever faced such fire. Horses went down right and left, and men were sometimes hurt in the joints of their armour. Some may even have been hurt through the armour itself. Later in the action the French King himself was slightly wounded in the neck by an arrow. The little English cannon added to the confusion. The only moment of peril was early in the action upon the English right and there units from the reserve quickly re-established the position. The great charge failed utterly.

The rest of the battle was no more than a confused surging of French units, arriving haphazard upon the field, against the strict English line. We hear of no manœuvring whatsoever. At midnight the last attacks ceased. There was no pursuit.

Edward continued his interrupted retreat to Calais and for a full year besieged that city until he took it. It was the one permanent fruit of the campaign.[3]

In 1356, ten years after Crécy, the campaign of Poitiers repeated most of the features of the earlier operation. In each case there was the strategic motive of diversion; the purpose of the move might be said to be the removal of French pressure upon a friendly force at the other end of France. In each case this motive was slight and the expedition was really no more than a great raid, penetrating haphazard and at leisure deep into France, next retreating hastily before superior French numbers, then defeating those superior numbers in a brilliant defence action, and finally continuing its interrupted retreat.

The commander at Poitiers was Edward the Black Prince, son to Edward III. Like his father, he was a good tactician, but lacked ability in planning a campaign. Unlike Edward III, he was headstrong, sometimes wasting invaluable time by sitting still, sometimes demanding so long a march from his men as to lay them up for several days.

The Prince based himself on Gascony, the district between the Garonne and the Pyrenees which was devoted to the Plantagenets. His force was small, more than ten but probably less than thirteen thousand. He had from 3500 to 4000 men-at-arms, most of them Gascon, with whom we must reckon at least an equal number of armed attendants. He had also from 2500 to 3000 English archers, fighting on foot but mounted for transportation, and 1000 lightly armed infantry. Since the French troops later mobilized against him were also far fewer than their predecessors at Crécy, we may suppose that the Black Death (the horrible pestilence which had swept Europe since that campaign) had so strained the economics of the time as to make it difficult to raise large forces.

With his little force, Prince Edward set out from Bergerac. During August he worked northward through Limousin and Berry, plundering as he went. He maintained a speed of about ten miles a day, and this even rate of advance was the one piece of strict method in his movements. Reaching Vierzon on August 28th he turned westward. On that same day, unknown of course

[3] Belloc, Crécy. See Plates 21 and 22.

to the Prince, King John of France arrived in the town of Chartres and began to concentrate troops there.

Shortly after leaving Vierzon the Black Prince delivered his only attack against a fortified place during the campaign. This was at Romorantin—the "Romo" of our American aviators in France in 1918—where the castle was held by a French detachment. It held out five days, the donjon surrendering September 3rd. On the day of that surrender King John, his concentration made, was marching south out of Chartres.

The Anglo-Gascon force was now operating in unfriendly country 200 miles from its base. From the first its commander had expected sooner or later to be attacked by superior numbers. Nevertheless, instead of turning southward, the Black Prince deliberately chose to run unnecessary risks by going on to the west. He may have hoped to get across the Loire and join the Plantagenet force operating north of that river. But on the other hand it had been reported to him that the bridges were cut; since he had this information it seems probable that he knew the river to be flooded too deep to ford. What makes his conduct harder to understand is that the point he made for was Tours, too large and strong a town for him to think of attacking. Worst of all, when from Romorantin five of his regular ten-mile marches had brought him to Tours on September 8th, he merely encamped before the town and sat idle until the 11th.

Meanwhile, although he did not know it, every hour increased his danger. Even as he reached Tours John was across the Loire at Blois, another French detachment was crossing at Amboise, and a third was preparing to cross at Tours itself.

When at last, on the 11th, the Prince learned his peril, he at once started southward by forced marches. In the race which now began he had in his favour the smallness of his force. On the other hand, he had against him the fact that he chose to cling to a long wagon train loaded with the booty of his raid, and the further fact that it is comparatively easy to scout forward in an advance and difficult to scout to the rear in a retreat. The Anglo-Gascons marched well, but the French marched better. On the evening of September 13th the pursued reached LaHaye des Cartes as the pursuers entered Loches twenty miles away. On the 14th the Prince did 15 miles and reached Châtellerault but the King did 20 and slept in LaHaye.

At this point, when only 15 miles separated him from his enemies the Prince took it into his head that he had shaken off pursuit. Accordingly he sat still in Châtellerault for two whole days—the 15th and 16th! Meanwhile John was acting far more vigorously but quite as strangely. After straining every nerve to pursue the English he was now only 15 miles behind them. He decided not to follow them further but to try to reach the neighbourhood of Poitiers ahead of them by a long detour eastward. He may have known of the extreme fatigue of the Anglo-Gascons, and if he did know it then his move was wise. On the other hand, if he feared to engage before joining the reinforcement which he knew awaited him in the considerable town of Poitiers, why had he already chased the English so hard? Had the pursued been able and willing to continue their march, then John's detour would have lost him his prey.

Two days' good marching carried the French to Chauvigny. They had passed to the eastward of the Anglo-Gascons, still motionless in Châtellerault, and both parties were now about equally distant from Poitiers, the French east and the Anglo-Gascons northeast of the town. On the third day, the 17th, the two forces blundered into contact with one another.

John's game was simple enough. It was merely to reach Poitiers, join his contingent there, and after that find the Prince and fight him. The Prince had a more difficult hand to play. Poitiers, which lay across his line of retreat, was too big and strong for him to tackle even could he have spared the time. Therefore he must make at least a small detour in passing the place. Furthermore he must guard as best he could against the chance of being attacked on the march, burdened as he was with his great wagon train of booty. His decision was to leave the main Paris-Bordeaux road which runs along the left bank of the river Clain between Châtellerault and Poitiers. Instead he would cross the Clain near Châtellerault and follow an old Roman road towards Poitiers up the right bank of that stream; within a few miles of Poitiers he would detour to the east of it through bypaths and strike the great Bordeaux road again south of the town. The plan would have been excellent had John been coming down from

the north. As matters really stood, with John marching westward from Chauvigny, the two armies were bound to pass close
together. In the event, with both armies going blind, as it were,

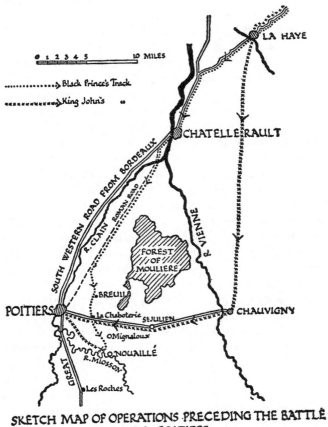

SKETCH MAP OF OPERATIONS PRECEDING THE BATTLE
OF POITIERS

PLATE 13.—OPERATIONS PRECEDING BATTLE OF POITIERS.

without distant reconnaissance, the Anglo-Gascon advance party
struck the French rear-guard when the latter was about 2½ miles
east of Poitiers.

The meeting, unexpected as it was to both sides, completely
upset the calculations of the Prince. Although the French rear-

guard soon drew off to Poitiers, still he knew that his chance of getting away without fighting was gone. His force was already tired with 16 miles of going, nevertheless he dragged it forward another two miles in order to be sure of at least a little leisure on the following morning. A reconnaissance towards Poitiers assured him that it was indeed John and the main French army that he had in his front. With dawn of the 18th he scouted forward another two miles, found a defensive position to which he led his tired force, and there awaited attack.

Given John's situation, a modern commander might well have moved south out of Poitiers by the great Bordeaux road. By such a move the French could easily have gotten south of the Prince, even had the latter abandoned his wagons, for he was forced to move by narrow country roads and winding lanes. Once south of the invader, the French could then have compelled him to battle on ground chosen by themselves. On the other hand, such a course would have been contrary to the habit of immediate combat bred by the short term of service of feudal troops. It might have shocked contemporary ideas of knightly honour. It would certainly have seemed unnatural to the intensity of the French blood. Apparently John never even thought of anything but finding his enemy and attacking him.

One day was spent in negotiations, and it is typical of the Middle Ages even in their decline that the intermediary in these was a Cardinal. For the sake of an unmolested retreat, the Prince was ready to free his prisoners without ransom and to make other concessions, but the negotiations broke down when the French insisted that he and a hundred designated knights must surrender as hostages. Meanwhile the Anglo-Gascons who had done over twenty miles the day before, were undoubtedly too tired to slip away southward, and the French who had done fifteen miles a day for three days running were likewise too tired to attack. On the morning of September 19th the French moved out to attack the Prince's position.

That position had been chosen with the idea of fighting a rearguard action to cover a retreat southward. Behind it the little river Miosson was crossed by a ford and a bridge which could be blocked by small detachments in order to check pursuit. Under the conditions of the times, the position was long for the force which had to hold it—almost exactly 1000 yards—but it was nevertheless extremely strong against frontal attack. In front it had a dip or draw about 30 feet deep, the southern slope of which was thickly covered by vineyards. In this part of France the vine is cultivated upon strong stakes about four feet high, set just far enough apart for the cultivator to slip between them, but much too close for horses or even for a regularly formed body of men on foot. At the top of the slope the vineyards were bounded by a hedge, and for passage through them there were only two sunken country lanes, one near the centre and the other to the left of the defenders. The steep slopes of the Miosson valley, together with a patch of marsh at the lower end of the draw, protected the left flank. The one weakness of the position was that the right flank was in the air.

In his dispositions the Black Prince did his utmost to remedy this weakness by covering the open flank with a wagon-park. He lined the hedge and the sunken lanes with archers and posted other archers as skirmishers among the vines. These formed an ideal cover for such troops, being just low enough to permit them to use their weapons while covering them against a charge. To support the archers he proposed to dismount his men-at-arms except for a small mounted reserve in rear of his exposed right flank.

I have said that the Prince had no mind to fight if he could help it. Early in the morning when no signs of a French attack were seen, he sent some of the most valuable loot-wagons, under a strong escort, back over the Miosson by the ford in rear of his left flank. He himself with his great banner rode down to superintend the crossing. Evidently if he were left alone he intended to draw off the rest of his army. If the French attack had been delayed until the whole Anglo-Gascon force was in column of route, it seems as if John would have had an easy victory. As luck would have it, the attack developed when most of the Black Prince's men were still standing to in their chosen position and he himself was still near by.

John had about twice as many men-at-arms as the Prince, say 8000, with what proportion of armed attendants we cannot say. The number of these last may have been at least 8000 more. To set against the 2500 English archers there were 2000 crossbowmen and 1000 mercenaries armed with the javelin.

The experience of Crécy had disposed the French to look for some new device with which to oppose the English. The dispositions finally adopted were suggested by a Scotchman long familiar with the Plantagenet tactics. John divided his army into four bodies formed in depth. The first was composed of all the missile infantry plus a small picked body of mounted knights. These last were to dash at the archers while the infantry engaged them in a fire fight. The main attack would then be delivered by the other three divisions composed—and here came in the striking innovation—of dismounted men-at-arms and other dismounted cavalry. The underlying idea here was that the horse was more vulnerable to arrow fire than the man. It was hard to armour him as thoroughly as his rider and if stung he became unmanageable. Why could not the man-at-arms attack on foot as he was accustomed to assault in siege warfare?

The idea was sound as far as it went, but it had the weak point of neglecting the factor of weight. Men too heavily armoured to skirmish and manœuvre freely on horseback could not march any distance on foot and then successfully engage fresh men who had been resting or standing still. Nor could they dismount close up to the hostile position for fear of a counter-stroke during the unfamiliar process of dismounting and forming up on foot.

When the French van came in sight of the Anglo-Gascon position they saw the Prince's great banner drawing off towards the Miosson and soon disappearing below the steep slope of the valley. From this the vanguard commanders correctly estimated that a retreat had begun. The sight was too much for their good judgment. One of them who objected that the hostile position was strong and that the first of their dismounted supporting divisions was still far behind was overruled by calling him coward. About nine o'clock, it has been estimated, the French van charged.

The mounted men could charge only four abreast up the two sunken lanes. They had to stand a terrible close fire from both flanks and in such a formation their charge was blocked by the first casualties. They were nearly all killed, but by concentrating upon themselves the English fire they gained for the French infantry a chance to close. Dodging forward through the grapestakes the crossbowmen and javelin men engaged the defenders of the position. At this point, however, the right of the assailants was enveloped and enfiladed at close quarters by the fire of a new body of defenders. These were the troops assigned as escorts to the advance party of wagons. The Prince had quickly ordered them back and they had naturally come into action in prolongation of the left of the original line at the hedge. Their unexpected appearance was decisive. All that was left of the French van—its infantry—broke.

Meanwhile the first of the French dismounted battalions had been struggling forward and was now ready to engage. It had been dismounted half a mile from the English position so that the effort of the mere approach march must have been a torture. Nevertheless its men managed to lumber forward up the slope through the vines and engaged the enemy at the hedge. Against them the arrow fire could do little. The Prince soon found it necessary to engage his reserve, keeping back only 400 men. The reinforcement made the defenders superior in number. Nevertheless the French fought so gallantly that only by the greatest effort was the position made good. It was about ten o'clock.

Now came the decisive phase of the action. The Anglo-Gascon line had been sorely tried and the second French dismounted division was now ready to engage. Had they shown the same spirit as their forerunners, victory must have been theirs. Instead, as the scanty remnants of the heroic first dismounted division dragged themselves back towards them they broke and fled without a blow struck!

It is right to call this piece of misconduct the decisive phase of the action for it prevented a decision in favour of the French, who seemed sure of winning. Except for their little reserve of 400, the Anglo-Gascons were badly fatigued. Some were carrying the wounded to the rear. Others were replacing broken swords or lances from the equipment of the fallen. The archers were looking everywhere for arrows, even pulling them out of the bodies of the dead and wounded. Still the fight was not yet over. Despite the failure of his leading units, the King of France was leading to the attack the last and largest of his three dismounted divisions. He had dismounted about a mile from the Prince's position and the fatigue of so long a march would somewhat compensate for the greater fatigue of the defenders. These last had now for the first time the advantage of numbers.

The Black Prince determined upon a general counter-attack.
He mounted his men-at-arms—their horses were still quite fresh—
and he put his reserve in the front rank. After shooting their last
few arrows the archers were to engage hand to hand. A small

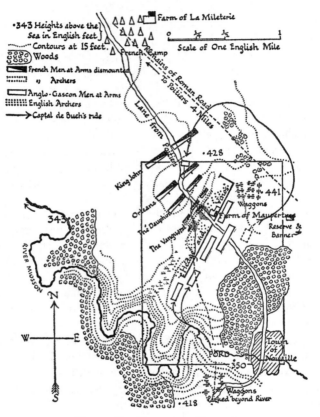

PLATE 14.—BATTLE OF POITIERS.

mounted detachment less than two hundred strong was to turn
the French left, keeping well out of sight. They would then charge
the hostile rear after the fighting in front had begun.

These dispositions made, the Prince advanced his main body.
The French took the shock well and for a long time the combat-
ants swayed to and fro. Then the flanking detachment engaged,
launching its charge suddenly from behind cover and displaying

a banner for the sake of the moral effect. The stratagem, for it was hardly more than that, succeeded. King John, after fighting with the greatest gallantry, was captured and the remnant of his army was destroyed.

Strategically the Prince made no use of his victory. He merely continued his interrupted retreat to Bordeaux, taking with him his prisoner. The treaty of Bretigny five years later, with its tripling of the Plantagenet holdings in France, was not the result of further military successes but of King John's dislike of captivity. He had been held all that time.[4]

After Poitiers, the rest of the Hundred Years War shows us no new developments of the art of war. From this time on commanders often dismounted their men-at-arms for an attack. In 1364 the combats of Cocherel and Auray show the practice followed, even when the defenders had so few archers that these last could not greatly have hindered a mounted charge. In 1367, at Navarette in Spain, the French auxiliaries of one Spanish faction dismounted their men-at-arms and so did the English supporters of the other faction. In 1385, at Aljubarotta in Portugal, the English contingent in the Portuguese army and the French serving with the Spanish invaders both did the same thing. In spite of so frequent a use of dismounted cavalry, true infantry never appears as the main reliance of armies during the Hundred Years War. Even the English archer was considered no more than an invaluable auxiliary to the men-at-arms.

Meanwhile if the long war failed to bring about the reappearance of infantry as the chief arm, it did make the professional mercenary soldier far more important than before, as compared with feudal troops. In all the engagements mentioned in the last paragraph, both the French and English forces were almost entirely mercenaries.

It should be noted that the increased importance of mercenaries was not due to a marked increase in the aggregate wealth of the time. On the contrary, after the terrible calamity of the Black Death the aggregate of wealth was not more but less than it had been for some generations. Hired men played a larger part because governmental centralization, especially on the financial side, was on the increase.

[4] Belloc, Poitiers. See Plates 23 and 24.

The fourteenth-century mercenaries treated their profession frankly as a means of raising money. They were called the "Free Companies" and they lived up to the name. Often they organized themselves democratically, like the Trade Gilds of the time, electing their officers for a certain term as Gild Magistrates were elected.[5] When unemployed they were a pest.

Before Aljubarotta was fought, the Hundred Years War had entered into a new phase. Between 1369 and 1374, without a single general action, the French Crown had narrowed down the Plantagenet holdings in France to the neighbourhood of Bordeaux and Bayonne. At bottom the reason for so much success was political. North of the Garonne the Plantagenets could inspire no loyalty.

On its military side, the recovery of so much territory by the French Crown was due to a new tactical method connected with the name of Du Guesclin. This man, who was Constable of France, and therefore Commander-in-Chief under the King, was free from the theatricalism of his time. To him victory was important and picturesque attitudes were not. Furthermore, he had grasped the fact that the strength of the Plantagenet tactics lay in the ability to defend a prepared position. Accordingly he took pains not to give them the kind of action in which they excelled.

Du Guesclin's resource was small war. He excelled in night attacks, ambuscades, and all sorts of stratagems. He was a skilful besieger, so much so that his assaults upon fortresses helped to give a new turn to fortification, as we shall see in the concluding paragraphs of this chapter dealing with military engineering. He loved to cut up convoys and to fall suddenly upon hostile detachments. To him, it was no shame whatsoever to retire without fighting when outnumbered. Joined with the favourable political factors, such methods achieved success after success.[6]

To follow the strict chronological order would now compel me to consider the achievements of the Swiss—that is, the reappearance of infantry as the chief arm. But for the sake of clearness I prefer first to describe the closing phases of the Hundred Years War.

Serious fighting began again in 1415, when Henry V of England

[5] Fortescue, Vol. 1, 51.   [6] Dict. du Mob., Vol. 6, 380–382.

landed an army of about 30,000 men at the mouth of the Seine and laid siege to Harfleur. He bombarded the place with cannon and took it after thirty-five days. Meanwhile dysentery, together with the casualties of the siege, destroyed one-third of the English effective, leaving him only 20,000 strong. As usual under the Valois, the French were slow to mobilize and consequently failed to relieve the place.

When at last Harfleur fell on September 18th, the season was far advanced. Although he knew that a hostile army greatly outnumbering his own would soon be in the field, a spirit of bravado led Henry to march across country towards Calais—a folly which invited the destruction of his entire force.

The campaign which followed shows us both sides tediously repeating the mistakes of Crécy and Poitiers.

Deliberately following the precedent of the Crécy campaign of seventy years before, Henry made for the ford of Blanchetaque at the mouth of the Somme. It was strongly guarded so that he was forced to work up the Somme looking for a chance to cross, but everywhere finding the bridges broken and all passages held by French detachments. Not until he reached Nesle was he able to cross by an undefended ford. He then turned north toward Calais, and at Agincourt on October 24th found his way blocked by the great French army. For nineteen days his force had kept up an average of over fourteen miles a day. Naturally so great an effort had told heavily upon it. In spite of systematic plundering, supply had been very difficult. Furthermore, the plundering had so angered the country people that they massacred all English stragglers. Accordingly Henry's effectives were reduced to about 15,000. The one thing in his favour was that his troops were well in hand.

The French, on their side, numbered about 60,000. They had mobilized slowly. Still full of feudal pride, their commander, Charles d'Albret, Constable of France, had refused to take with him 6000 crossbowmen of the Parisian municipal militia who volunteered for the expedition. "What need have we of these shopkeepers? " said the nobles.[7]

Had the huge but clumsy French force been able to bring its overwhelming numbers to bear, Henry must have been wiped

[7] Boutaric, 212.

out. He was ready to negotiate on any but the most humiliating terms. As it was, the Constable committed every possible fault. Finding himself across the English line of march, he failed to attack at once and put off the action until the following day, October 25th. He then engaged on a narrow front, scarcely over 1000 yards, flanked on both sides by thick woods through which it was impossible to take formed bodies of troops. These woods he failed to reconnoitre. Finally, he did not even try to use his archers and crossbowmen, but in each division of his army he masked them by forming them behind his men-at-arms. Naturally, on so narrow a front, his three divisions were arranged in depth. In the first two of them the greater part of the men-at-arms were dismounted, with mounted units covering the wings.

The different French units failed to support one another. Lack of reconnaissance permitted the English to push forward strong flanking parties of archers who fired upon both flanks from the cover of the woods. A heavy rain which had turned the ground into mud made the heavily weighted fifteenth-century men-at-arms, clumsy enough at best, almost helpless. The lightly armed English archers, on the other hand, were far better able to move about. Henry had ordered them to carry stakes which could be hastily driven into the ground to serve as a palisade. But when they had shot all their arrows they were able to close successfully with the lumbering French men-at-arms.

Although the victory greatly increased English prestige, it had no direct strategic result whatsoever. Henry's little force, exhausted by its own efforts, merely continued its retreat on Calais.[8]

After Agincourt (1415) the long succession of English victories (which lasted until 1429 and brought about the occupation of practically all France north of the Loire) resulted more from the political factions of the French than from any other cause. While the factions fought each other, the small well-disciplined English forces could do much as they pleased. Furthermore, the mercenary adventurers in the French service were willing enough to have the war drag on, because they feared to see their occupation gone at the peace.

At the siege of Orleans in 1428–29, the English were too few even

[8] Dict. du Mob., Vol. 6, 382–387; Fortescue, Vol. 1, 54–62.

to blockade the place properly. Like de Montfort before Toulouse in 1218, all they could do was to set up a partial blockade by establishing themselves in redoubts known as bastiles, opposite a part of the circumferences of the defences. Their one hope was to wear down the morale of the garrison and citizens. In this their great asset was the terror of their name and the corresponding discouragement of the French.

During the first phase of the siege of Orleans, the skirmish known as the battle of the Herrings shows no tactical advance on either side. A French force based upon Orleans was trying to intercept an English convoy approaching by the great Paris-Étampes road with lenten provisions of fish for the besiegers. The French had a chance to surprise the convoy, or at the very least to strike it while in column of route, but this chance was deliberately thrown away by a bad command which postponed the attack. When the attack was finally delivered, the escort was ready to meet it—deployed in the time-honoured English prepared defensive position with men-at-arms dismounted and archers protected by their sharp stakes. The French made their usual bull-headed frontal attack and were broken with heavy loss. After seventy years' experience of the English tactics it was a miserable showing.

When Joan of Arc appeared, the whole situation changed. As soon as the morale and activity of the French were restored under her inspiration, their superior numbers were bound to tell. In the fighting at the St. Loup redoubt the French were 1500 to 400. At Les Tourelles redoubt the odds were even greater, 5000 to 400 or 500. There was nothing for the English but retreat. Their prestige once broken, the operation became hopeless.

Joan's victory of Patay, which cleared the English out of the Loire valley, was won partly by the new French spirit of enterprise, partly by a piece of indiscipline on the part of the enemy. The strict discipline which had been such an asset throughout the long war was now weakening. At Patay the French knew that the English were advancing southward but did not know their exact position, which was covered by a wood. A stag blundered in among the English, and the loud sportsman's halloo which they raised told the French exactly where they were. Attacked unexpectedly with no time to prepare a position and before the archers had had time to plant their pointed stakes, the invaders were helpless. They were swept away by a vigorous cavalry charge.[9]

The new spirit with which Joan had inspired the French did not die with her death. It spread to the peasants, who kept up a steady guerrilla warfare against the English. Under such circumstances the invaders steadily lost ground. All the calculations of the soldiers of the time were upset by so new and unexpected a thing as a genuine popular resistance. There was no precedent for it except the English popular resistance under John two centuries before—an incident probably long forgotten. Along with the new spirit among the French peasantry there was a lull in the factional quarrels of the French nobles.

The final expulsion of the English from France (except Calais) came about in 1453. From this time on the English archer has no further lesson to teach us. Archers played a considerable part in the English civil wars known as the Wars of the Roses, but these wars have little interest for the military student. Their long survival in England—we find archers among the troops raised to resist a possible landing from the Spanish Armada in 1588—did not affect the art of war.

Important French military reforms helped to bring about the end of the long war. Chief among these was the establishment by the French Crown of a permanent, regularly paid, professional army. West of the Adriatic such a thing had not been seen in Christendom since the decline of Rome.

This momentous change was effected by two royal decrees of Charles VII (1422–1461), the first passed at the request of the States General (i. e., Parliament) in 1439, the second on initiative of the Crown in 1444. For our purposes the two decrees may be treated as one. The crying need for reform sprang from the disturbances caused by the "Free Companies" of mercenary adventurers. Accordingly the Crown took upon itself the appointment of all captains of companies, and expressly forbade the raising of troops by unauthorized persons. Fifteen "Compagnies des Ordonnances du Roi," i. e., "Of the King's Servants" or "For the King's Service," were raised. It is interesting to note that the legislator seems to fear that it may be difficult to keep the size of the companies within bounds. Each of them was strictly limited

[9] Anatole France, Joan of Arc.

to 100 "lances," the term lance being understood as a man-at-arms, his squire, his groom (who is to be armed with a cutlass), and three archers. The total enlisted strength was thus fixed at 18,000.[10]

These Ordonnance Companies were to serve as an example for Christendom. The type of army represented by them was to dominate European warfare until the French Revolution imagined the armed nation. To this day the United States Regular Army is a professional force nationally recruited, and so is the post-war army of the German Reich, while the British army is of the same sort plus a considerable barbarian element. Another provision in the same decree made for discipline and centralization under the Crown by providing that all nobles must be responsible to the King for the acts of their own vassals when on royal service, exactly as the King's hired captains had always been held responsible for their commands.

Besides the decree establishing the Ordonnance Companies, Charles VII's reign saw two other major innovations. A permanent artillery department was organized and in 1436 the first chief of the French artillery, with the title of "Master of the Artillery" was commissioned and took the oath.[11]

In 1448 the Crown tried to establish an organized militia force throughout the Kingdom. The officers of the King were to choose out of every parish a man to serve in the new body. They were called "Francs (i. e., free) Archers" because they were exempted from certain taxes, and because most of them were armed with the bow. Inspired by the patriotic desire to get rid of the English, they did some good service in the last battles of the Hundred Years War. But on the whole their record was decidedly spotty, as might have been expected from such a force. Their chief importance was that their establishment showed a desire to give some sort of organization to infantry and to carry forward the principle of centralization under the Crown.[12]

The natural opposition of the nobles to the new state of things was lessened by the fact that enlistment in the Ordonnance Companies offered a career to the more active and ambitious individuals among the nobility itself. Even the chance of becoming an archer in an Ordonnance Company was a stepping stone to greater things.

[10] Boutaric, 308–317.   [11] Dict. du Mob., 392.   [12] Boutaric, 317–335.

In France, the middle and end of the fifteenth century, which saw such notable reforms in military organization, saw no corresponding development in tactics. There was a reaction against the headstrong folly and blind belief in the man-at-arms which had lost so many battles, but that reaction produced no new thought-out system of its own. In tactical doctrine, especially as to the relation between infantry and cavalry, the period is one of confusion.

As instances of this confusion, I shall quote two passages from de Comines, for many years a councillor to Louis XI of France; together with a royal decree of Charles VIII, Louis' successor.

In the first passage, de Comines discusses the conduct of the Burgundians at the battle of Montlhéry in 1465:

> It was at first proposed that everyone without exception, should dismount; and afterwards this proposal was modified, for almost all the men-at-arms mounted. Several good knights and esquires were commanded to remain afoot . . . for among the Burgundians at that time those who dismounted with the archers were the most honoured (of all), and always a great number of men of good condition followed this custom, so that the people should be encouraged and should fight better. And this custom they learned from the English in whose company Duke Philip in his youth had made war in France. . . .[13]

This passage shows clearly that the connexion of the English habit of dismounting their men-at-arms with their inveterate preference for defensive tactics had not been grasped at all. Evidently neither the Burgundians nor any other French faction had reasoned the matter out. As late as 1465, in this same haphazard battle of Montlhéry, we find certain units of Burgundian men-at-arms riding down their own archers after the abominable fashion of Courtrai (1302) and Crécy (1346).[14]

---

[13] De Comines: Memoirs, Bk. I, Ch. III.
"De prime face fut advisé que tout se mettroit à pied, sans nul excepter; et depuis muerent propos, car presque tous ces hommes d'armes monterent à cheval. Plusieurs bons chevaliers et escuyers furent ordonnés a demourer à pied, . . . car entre les Bourguignons lors estoient les plus honorés ceux qui descendoient avec les archiers; et toujours s'y mettoit grande quantité de gens de bien, afin que le peuple en fust plus assuré et combatist mieux, et tenoient cela des Anglois, avec les quels le duc Phillipe avoit fait la guerre en France, durant sa jeunesse. . . ."
[14] Dict. du Mob., Vol. 6, 396, 399.

In the second passage from de Comines, that highly placed and experienced man quaintly expresses his own idea of tactics as follows:

> . . . my opinion is that the sovereign thing in the world for battles is to have archers; but they should number thousands, for in small numbers they are worth nothing, and they should be ill mounted, so that they may have no regret whatsoever at losing their horses, or else they should have no horses at all. . . .[15]

Before commenting on this opinion of de Comines, I prefer to contrast with it a decree of Charles VIII (1483–1498) issued in 1485. The purpose of the decree is to re-establish the Francs Archers, for it seems that that militia infantry had died out since its creation in 1448. The preamble runs as follows:

> Whereas it is necessary, together with . . . our ordonnance (sc. companies) who are all mounted, to have . . . a number of infantry . . . whereas mounted men cannot easily accomplish great exploits without infantry . . .[16]

On comparing this passage with de Comines' on archers, the confusion of late fifteenth-century tactical doctrine is clear. While de Comines rates archers above men-at-arms, Charles VIII makes them only a necessary auxiliary arm, a statement which might have been truly made at any time during the long supremacy of cavalry.

The source of such a confusion is to be found in the experience of the Hundred Years War. While fire superiority had always been important in supporting attacks against an immobile defensive and in helping to repel attacks against such a defensive, nevertheless the English longbow had made it more important still. Fur-

---

[15] De Comines: Memoirs, Bk. I, Ch. IV.
". . . mon advis est, que la souveraine chose du monde pour les batailles, sont les archiers mais qu'ils soient à milliers, car en petit nombre ne valent rien, et que ce soient gens mal montés, a ce qu'ils n'ayent point le regret de perdre leurs chevaux, ou du tout n'en ayent point; . . ."
[16] Ordonnance (i. e., decree) du 8 Decembre, 1485; Godefroy, Charles VIII, 502, quoted Boutaric, 329.
"Attendu qu'il serait necessaire, avec . . . nos ordonnances, qui sont tous à cheval, avoir . . . quelques nombres de gens de guerre à pied, . . . attendu que, gens de cheval ne peuvent aisément faire grand exploit sans gens de pied . . ."

thermore, the increasing weight and clumsiness of plate armour had deprived the armoured horseman of the rapidity and suppleness of movement which would have helped him to cope with the English tactics.

On the other hand, archers were not tactically self-sufficient. In an action between two mounted bodies they were not worth while. In the open they could not stand on the defensive without strong supports of dismounted men-at-arms to take the shock of the hostile charge. Whenever they could they covered themselves with stakes or some other form of entrenchment. Most important of all, they lacked offensive power because (under normal conditions) they could not close. It needed the heavy mud of Agincourt to enable them to do so—even in support of their own men-at-arms. All told then, the English archers never made infantry the chief arm. The Hundred Years War shows us the decadence of mediæval cavalry. Despite de Comines, it does not mark the beginning of the superiority of infantry.

The first nation to astonish Europe with an infantry of real offensive power were the Swiss. As with the Scotch, poverty forbade these mountaineers to develop a numerous and efficient cavalry. Moreover, the mountainous nature of the country, as in ancient Greece, tended to limit mounted action. Therefore the Swiss were footmen not by choice but by neccessity.

The same cause—poverty—forbade the Swiss complete armour, and this again suited their rough country since an unarmoured man can better scramble over difficult ground.

Military genius enabled the fourteenth- and fifteenth-century Swiss to get over the foregoing limitations—as the Scotch, for instance, never did. The problem was the same as that of the professional Roman army in the fourth century. Its general terms had remained unchanged for a thousand years. For a fuller discussion I refer my readers to my account of the fourth century and also to my general discussion of mediæval war. Suffice it here that once the cavalryman was provided with a shaped saddle and stirrups, together with armour both for himself and for his horse, the infantryman found it necessary to have a weapon long enough to keep him at a distance. Hence the pike. Whether, granted a higher standard of discipline plus individual initiative, the sword and buckler man (such as the old Roman legionary) would have survived and done better than the pikeman, we cannot tell. It seems possible. The offensive weakness of the pike was that to use it it had to be levelled, and once levelled it could not be traversed freely from side to side because of the close deep formations necessitated by its use. Hence pikemen can be used only in regular formations of the strictest sort and have great difficulty in making good any gap which may appear in their ranks. Once a bad gap does appear, they are at the mercy of cavalry or of resolute infantry armed with the sword.

Now anyone who has drilled or watched other men drilling knows how extraordinarily hard it is to advance in close order and still maintain a regular front. Take even so small a unit as a war-strength company. Put them on a level parade ground in the midst of profound peace and tell them to advance in company front for a hundred yards. Their line will ripple to and fro constantly as they try to correct the beginnings of little dislocations. It is astonishing how much practice the thing takes. Imagine then a body of several thousand pikemen advancing in action, and remember that the penetration of a single bad gap by the enemy may well mean disaster. Then you will have an idea of the extraordinary perfection of drill and discipline required for such a movement.

This necessary perfection the Swiss achieved; and to that achievement (not to the equipment, which was only the instrument with which the thing was done) they owed their unique position in fifteenth-century Europe. Even to-day, in the military exercise of rifle shooting their whole citizenry, in their spare time, show a continuous application unequalled in the world. They are always at it. Just so in the late mediæval period we are not surprised to learn that from childhood they were always practising the advance in close order. Boys too young to carry a man's-size pike received little pikes with which to drill. Military drills and reviews took place on holidays and Fair days. They were even used at the celebration of weddings.[17]

The Swiss perfection of drill and discipline was well served by a highly specialized equipment. They developed a pike with an

[17] For the intense Swiss application and for their march music, see Fortescue, Vol. 1, 83–84. For their equipment and formations see Dodge: Gustavus Adolphus, 11–13.

18-foot shaft and beyond that a 3-foot iron shank to keep the head from being cut off by a sword stroke. In all history such a monster can be compared only with the Macedonian sarissa, and even under Alexander we never hear of the Macedonian phalanx either repulsing or delivering flank attacks like the Swiss. It gave them no less than four rows of points protruding beyond the front. We know that they marched in cadence to music—apparently they were the first modern men to do so. Besides pikemen they had halberdiers, evidently to finish the job after the pikemen. The halberd was a battle-axe with a handle no less than eight feet long, and like the long pike must have taken great strength and endless practice to wield. In the hands of a powerful veteran it was probably more effective against the perfected plate armour of the day than any other infantry or cavalry weapon—it could even decapitate a horse. Besides pikemen and halberdiers the Swiss had a small proportion of missile troops used for skirmishing. These were at first crossbowmen, later arquebusiers, but were never of first-rate importance.

A Swiss army was usually formed in three masses. It might attempt to envelop a flank or to pierce the opposing centre by means of the time-honoured wedge formation. When threatened with envelopment they formed square, not the earlier mediæval circle. The missile troops, and apparently the halberdiers, were posted at the corners. The Swiss infantry could move rapidly without losing formation, an ominous fact for the increasingly cumbrous cavalry of the time.

The Swiss campaigns divide into two phases. In the first (1315–1476) we find them defending their independence first against the House of Austria and then against that of Burgundy. In the second phase, from 1476 on, war became the chief industry of the country and the Swiss hired themselves out as soldiers in a purely commercial spirit.

The first of the Swiss victories was at Morgarten in 1315. In it we find few of the characteristic features of later Swiss tactics. A large Austrian army from 15,000 to 20,000 strong, relying chiefly upon its men-at-arms, invaded the Swiss valleys and foolishly involved themselves in an icy mountain pass between a lake and a precipice. The Swiss numbered only 1300 to 1500 unarmoured foot but on such a terrain they had it all their own way. From above they riddled the Austrian formation by rolling down tree-trunks and boulders upon it. In the panic which ensued, the mountaineers attacked with the halberd and destroyed their opponents.

At Laupen in 1339, the first signs of offensive power on the part of the Swiss infantry appear. Here the Swiss drove the hostile infantry from the field, and then successfully stood off the charges of the men-at-arms.

The important victory of Sempach (1386) finally freed the Swiss from the Austrian House of Hapsburg. Here again the mountaineers were outnumbered, although not so heavily as at Morgarten. At Sempach they had between 1500 and 1600 men against 6000 Austrians. The terrain was sloping meadowland cut up by hedges and streams. I would remind the reader that open field agriculture had been from the beginning an important factor in the supremacy of cavalry. The Austrians therefore dismounted their men-at-arms and at the first shock they drove back the Swiss. Their success, however, was short-lived. We have already seen how impossible it was to advance for any distance on foot while wearing the heavy plate armour of the time, without extreme fatigue. In this case the difficulty of the ground and still more the sun of a hot July day made the task of the cumbrous Austrian men-at-arms still harder. Meanwhile the Swiss, unburdened by armour, charged again and again. At last the Hapsburg troops broke and their commander was killed.

Sempach taught the Swiss their strength. Two years later at Näfels a mere handful of them defeated another Austrian army.

Perhaps the most striking of all their feats of arms is the battle fought near Basle in 1444. At this time the Hundred Years War was drawing to a close, and consequently there were great numbers of unemployed mercenary adventurers known as Free-Lances—men ready to sell their swords to the highest bidder. With their aid the Hapsburgs made a last attempt to conquer the Swiss. The Free-Lances were from 30,000 to 50,000 strong. Either in bravado or (more probably) in desperation, a tiny Swiss force of from 1200 to 1600 men met them in the field. It is not surprising that so large a body of professional soldiers was able to destroy such a handful of opponents. The point is that the Swiss handful did so well and inflicted such heavy losses on the overwhelming force of freebooters that these last decided they had had enough. Instead of persisting in their invasion they were glad to retire.

The fame of the Swiss was raised to its highest point by their war against Charles the Rash, Duke of Burgundy—at the time one of the most powerful princes in Christendom. Hostilities began after a complicated series of intrigues between the French Crown, the Hapsburgs, the Duke and the Swiss.

The first battle was fought in March, 1476, near the town of Grandson whose castle Charles had just retaken from the Swiss. The Swiss were moving to relieve the place, but when they heard of its fall they nevertheless continued their advance. Their formation was in two separate bodies, one of which was to attack the Burgundian entrenched camp in front. Meanwhile the other was to make a turning movement out of sight behind some high hills and suddenly attack the camp in flank. Learning of the approach of the Swiss, Charles seems to have thought that the first of their two bodies was their entire army. At all events he pushed forward his cavalry over an unfavourable terrain, charged, and was sharply repulsed.

The mobility of the Swiss now came into play with decisive effect. Charles ordered his cavalry to retreat towards the camp, intending to renew the fight on better ground. Had he been opposed by mediæval infantry of the normal type he would have had ample time to make new dispositions. As it was, the Swiss pressed him so hotly that his retreating troops, in order to break contact, had to turn their retreat into a flight and arrived at the camp in confusion with the Swiss still close at their heels. Just at this point the sudden and unexpected appearance of the second body of Swiss (who had now completed their turning movement), threw the whole Burgundian army into a panic. Practically without resistance they abandoned their camp with its entrenchments and artillery and fled in disorder. Throughout the action the Burgundians had been so nonplussed by the hostile tactics that the losses of both sides were insignificant.

In June of the same year—1476—about three months after Grandson, the Swiss again defeated Charles at the far bloodier battle of Morat. After a considerable effort to raise troops the Duke had with him rather more than 20,000 men including 3000 English archers. With this force, supported by a formidable artillery, he laid siege to the little town of Morat. The Swiss moved to raise the siege with 35,000 men, of whom 4000 were cavalry—an unusually high proportion of this arm for a Swiss army. Of the infantry 11,000 were pikemen and 10,000 had halberds. Ten thousand carried the crude infantry firearms of the time.

The Swiss took position on some rising ground overlooking Charles' camp and there waited to be attacked. The Duke however had learned caution at Grandson. He drew up his troops on level ground below the Swiss position, held them there motionless for some hours under a heavy rain, and finally withdrew behind his entrenchments. The Swiss then determined to take the offensive. As at Grandson, they sent a good-sized detachment to make a turning movement behind cover. Their frontal attack was checked (indeed their long pikes were not suited to assaulting entrenchments) but at least it succeeded in concentrating the enemy's attention against itself. The flank attack together with a brisk sortie from the town succeeded in carrying the Burgundian palisades after heavy losses on both sides. The rain probably softened the bowstrings of the English archers and this may have prevented them from doing themselves justice.[18]

In 1477 the Swiss for the first time sent an army away from their native mountains. Acting in concert with certain lowland cities allied with them against Charles, they advanced to Nancy and there destroyed the Duke's last army. As at Grandson and Morat, it was their manœuvring power and mobility which obtained the decision by means of a combined front and flank attack.

Already, in 1474, the Swiss had begun the practice of hiring themselves out as soldiers to foreign governments; and for over a century they were so much in demand that war became the chief industry of the country.

The fortunes of the Swiss on the battlefields of the sixteenth century do not concern this chapter. Let it here suffice that having begun as brilliant and daring innovators in tactics, they were extremely slow to keep pace with later improvements introduced in the infantry of other nations. In particular they long persisted in the extremely broad and deep phalanx formation with which their first victories were won, and they never excelled in fire power.

[18] Dict. du Mob., Vol. 6, 400–402.

Nevertheless it remains their great achievement that they were the first since the Romans to develop a real attacking infantry.

At the close of the fifteenth century, Christendom had not yet learned the Swiss lesson. The age of cavalry was closing but had not yet completely closed. It was left for the infantry footmen of the sixteenth century to re-establish infantry as the chief arm.

I will close this chapter by considering briefly late-mediæval fortification and the influence of gunpowder.

The chief improvement introduced into fortification by the engineers of the fourteenth century was stone machicolation. We have seen that the chief problem of the mediæval military architect was defence against sapping or battering the base of his walls. We have seen also that the men of the twelfth and thirteenth centuries attempted a solution by means of overhanging wooden galleries known as "hoards" or "hoardings." However, it was the weakness of a hoarding that it might be burned. As the improvement in combustibles increased the seriousness of this danger, the fourteenth-century engineers replaced the hoarding with an overhang all of stone which permitted a direct command of the wall base.

It is true that long before the fourteenth century, stone machicolations were to be found in the crusading castles built in the treeless country of Syria. It is also true that exceptional instances of it are found in the West. Thus the Castle of Ghent, built as early as 1180, shows an imperfect and non-continuous form of it. The donjon of Château Gaillard (1198) has it in a very perfect form. Despite such exceptions, the use of stone machicolation did not become general before 1300. The thirteenth-century architect of Coucy compromised by having wooden hoardings carried on stone brackets.

In the fifteenth century, pre-gunpowder fortifications culminated in the establishment of easy lateral communication throughout the perimeter of the defence. At first glance this seems obvious enough. In the U. S. Army Field Service Regulations of 1914, Section 193, "good communications throughout the position" are laid down axiomatically as one of the requisites to be sought in a defensive position, and in permanent fortifications the same principle obtains. Therefore its late appearance in mediæval military engineering deserves explanation. The reason was that mediæval engineers so feared surprise that they were willing to sacrifice communication in order to delay a besieger by making each part of their fortresses as independent as possible. For instance, the fourteenth-century walls of Avignon have stone machicolation, but there the towers still interrupt the curtain walls. To pass through a tower from one curtain to another sometimes one had to cross little drawbridges, and always to pass through narrow doors and go up and down steps. This system was intended to compel the besiegers to take the castle stone by stone, each tower being an independent redoubt. But it had the disadvantage of demanding a numerous garrison and the exercise of the greatest vigilance at all points, for if the besiegers could get a foothold anywhere it was hard to concentrate the garrison against them because of the difficult lateral communications of the defence. If a tower could be surprised and suddenly rushed, the assailants could be dislodged only with difficulty. With the longbows and powerful crossbows of the second half of the fourteenth century, and with the increasing proportion of trained and disciplined mercenary troops in the armies of the time, an energetic leader like Du Guesclin could often rush twelfth- and thirteenth-century works. The curtains, which were lower than the towers, could frequently be escaladed with ladders. Accordingly we find that by 1400 a new system of defence was put in force.

The castle of Pierrefonds is perhaps the best example of the new system. First, there is a low outwork, without flankments. This runs close under three sides of the castle proper, which is a parallelogram a little over 100 yards on its long sides and about 75 yards on the ends. The curtains are over 100 feet high and the entire circuit of the defence can be made on the same level. Stone machicolations and two stages of battlements run all around. The better to resist mining, the lower walls have no loop-holes but are solid throughout, except for a small sally port on the side opposite to the main entrance. Viollet-le-Duc estimates that the ends could be defended with 40 men each and the sides with 60 men each, while to attack effectively on two sides at once would necessitate a besieging army of at least 2000 men and probably many more.[19]

At this point matters stood when the influence of gunpowder

[19] For machicolation and for fifteenth-century fortification, see Dict. de l'Arch.

began to be felt in sieges. The time and place of its invention, and whether or not it had anything to do with incendiary mixtures such as Greek fire, are equally unknown. That the Chinese or Mohammedans first used it has been alleged but never proved. Roger Bacon (1214–1294), the Oxford Franciscan, in his "De Mirabili Potestate Artis et Naturæ," written in 1242, gives a receipt for making gunpowder, says it was already known in his time, and treats of it solely as an explosive, not as a propellant. The first well-authenticated case of its use in war was in Edward III's Crécy campaign in 1346.

Fourteenth-century cannon were small and of no great power. Early in the following century they became larger and more serious affairs. In 1415 they played an important part in Henry V's siege of Harfleur. Here they seem to have been used principally in harassing fire; the inhabitants begged Henry to accept their surrender . . . "for the fire was to them intolerable."[20]

In the last of the great mediæval sieges, that of Constantinople by the Turks in 1453, the garrison numbered only 9000 men to defend a land front of about 9500 yards and a sea front of nearly 30,000. The defences were so strong that behind them this tiny force resisted for 55 days an enormous Turkish army equipped with the finest siege artillery hitherto known. In particular there were three enormous 25-inch cannon cast by a Christian renegade in the service of the Sultan. Their huge stone bullets, weighing from 1200 to 1500 pounds, when fired at a high angle could range a mile and then bury themselves six feet in the earth. Some of them are still to be seen. These guns had no carriages. They had to be laboriously wedged into position on the ground by means of rocks and lumber, and their rate of fire was only seven shots per day and one per night. Nevertheless they were powerful enough to keep the entire besieged population repairing the damage done, and they ended by making an enormous breach through which the Turks entered on the fifty-fifth day of the siege.[21]

Evidently, when the strongest city in the world could hold out less than two months, gunpowder had revolutionized military

[20] Fortescue: History of the British Army, Vol. I, 55. From the "Gesta Henrici Quinti" and Monstrelet.
[21] Schlumberger.

engineering. In general, from the middle of the century on, sieges tended to become shorter and shorter. By 1500 artillery had established a complete superiority over the fortification of the day, the reason being that mediæval fortresses had no provision for emplacements in which cannon of any size could be mounted for counter-battery work.

While the fifteenth-century cannon were revolutionizing siege-work and position warfare in general, firearms of all sorts were without effect upon open warfare. The early hand-firearms, in particular, were so crude that their effect upon tactics was negligible.

The reason for the impotence of early artillery in mobile warfare is to be found in the imperfection of the gun-carriages. Not until near the end of our period was a carriage devised which made possible a reasonably rapid adjustment of fire. The French artillerists seem to have been its inventors. In 1494 the army of Charles VIII of France astonished Italy with its field-guns unlimbering for action like modern pieces. These cannon had two wheels and a trail. They were even capable of a few degrees of elevation or depression obtained as follows: the trail was divided into an upper and a lower section, hinged together in front. The gun itself was solidly set in the upper section. At the rear end of the lower section was a stepped bracket for maintaining the upper section (and hence the gun) at the elevation desired. Since the weight of the gun bore heavily on the bracket and hinge, it was a slow, hard job to change elevation. Nevertheless the fact that it could be done at all marks a notable advance.[22]

Indeed the appearance of true field artillery in Charles VIII's Italian expedition in 1494 makes of that campaign a convenient point at which to end an account of the Mediæval Art of War.

In closing let us briefly run over the new factors about to put an end to the long supremacy of cavalry. First of all, cavalry itself had for two centuries been stiff and overburdened with the great weight of plate armour. Second, the French had now set up a permanent, disciplined, professional army. The Swiss had so perfected their drill as to develop a true attacking infantry. The French, again, had produced field artillery. These new things (together with the invention of efficient hand-firearms which was to come in the near future) were to revolutionize the Art of War.

[22] Dict. de l'Arch., Vol. 5, 246–260.

BIBLIOGRAPHY

AMMIANUS MARCELLINUS, *Roman History*.
Ammianus was born about 325–330 and lived until after 391. He was therefore a contemporary of Julian, Valens, and Theodosius. He was a professional soldier, saw much active service, and seems to have served on Julian's staff in that emperor's campaigns. Hence he was probably present at the battle of Strassburg.

ANGLADE, PROFESSEUR JOSEPH, *La Bataille de Muret*. Toulouse, 1913.
Valuable for voluminous quotations from the sources, the more important being given in full.

ASTRUC, REV. PROFESSEUR J., *La Conquête de la Vicomté de Carcassonne par Simon de Montfort*. Pamphlet, Carcassonne, 1912.
Incidental mention.

AUSSARESSES, F., *L'Armée byzantine à la fin du VIème siècle d'après la Strategicon de l'Empereur Maurice*. Paris, 1909.

BELLOC, HILAIRE, *Book of the Bayeux Tapestry*. New York, 1914.
Complete reproduction of the Tapestry which is our chief source of knowledge of the equipment of the time.

BELLOC, HILAIRE, *Crécy*. London, 1912.
Monograph on the campaign and battle, with an introduction on Mediæval Warfare in general and the difficulties of its study.

BELLOC, HILAIRE, *Poitiers*. London, 1913.
Monograph on the campaign and battle.

BELLOC, HILAIRE, *The Stane Street*. London, 1913.
Incidental reference.

BELLOC, HILAIRE, *Warfare in England*. London.
Small book, three-quarters of which covers the mediæval period. Concerned chiefly with strategy and the influence of geography thereon. Very little on tactics. The only good account of John's fine campaign of 1216.

BOUTARIC, EDGARD, *Institutions militaires de la France avant les armées permanentes*. Paris, 1863.
The classic on its subject. Needs correction on the Dark Ages because of its old-fashioned exaggeration of Teutonic influence.

BURY, PROFESSOR J. B., *History of the Later Roman Empire, 395–800 A. D.* 2 vol. London and New York, 1889.
Less full but more accurate and critical than Hodgkin.

BURY, PROFESSOR J. B., *History of the Eastern Roman Empire, 802–867 A. D.* London and New York, 1912.
Incidental reference.

CAGNAT, R., *Les Deux camps de la Légion IIIe Auguste à Lambese d'après les fouilles récentes*. Paris, 1918.
Monograph shedding considerable light on Roman garrison life, the legionary staff, and the various bodies of special duty men.

CAGNAT, R., *La Frontière militaire de la Tripolitaine à l'époque romaine*. Paris, 1912.
Monograph on the remains of Roman frontier posts along the edge of the desert.

CHEESMAN, G. L., *The Auxilia of the Roman Imperial Army*. Oxford, 1914.
Particularly good on recruitment and frontier defence. Unfortunately he ends about 300 A. D.

COULANGES, FUSTEL DE, *Histoire des institutions politiques de l'ancienne France: L'Invasion germanique et la fin de l'Empire*. Paris, 1891.
Concerns itself only incidentally with events outside Gaul, but is, nevertheless, the best account of the process by which centralized Roman government was originally lost in the West.

DEAN, BASHFORD, *Helmets and Body Armor in Modern Warfare*. New Haven, Conn., 1920.
The introduction (pp. 25–50) has a good outline of the use of armour in the mediæval and early modern period, giving weights, illustrations, etc.

DELPECH, HENRI, *La Tactique au 13me siècle*. 2 vol., Paris, 1886.
Still the best study of Mediæval Tactics. Gives the theoretical background on Vegetius, the increased skill and flexibility in cavalry tactics up to about 1270 A. D., and indicates the loss of manœuvring power through the excessive weight of plate armour. (See Dieulafoy for Muret.)

DIEULAFOY, MARCEL, *Le Bataille de Muret*. Paris, 1899.
Supersedes Delpech on Muret, gives a number of quotations of original sources, but is unduly contemptuous of the Middle Ages.

DIEULAFOY, MARCEL, *La Château Gaillard et l'architecture militaire au XIIIe siècle*. Paris, 1898.
Monograph containing detailed description and a number of valuable plates. Attempts the hopeless task of proving a Persian origin for mediæval military architecture.

DION CASSIUS, *Roman History*.
Dion Cassius lived about 150–235 A. D. A lawyer by profession, he rose to high political office, including the government of the provinces of Dalmatia, Africa, and Pannonia. As such he must have exercised military command. He was an intimate friend of the able and soldierly Emperor Septimius Severus (reigned 192–211).

DODGE, LT. COL. THEODORE AYRAULT, *Cæsar*. Boston, 1900.
The last chapter, XLVI, gives an outline of the Art of War of the Roman Empire.

DODGE, LT. COL. THEODORE AYRAULT, *Gustavus Adolphus*. Boston, 1896.
Chap. I, "The Era of Cavalry," outlines (roughly and most insufficiently) the Art of War, A. D. 378–1315. Chap. II, "The Reap-

pearance of Infantry," attempts to outline the Art of War, A. D. 1315–1500. The best of this chapter is the discussion of the Swiss. *Encyclopædia Britannica* (E. B.), 11th Edition.

FERRERO, GUGLIELMO, *Greatness and Decline of Rome*, Vol. 5, "The Republic of Augustus." New York, 1909.
  Describes the strategy of the Pannonian revolt and the invasion of Germany.

FERRERO, GUGLIELMO, *Ruin of Ancient Civilization and Triumph of Christianity*. New York, 1921.
  Analyzes the third-century decline, showing it to have been political, financial, social, and religious rather than military.

FORTESCUE, JOHN W., *History of the British Army*. 10 vol., London and New York, 1899.
  The standard work on the subject. Occasionally suffers from undue nationalist partiality.

FRANCE, ANATOLE, *Joan of Arc*. London and New York, 1909.
  Full account of the siege of Orleans and Joan's campaigns.

GIBBON, EDWARD, *History of the Decline and Fall of the Roman Empire* (Harper edition). 6 vol., New York, 1900.
  Incidental reference.

HAVERFIELD, PROF. FRANCIS J., "Britain" and "Roman Army," articles in *Encyclopædia Britannica*, 11th Edition.
  Incidental reference.

HODGKIN, THOMAS, *Italy and Her Invaders*. 8 vol., Oxford, 1892.
  Old-fashioned but full account of Italian affairs, 363–814 A. D. Needs checking by more recent writers, but is still valuable on account of the mass of detail given.

JOSEPHUS, FLAVIUS, *Jewish War*.
  Josephus held high command among the Jewish rebels at the beginning of the war. Later he went over to the Romans and accompanied Titus' army during the siege of Jerusalem.

MANGIN, LIEUTENANT COLONEL, *La Force Noire*. Paris.
  General Mangin, as he now is, is virtually the founder of the French black army, and was among the French army commanders during the recent war. Chapters i and ii of Book 2 discuss the use of negro troops by the Moors in Spain and incidentally contain information as to this little known period.

MONCRIEFF, CHARLES SCOTT, *The Song of Roland*, verse translation. New York, 1920.
  Incidental reference.

NICKERSON, HOFFMAN, *The Inquisition: A Political and Military History of Its Establishment*. Boston, 1923.
  Contains an account of the Albigensian War.

NORGATE, KATE, *John Lackland*. London and New York, 1902.
  Valuable for occasional detail, although no attempt to analyze military affairs is made, and the author entirely misses John's high strategic ability.

OMAN, PROF. CHARLES, *History of the Art of War in the Middle Ages, A. D. 378–1485.* 2 vol., London, 1924.

The only survey of the entire field including fortification; hence its value to the student.

SCHLUMBERGER, G., *Le Siège de Constantinople en 1453.* Paris, 1914.

A full account of the siege, with special reference to the Turkish big guns.

TACITUS, CORNELIUS, *Annals, History, Agricola.*

Tacitus lived about 55–120 A. D. He was a Roman of good family who held high political office, and had every opportunity of learning about military affairs from officers who had participated in them. There is no evidence to show that he ever held high military command, and he shows little interest in the technical, as opposed to the moral and social aspects of war.

VIOLLET-LE-DUC, E., *Dictionnaire du mobilier français* ("Dict. du Mob."), vol. 5 and 6.

Vol. 6, article "Tactique," is particularly good on Poitiers and Agincourt; notices the late Roman period and gives accounts of Hastings, Bouvines, Crécy, Joan of Arc and a notice of fifteen-sixteenth century infantry. The rest of Vol. 6, together with Vol. 5, is the fullest account of mediæval armour, weapons, and equipment. Copiously illustrated.

VIOLLET-LE-DUC, E., *Dictionnaire de l'architecture français* ("Dict. de l'arch."). 10 vol.

Articles and illustrations scattered through this inexhaustible work, together compose the best account of mediæval fortification and siegework.

YOUNG, BRIGADIER GENERAL G. F., *East and West Through Fifteen Centuries,* 2 vol., London and New York, 1916.

The author is a professional soldier who has seen active service in the East. Although not abreast of modern scholarship, he is occasionally useful because of his common-sense view of military operations.

INDEX

Adiutrix, designation of Roman legion, 23, 37
Adrianople, campaign of, 61
Agincourt, battle of, 201
Ala, Roman cavalry unit, 7, 69, 153
Albigensian Crusade, 146
Alemanni, 72
Aljubarotta, battle of, 199
Antioch, battle of, 135
Armour, Mediæval, 107, 113, 132, 133, 156, 173, 174, 177, 179, 189, 196, 208; Roman, 7, 52, 62, 69, 87, 107
  Chain, 7, 87, 113, 132, 174; plate, 7, 132, 173, 174, 177, 179, 189
  Horse, 132, 189, 196, 208
  Gambeson, 132; helmet, 7, 113, 132, 133; shield, 113
  Weight, 107, 108, 189
Arms of service, chiefs of, 48
Army
  Roman, under Augustus, 3; organization, 5; life service, 6; early Empire, 9; value of professional, 77; of Emperor Maurice, 79
  Feudal, appearance in western Europe, 92; description, 100; compared with Roman, 101
  French, establishment of standing, 204
Arsouf, battle of, 138
Artillery, mediæval, 124; range, catapult, 125; at Crécy, 185; first organized in France, 205; at siege of Constantinople (1453), 216; rate of fire, 15th century, 216; field carriages, 15th century, 217
Attila, 257
Augustus, Roman Emperor, 1
Auxiliaries, in Roman army, 5, 7

Baldwin I, King of Jerusalem, 135
Ballista, 124
Band, troop unit, 79, 81
Bannockburn, battle of, 183
Basle, battle of, 211
Beacon fires, Byzantine use of, 88
Belisarius, 73
Benevento, battle of, 172
Black Prince, the, 190
Boadicea, British tribal queen, 21
Bonus, military, Roman, 3, 5
Bouvines, battle of, 157
Britain, Roman invasions of, 17; strategic location of Roman troops in, 18
Bucelaries, class of imperial Roman troops, 79
Buffer states, Roman system of, 52, 66
Byzantine Empire, military system of, 86

Camel corps, Roman, 42
Camp-followers, imperial Roman armies, 79
Camp, Roman, 25. See also *Fortifications*
Canal, Rhine to North Sea (13 B.C.), 11
Castles, see *Fortifications*
Cataphractos, East Roman heavy cavalryman, 87
Catapult, 8; see also *Artillery*
Cavalry, forms part of Roman legion under Augustus, 4; Roman, increase of importance under Empire, 42, 52, 55, 63, 69; light and heavy, 70; first use of stirrups, 80; principal arm in Byzantine armies, 81, 88, 91; during Middle Ages, 105, 108; use dismounted in Middle

A CATALOG OF SELECTED
DOVER BOOKS
IN ALL FIELDS OF INTEREST

A CATALOG OF SELECTED DOVER
BOOKS IN ALL FIELDS OF INTEREST

CONCERNING THE SPIRITUAL IN ART, Wassily Kandinsky. Pioneering work by father of abstract art. Thoughts on color theory, nature of art. Analysis of earlier masters. 12 illustrations. 80pp. of text. 5⅜ x 8½. 23411-8

ANIMALS: 1,419 Copyright-Free Illustrations of Mammals, Birds, Fish, Insects, etc., Jim Harter (ed.). Clear wood engravings present, in extremely lifelike poses, over 1,000 species of animals. One of the most extensive pictorial sourcebooks of its kind. Captions. Index. 284pp. 9 x 12. 23766-4

CELTIC ART: The Methods of Construction, George Bain. Simple geometric techniques for making Celtic interlacements, spirals, Kells-type initials, animals, humans, etc. Over 500 illustrations. 160pp. 9 x 12. (Available in U.S. only.) 22923-8

AN ATLAS OF ANATOMY FOR ARTISTS, Fritz Schider. Most thorough reference work on art anatomy in the world. Hundreds of illustrations, including selections from works by Vesalius, Leonardo, Goya, Ingres, Michelangelo, others. 593 illustrations. 192pp. 7⅛ x 10¼. 20241-0

CELTIC HAND STROKE-BY-STROKE (Irish Half-Uncial from "The Book of Kells"): An Arthur Baker Calligraphy Manual, Arthur Baker. Complete guide to creating each letter of the alphabet in distinctive Celtic manner. Covers hand position, strokes, pens, inks, paper, more. Illustrated. 48pp. 8¼ x 11. 24336-2

EASY ORIGAMI, John Montroll. Charming collection of 32 projects (hat, cup, pelican, piano, swan, many more) specially designed for the novice origami hobbyist. Clearly illustrated easy-to-follow instructions insure that even beginning papercrafters will achieve successful results. 48pp. 8¼ x 11. 27298-2

THE COMPLETE BOOK OF BIRDHOUSE CONSTRUCTION FOR WOODWORKERS, Scott D. Campbell. Detailed instructions, illustrations, tables. Also data on bird habitat and instinct patterns. Bibliography. 3 tables. 63 illustrations in 15 figures. 48pp. 5¼ x 8½. 24407-5

BLOOMINGDALE'S ILLUSTRATED 1886 CATALOG: Fashions, Dry Goods and Housewares, Bloomingdale Brothers. Famed merchants' extremely rare catalog depicting about 1,700 products: clothing, housewares, firearms, dry goods, jewelry, more. Invaluable for dating, identifying vintage items. Also, copyright-free graphics for artists, designers. Co-published with Henry Ford Museum & Greenfield Village. 160pp. 8¼ x 11. 25780-0

HISTORIC COSTUME IN PICTURES, Braun & Schneider. Over 1,450 costumed figures in clearly detailed engravings—from dawn of civilization to end of 19th century. Captions. Many folk costumes. 256pp. 8⅜ x 11¾. 23150-X

STICKLEY CRAFTSMAN FURNITURE CATALOGS, Gustav Stickley and L. & J. G. Stickley. Beautiful, functional furniture in two authentic catalogs from 1910. 594 illustrations, including 277 photos, show settles, rockers, armchairs, reclining chairs, bookcases, desks, tables. 183pp. 6½ x 9¼. 23838-5

AMERICAN LOCOMOTIVES IN HISTORIC PHOTOGRAPHS: 1858 to 1949, Ron Ziel (ed.). A rare collection of 126 meticulously detailed official photographs, called "builder portraits," of American locomotives that majestically chronicle the rise of steam locomotive power in America. Introduction. Detailed captions. xi+ 129pp. 9 x 12. 27393-8

AMERICA'S LIGHTHOUSES: An Illustrated History, Francis Ross Holland, Jr. Delightfully written, profusely illustrated fact-filled survey of over 200 American lighthouses since 1716. History, anecdotes, technological advances, more. 240pp. 8 x 10¾. 25576-X

TOWARDS A NEW ARCHITECTURE, Le Corbusier. Pioneering manifesto by founder of "International School." Technical and aesthetic theories, views of industry, economics, relation of form to function, "mass-production split" and much more. Profusely illustrated. 320pp. 6⅛ x 9¼. (Available in U.S. only.) 25023-7

HOW THE OTHER HALF LIVES, Jacob Riis. Famous journalistic record, exposing poverty and degradation of New York slums around 1900, by major social reformer. 100 striking and influential photographs. 233pp. 10 x 7⅞. 22012-5

FRUIT KEY AND TWIG KEY TO TREES AND SHRUBS, William M. Harlow. One of the handiest and most widely used identification aids. Fruit key covers 120 deciduous and evergreen species; twig key 160 deciduous species. Easily used. Over 300 photographs. 126pp. 5⅜ x 8½. 20511-8

COMMON BIRD SONGS, Dr. Donald J. Borror. Songs of 60 most common U.S. birds: robins, sparrows, cardinals, bluejays, finches, more–arranged in order of increasing complexity. Up to 9 variations of songs of each species.
Cassette and manual 99911-4

ORCHIDS AS HOUSE PLANTS, Rebecca Tyson Northen. Grow cattleyas and many other kinds of orchids–in a window, in a case, or under artificial light. 63 illustrations. 148pp. 5⅜ x 8½. 23261-1

MONSTER MAZES, Dave Phillips. Masterful mazes at four levels of difficulty. Avoid deadly perils and evil creatures to find magical treasures. Solutions for all 32 exciting illustrated puzzles. 48pp. 8¼ x 11. 26005-4

MOZART'S DON GIOVANNI (DOVER OPERA LIBRETTO SERIES), Wolfgang Amadeus Mozart. Introduced and translated by Ellen H. Bleiler. Standard Italian libretto, with complete English translation. Convenient and thoroughly portable–an ideal companion for reading along with a recording or the performance itself. Introduction. List of characters. Plot summary. 121pp. 5¼ x 8½. 24944-1

TECHNICAL MANUAL AND DICTIONARY OF CLASSICAL BALLET, Gail Grant. Defines, explains, comments on steps, movements, poses and concepts. 15-page pictorial section. Basic book for student, viewer. 127pp. 5⅜ x 8½. 21843-0

THE CLARINET AND CLARINET PLAYING, David Pino. Lively, comprehensive work features suggestions about technique, musicianship, and musical interpretation, as well as guidelines for teaching, making your own reeds, and preparing for public performance. Includes an intriguing look at clarinet history. "A godsend," *The Clarinet,* Journal of the International Clarinet Society. Appendixes. 7 illus. 320pp. 5⅜ x 8½. 40270-3

HOLLYWOOD GLAMOR PORTRAITS, John Kobal (ed.). 145 photos from 1926-49. Harlow, Gable, Bogart, Bacall; 94 stars in all. Full background on photographers, technical aspects. 160pp. 8⅜ x 11¼. 23352-9

THE ANNOTATED CASEY AT THE BAT: A Collection of Ballads about the Mighty Casey/Third, Revised Edition, Martin Gardner (ed.). Amusing sequels and parodies of one of America's best-loved poems: Casey's Revenge, Why Casey Whiffed, Casey's Sister at the Bat, others. 256pp. 5⅜ x 8½. 28598-7

THE RAVEN AND OTHER FAVORITE POEMS, Edgar Allan Poe. Over 40 of the author's most memorable poems: "The Bells," "Ulalume," "Israfel," "To Helen," "The Conqueror Worm," "Eldorado," "Annabel Lee," many more. Alphabetic lists of titles and first lines. 64pp. 5₃⁄₁₆ x 8¼. 26685-0

PERSONAL MEMOIRS OF U. S. GRANT, Ulysses Simpson Grant. Intelligent, deeply moving firsthand account of Civil War campaigns, considered by many the finest military memoirs ever written. Includes letters, historic photographs, maps and more. 528pp. 6⅛ x 9¼. 28587-1

ANCIENT EGYPTIAN MATERIALS AND INDUSTRIES, A. Lucas and J. Harris. Fascinating, comprehensive, thoroughly documented text describes this ancient civilization's vast resources and the processes that incorporated them in daily life, including the use of animal products, building materials, cosmetics, perfumes and incense, fibers, glazed ware, glass and its manufacture, materials used in the mummification process, and much more. 544pp. 6⅛ x 9¼. (Available in U.S. only.) 40446-3

RUSSIAN STORIES/RUSSKIE RASSKAZY: A Dual-Language Book, edited by Gleb Struve. Twelve tales by such masters as Chekhov, Tolstoy, Dostoevsky, Pushkin, others. Excellent word-for-word English translations on facing pages, plus teaching and study aids, Russian/English vocabulary, biographical/critical introductions, more. 416pp. 5⅜ x 8½. 26244-8

PHILADELPHIA THEN AND NOW: 60 Sites Photographed in the Past and Present, Kenneth Finkel and Susan Oyama. Rare photographs of City Hall, Logan Square, Independence Hall, Betsy Ross House, other landmarks juxtaposed with contemporary views. Captures changing face of historic city. Introduction. Captions. 128pp. 8¼ x 11. 25790-8

AIA ARCHITECTURAL GUIDE TO NASSAU AND SUFFOLK COUNTIES, LONG ISLAND, The American Institute of Architects, Long Island Chapter, and the Society for the Preservation of Long Island Antiquities. Comprehensive, well-researched and generously illustrated volume brings to life over three centuries of Long Island's great architectural heritage. More than 240 photographs with authoritative, extensively detailed captions. 176pp. 8¼ x 11. 26946-9

NORTH AMERICAN INDIAN LIFE: Customs and Traditions of 23 Tribes, Elsie Clews Parsons (ed.). 27 fictionalized essays by noted anthropologists examine religion, customs, government, additional facets of life among the Winnebago, Crow, Zuni, Eskimo, other tribes. 480pp. 6⅛ x 9¼. 27377-6

FRANK LLOYD WRIGHT'S DANA HOUSE, Donald Hoffmann. Pictorial essay of residential masterpiece with over 160 interior and exterior photos, plans, elevations, sketches and studies. 128pp. 9¼ x 10¾. 29120-0

THE MALE AND FEMALE FIGURE IN MOTION: 60 Classic Photographic Sequences, Eadweard Muybridge. 60 true-action photographs of men and women walking, running, climbing, bending, turning, etc., reproduced from rare 19th-century masterpiece. vi + 121pp. 9 x 12. 24745-7

1001 QUESTIONS ANSWERED ABOUT THE SEASHORE, N. J. Berrill and Jacquelyn Berrill. Queries answered about dolphins, sea snails, sponges, starfish, fishes, shore birds, many others. Covers appearance, breeding, growth, feeding, much more. 305pp. 5¼ x 8¼. 23366-9

ATTRACTING BIRDS TO YOUR YARD, William J. Weber. Easy-to-follow guide offers advice on how to attract the greatest diversity of birds: birdhouses, feeders, water and waterers, much more. 96pp. 5³⁄₁₆ x 8¼. 28927-3

MEDICINAL AND OTHER USES OF NORTH AMERICAN PLANTS: A Historical Survey with Special Reference to the Eastern Indian Tribes, Charlotte Erichsen-Brown. Chronological historical citations document 500 years of usage of plants, trees, shrubs native to eastern Canada, northeastern U.S. Also complete identifying information. 343 illustrations. 544pp. 6½ x 9¼. 25951-X

STORYBOOK MAZES, Dave Phillips. 23 stories and mazes on two-page spreads: Wizard of Oz, Treasure Island, Robin Hood, etc. Solutions. 64pp. 8¼ x 11. 23628-5

AMERICAN NEGRO SONGS: 230 Folk Songs and Spirituals, Religious and Secular, John W. Work. This authoritative study traces the African influences of songs sung and played by black Americans at work, in church, and as entertainment. The author discusses the lyric significance of such songs as "Swing Low, Sweet Chariot," "John Henry," and others and offers the words and music for 230 songs. Bibliography. Index of Song Titles. 272pp. 6½ x 9¼. 40271-1

MOVIE-STAR PORTRAITS OF THE FORTIES, John Kobal (ed.). 163 glamor, studio photos of 106 stars of the 1940s: Rita Hayworth, Ava Gardner, Marlon Brando, Clark Gable, many more. 176pp. 8⅜ x 11¼. 23546-7

BENCHLEY LOST AND FOUND, Robert Benchley. Finest humor from early 30s, about pet peeves, child psychologists, post office and others. Mostly unavailable elsewhere. 73 illustrations by Peter Arno and others. 183pp. 5⅜ x 8½. 22410-4

YEKL and THE IMPORTED BRIDEGROOM AND OTHER STORIES OF YIDDISH NEW YORK, Abraham Cahan. Film Hester Street based on *Yekl* (1896). Novel, other stories among first about Jewish immigrants on N.Y.'s East Side. 240pp. 5⅜ x 8½. 22427-9

SELECTED POEMS, Walt Whitman. Generous sampling from *Leaves of Grass*. Twenty-four poems include "I Hear America Singing," "Song of the Open Road," "I Sing the Body Electric," "When Lilacs Last in the Dooryard Bloom'd," "O Captain! My Captain!"—all reprinted from an authoritative edition. Lists of titles and first lines. 128pp. 5³⁄₁₆ x 8¼. 26878-0

THE BEST TALES OF HOFFMANN, E. T. A. Hoffmann. 10 of Hoffmann's most important stories: "Nutcracker and the King of Mice," "The Golden Flowerpot," etc. 458pp. 5⅜ x 8½. 21793-0

FROM FETISH TO GOD IN ANCIENT EGYPT, E. A. Wallis Budge. Rich detailed survey of Egyptian conception of "God" and gods, magic, cult of animals, Osiris, more. Also, superb English translations of hymns and legends. 240 illustrations. 545pp. 5⅜ x 8½. 25803-3

FRENCH STORIES/CONTES FRANÇAIS: A Dual-Language Book, Wallace Fowlie. Ten stories by French masters, Voltaire to Camus: "Micromegas" by Voltaire; "The Atheist's Mass" by Balzac; "Minuet" by de Maupassant; "The Guest" by Camus, six more. Excellent English translations on facing pages. Also French-English vocabulary list, exercises, more. 352pp. 5⅜ x 8½. 26443-2

CHICAGO AT THE TURN OF THE CENTURY IN PHOTOGRAPHS: 122 Historic Views from the Collections of the Chicago Historical Society, Larry A. Viskochil. Rare large-format prints offer detailed views of City Hall, State Street, the Loop, Hull House, Union Station, many other landmarks, circa 1904-1913. Introduction. Captions. Maps. 144pp. 9⅜ x 12¼. 24656-6

OLD BROOKLYN IN EARLY PHOTOGRAPHS, 1865-1929, William Lee Younger. Luna Park, Gravesend race track, construction of Grand Army Plaza, moving of Hotel Brighton, etc. 157 previously unpublished photographs. 165pp. 8⅞ x 11¾. 23587-4

THE MYTHS OF THE NORTH AMERICAN INDIANS, Lewis Spence. Rich anthology of the myths and legends of the Algonquins, Iroquois, Pawnees and Sioux, prefaced by an extensive historical and ethnological commentary. 36 illustrations. 480pp. 5⅜ x 8½. 25967-6

AN ENCYCLOPEDIA OF BATTLES: Accounts of Over 1,560 Battles from 1479 B.C. to the Present, David Eggenberger. Essential details of every major battle in recorded history from the first battle of Megiddo in 1479 B.C. to Grenada in 1984. List of Battle Maps. New Appendix covering the years 1967-1984. Index. 99 illustrations. 544pp. 6½ x 9¼. 24913-1

SAILING ALONE AROUND THE WORLD, Captain Joshua Slocum. First man to sail around the world, alone, in small boat. One of great feats of seamanship told in delightful manner. 67 illustrations. 294pp. 5⅜ x 8½. 20326-3

ANARCHISM AND OTHER ESSAYS, Emma Goldman. Powerful, penetrating, prophetic essays on direct action, role of minorities, prison reform, puritan hypocrisy, violence, etc. 271pp. 5⅜ x 8½. 22484-8

MYTHS OF THE HINDUS AND BUDDHISTS, Ananda K. Coomaraswamy and Sister Nivedita. Great stories of the epics; deeds of Krishna, Shiva, taken from puranas, Vedas, folk tales; etc. 32 illustrations. 400pp. 5⅜ x 8½. 21759-0

THE TRAUMA OF BIRTH, Otto Rank. Rank's controversial thesis that anxiety neurosis is caused by profound psychological trauma which occurs at birth. 256pp. 5³⁄₈ x 8½. 27974-X

A THEOLOGICO-POLITICAL TREATISE, Benedict Spinoza. Also contains unfinished Political Treatise. Great classic on religious liberty, theory of government on common consent. R. Elwes translation. Total of 421pp. 5⅜ x 8½. 20249-6

CATALOG OF DOVER BOOKS

MY BONDAGE AND MY FREEDOM, Frederick Douglass. Born a slave, Douglass became outspoken force in antislavery movement. The best of Douglass' autobiographies. Graphic description of slave life. 464pp. 5⅜ x 8½. 22457-0

FOLLOWING THE EQUATOR: A Journey Around the World, Mark Twain. Fascinating humorous account of 1897 voyage to Hawaii, Australia, India, New Zealand, etc. Ironic, bemused reports on peoples, customs, climate, flora and fauna, politics, much more. 197 illustrations. 720pp. 5⅜ x 8½. 26113-1

THE PEOPLE CALLED SHAKERS, Edward D. Andrews. Definitive study of Shakers: origins, beliefs, practices, dances, social organization, furniture and crafts, etc. 33 illustrations. 351pp. 5⅜ x 8½. 21081-2

THE MYTHS OF GREECE AND ROME, H. A. Guerber. A classic of mythology, generously illustrated, long prized for its simple, graphic, accurate retelling of the principal myths of Greece and Rome, and for its commentary on their origins and significance. With 64 illustrations by Michelangelo, Raphael, Titian, Rubens, Canova, Bernini and others. 480pp. 5⅜ x 8½. 27584-1

PSYCHOLOGY OF MUSIC, Carl E. Seashore. Classic work discusses music as a medium from psychological viewpoint. Clear treatment of physical acoustics, auditory apparatus, sound perception, development of musical skills, nature of musical feeling, host of other topics. 88 figures. 408pp. 5⅜ x 8½. 21851-1

THE PHILOSOPHY OF HISTORY, Georg W. Hegel. Great classic of Western thought develops concept that history is not chance but rational process, the evolution of freedom. 457pp. 5⅜ x 8½. 20112-0

THE BOOK OF TEA, Kakuzo Okakura. Minor classic of the Orient: entertaining, charming explanation, interpretation of traditional Japanese culture in terms of tea ceremony. 94pp. 5⅜ x 8½. 20070-1

LIFE IN ANCIENT EGYPT, Adolf Erman. Fullest, most thorough, detailed older account with much not in more recent books, domestic life, religion, magic, medicine, commerce, much more. Many illustrations reproduce tomb paintings, carvings, hieroglyphs, etc. 597pp. 5⅜ x 8½. 22632-8

SUNDIALS, Their Theory and Construction, Albert Waugh. Far and away the best, most thorough coverage of ideas, mathematics concerned, types, construction, adjusting anywhere. Simple, nontechnical treatment allows even children to build several of these dials. Over 100 illustrations. 230pp. 5⅜ x 8½. 22947-5

THEORETICAL HYDRODYNAMICS, L. M. Milne-Thomson. Classic exposition of the mathematical theory of fluid motion, applicable to both hydrodynamics and aerodynamics. Over 600 exercises. 768pp. 6⅛ x 9¼. 68970-0

SONGS OF EXPERIENCE: Facsimile Reproduction with 26 Plates in Full Color, William Blake. 26 full-color plates from a rare 1826 edition. Includes "The Tyger," "London," "Holy Thursday," and other poems. Printed text of poems. 48pp. 5¼ x 7. 24636-1

OLD-TIME VIGNETTES IN FULL COLOR, Carol Belanger Grafton (ed.). Over 390 charming, often sentimental illustrations, selected from archives of Victorian graphics—pretty women posing, children playing, food, flowers, kittens and puppies, smiling cherubs, birds and butterflies, much more. All copyright-free. 48pp. 9¼ x 12¼. 27269-9

CATALOG OF DOVER BOOKS

PERSPECTIVE FOR ARTISTS, Rex Vicat Cole. Depth, perspective of sky and sea, shadows, much more, not usually covered. 391 diagrams, 81 reproductions of drawings and paintings. 279pp. 5⅜ x 8½. 22487-2

DRAWING THE LIVING FIGURE, Joseph Sheppard. Innovative approach to artistic anatomy focuses on specifics of surface anatomy, rather than muscles and bones. Over 170 drawings of live models in front, back and side views, and in widely varying poses. Accompanying diagrams. 177 illustrations. Introduction. Index. 144pp. 8⅜ x11¼. 26723-7

GOTHIC AND OLD ENGLISH ALPHABETS: 100 Complete Fonts, Dan X. Solo. Add power, elegance to posters, signs, other graphics with 100 stunning copyright-free alphabets: Blackstone, Dolbey, Germania, 97 more–including many lower-case, numerals, punctuation marks. 104pp. 8⅛ x 11. 24695-7

HOW TO DO BEADWORK, Mary White. Fundamental book on craft from simple projects to five-bead chains and woven works. 106 illustrations. 142pp. 5⅜ x 8. 20697-1

THE BOOK OF WOOD CARVING, Charles Marshall Sayers. Finest book for beginners discusses fundamentals and offers 34 designs. "Absolutely first rate . . . well thought out and well executed."–E. J. Tangerman. 118pp. 7¾ x 10⅝. 23654-4

ILLUSTRATED CATALOG OF CIVIL WAR MILITARY GOODS: Union Army Weapons, Insignia, Uniform Accessories, and Other Equipment, Schuyler, Hartley, and Graham. Rare, profusely illustrated 1846 catalog includes Union Army uniform and dress regulations, arms and ammunition, coats, insignia, flags, swords, rifles, etc. 226 illustrations. 160pp. 9 x 12. 24939-5

WOMEN'S FASHIONS OF THE EARLY 1900s: An Unabridged Republication of "New York Fashions, 1909," National Cloak & Suit Co. Rare catalog of mail-order fashions documents women's and children's clothing styles shortly after the turn of the century. Captions offer full descriptions, prices. Invaluable resource for fashion, costume historians. Approximately 725 illustrations. 128pp. 8⅜ x 11¼. 27276-1

THE 1912 AND 1915 GUSTAV STICKLEY FURNITURE CATALOGS, Gustav Stickley. With over 200 detailed illustrations and descriptions, these two catalogs are essential reading and reference materials and identification guides for Stickley furniture. Captions cite materials, dimensions and prices. 112pp. 6½ x 9¼. 26676-1

EARLY AMERICAN LOCOMOTIVES, John H. White, Jr. Finest locomotive engravings from early 19th century: historical (1804–74), main-line (after 1870), special, foreign, etc. 147 plates. 142pp. 11⅜ x 8¼. 22772-3

THE TALL SHIPS OF TODAY IN PHOTOGRAPHS, Frank O. Braynard. Lavishly illustrated tribute to nearly 100 majestic contemporary sailing vessels: Amerigo Vespucci, Clearwater, Constitution, Eagle, Mayflower, Sea Cloud, Victory, many more. Authoritative captions provide statistics, background on each ship. 190 black-and-white photographs and illustrations. Introduction. 128pp. 8⅞ x 11¾. 27163-3

LITTLE BOOK OF EARLY AMERICAN CRAFTS AND TRADES, Peter Stockham (ed.). 1807 children's book explains crafts and trades: baker, hatter, cooper, potter, and many others. 23 copperplate illustrations. 140pp. 4⅝ x 6. 23336-7

VICTORIAN FASHIONS AND COSTUMES FROM HARPER'S BAZAR, 1867–1898, Stella Blum (ed.). Day costumes, evening wear, sports clothes, shoes, hats, other accessories in over 1,000 detailed engravings. 320pp. 9⅜ x 12¼. 22990-4

GUSTAV STICKLEY, THE CRAFTSMAN, Mary Ann Smith. Superb study surveys broad scope of Stickley's achievement, especially in architecture. Design philosophy, rise and fall of the Craftsman empire, descriptions and floor plans for many Craftsman houses, more. 86 black-and-white halftones. 31 line illustrations. Introduction 208pp. 6½ x 9¼. 27210-9

THE LONG ISLAND RAIL ROAD IN EARLY PHOTOGRAPHS, Ron Ziel. Over 220 rare photos, informative text document origin (1844) and development of rail service on Long Island. Vintage views of early trains, locomotives, stations, passengers, crews, much more. Captions. 8⅞ x 11¾. 26301-0

VOYAGE OF THE LIBERDADE, Joshua Slocum. Great 19th-century mariner's thrilling, first-hand account of the wreck of his ship off South America, the 35-foot boat he built from the wreckage, and its remarkable voyage home. 128pp. 5⅜ x 8½. 40022-0

TEN BOOKS ON ARCHITECTURE, Vitruvius. The most important book ever written on architecture. Early Roman aesthetics, technology, classical orders, site selection, all other aspects. Morgan translation. 331pp. 5⅜ x 8½. 20645-9

THE HUMAN FIGURE IN MOTION, Eadweard Muybridge. More than 4,500 stopped-action photos, in action series, showing undraped men, women, children jumping, lying down, throwing, sitting, wrestling, carrying, etc. 390pp. 7⅞ x 10⅝. 20204-6 Clothbd.

TREES OF THE EASTERN AND CENTRAL UNITED STATES AND CANADA, William M. Harlow. Best one-volume guide to 140 trees. Full descriptions, woodlore, range, etc. Over 600 illustrations. Handy size. 288pp. 4½ x 6⅜. 20395-6

SONGS OF WESTERN BIRDS, Dr. Donald J. Borror. Complete song and call repertoire of 60 western species, including flycatchers, juncoes, cactus wrens, many more–includes fully illustrated booklet. Cassette and manual 99913-0

GROWING AND USING HERBS AND SPICES, Milo Miloradovich. Versatile handbook provides all the information needed for cultivation and use of all the herbs and spices available in North America. 4 illustrations. Index. Glossary. 236pp. 5⅜ x 8½. 25058-X

BIG BOOK OF MAZES AND LABYRINTHS, Walter Shepherd. 50 mazes and labyrinths in all–classical, solid, ripple, and more–in one great volume. Perfect inexpensive puzzler for clever youngsters. Full solutions. 112pp. 8⅛ x 11. 22951-3

CATALOG OF DOVER BOOKS

PIANO TUNING, J. Cree Fischer. Clearest, best book for beginner, amateur. Simple repairs, raising dropped notes, tuning by easy method of flattened fifths. No previous skills needed. 4 illustrations. 201pp. 5⅜ x 8½.   23267-0

HINTS TO SINGERS, Lillian Nordica. Selecting the right teacher, developing confidence, overcoming stage fright, and many other important skills receive thoughtful discussion in this indispensible guide, written by a world-famous diva of four decades' experience. 96pp. 5⅜ x 8½.   40094-8

THE COMPLETE NONSENSE OF EDWARD LEAR, Edward Lear. All nonsense limericks, zany alphabets, Owl and Pussycat, songs, nonsense botany, etc., illustrated by Lear. Total of 320pp. 5⅜ x 8½. (Available in U.S. only.)   20167-8

VICTORIAN PARLOUR POETRY: An Annotated Anthology, Michael R. Turner. 117 gems by Longfellow, Tennyson, Browning, many lesser-known poets. "The Village Blacksmith," "Curfew Must Not Ring Tonight," "Only a Baby Small," dozens more, often difficult to find elsewhere. Index of poets, titles, first lines. xxiii + 325pp. 5⅜ x 8¼.   27044-0

DUBLINERS, James Joyce. Fifteen stories offer vivid, tightly focused observations of the lives of Dublin's poorer classes. At least one, "The Dead," is considered a masterpiece. Reprinted complete and unabridged from standard edition. 160pp. 5³⁄₁₆ x 8¼.   26870-5

GREAT WEIRD TALES: 14 Stories by Lovecraft, Blackwood, Machen and Others, S. T. Joshi (ed.). 14 spellbinding tales, including "The Sin Eater," by Fiona McLeod, "The Eye Above the Mantel," by Frank Belknap Long, as well as renowned works by R. H. Barlow, Lord Dunsany, Arthur Machen, W. C. Morrow and eight other masters of the genre. 256pp. 5⅜ x 8½. (Available in U.S. only.)   40436-6

THE BOOK OF THE SACRED MAGIC OF ABRAMELIN THE MAGE, translated by S. MacGregor Mathers. Medieval manuscript of ceremonial magic. Basic document in Aleister Crowley, Golden Dawn groups. 268pp. 5⅜ x 8½.   23211-5

NEW RUSSIAN-ENGLISH AND ENGLISH-RUSSIAN DICTIONARY, M. A. O'Brien. This is a remarkably handy Russian dictionary, containing a surprising amount of information, including over 70,000 entries. 366pp. 4½ x 6⅛.   20208-9

HISTORIC HOMES OF THE AMERICAN PRESIDENTS, Second, Revised Edition, Irvin Haas. A traveler's guide to American Presidential homes, most open to the public, depicting and describing homes occupied by every American President from George Washington to George Bush. With visiting hours, admission charges, travel routes. 175 photographs. Index. 160pp. 8¼ x 11.   26751-2

NEW YORK IN THE FORTIES, Andreas Feininger. 162 brilliant photographs by the well-known photographer, formerly with *Life* magazine. Commuters, shoppers, Times Square at night, much else from city at its peak. Captions by John von Hartz. 181pp. 9¼ x 10¾.   23585-8

INDIAN SIGN LANGUAGE, William Tomkins. Over 525 signs developed by Sioux and other tribes. Written instructions and diagrams. Also 290 pictographs. 111pp. 6⅛ x 9¼.   22029-X

CATALOG OF DOVER BOOKS

ANATOMY: A Complete Guide for Artists, Joseph Sheppard. A master of figure drawing shows artists how to render human anatomy convincingly. Over 460 illustrations. 224pp. 8⅜ x 11¼. 27279-6

MEDIEVAL CALLIGRAPHY: Its History and Technique, Marc Drogin. Spirited history, comprehensive instruction manual covers 13 styles (ca. 4th century through 15th). Excellent photographs; directions for duplicating medieval techniques with modern tools. 224pp. 8⅜ x 11¼. 26142-5

DRIED FLOWERS: How to Prepare Them, Sarah Whitlock and Martha Rankin. Complete instructions on how to use silica gel, meal and borax, perlite aggregate, sand and borax, glycerine and water to create attractive permanent flower arrangements. 12 illustrations. 32pp. 5⅜ x 8½. 21802-3

EASY-TO-MAKE BIRD FEEDERS FOR WOODWORKERS, Scott D. Campbell. Detailed, simple-to-use guide for designing, constructing, caring for and using feeders. Text, illustrations for 12 classic and contemporary designs. 96pp. 5⅜ x 8½. 25847-5

SCOTTISH WONDER TALES FROM MYTH AND LEGEND, Donald A. Mackenzie. 16 lively tales tell of giants rumbling down mountainsides, of a magic wand that turns stone pillars into warriors, of gods and goddesses, evil hags, powerful forces and more. 240pp. 5⅜ x 8½. 29677-6

THE HISTORY OF UNDERCLOTHES, C. Willett Cunnington and Phyllis Cunnington. Fascinating, well-documented survey covering six centuries of English undergarments, enhanced with over 100 illustrations: 12th-century laced-up bodice, footed long drawers (1795), 19th-century bustles, l9th-century corsets for men, Victorian "bust improvers," much more. 272pp. 5⅜ x 8¼. 27124-2

ARTS AND CRAFTS FURNITURE: The Complete Brooks Catalog of 1912, Brooks Manufacturing Co. Photos and detailed descriptions of more than 150 now very collectible furniture designs from the Arts and Crafts movement depict davenports, settees, buffets, desks, tables, chairs, bedsteads, dressers and more, all built of solid, quarter-sawed oak. Invaluable for students and enthusiasts of antiques, Americana and the decorative arts. 80pp. 6½ x 9¼. 27471-3

WILBUR AND ORVILLE: A Biography of the Wright Brothers, Fred Howard. Definitive, crisply written study tells the full story of the brothers' lives and work. A vividly written biography, unparalleled in scope and color, that also captures the spirit of an extraordinary era. 560pp. 6⅛ x 9¼. 40297-5

THE ARTS OF THE SAILOR: Knotting, Splicing and Ropework, Hervey Garrett Smith. Indispensable shipboard reference covers tools, basic knots and useful hitches; handsewing and canvas work, more. Over 100 illustrations. Delightful reading for sea lovers. 256pp. 5⅜ x 8½. 26440-8

FRANK LLOYD WRIGHT'S FALLINGWATER: The House and Its History, Second, Revised Edition, Donald Hoffmann. A total revision—both in text and illustrations—of the standard document on Fallingwater, the boldest, most personal architectural statement of Wright's mature years, updated with valuable new material from the recently opened Frank Lloyd Wright Archives. "Fascinating"—*The New York Times*. 116 illustrations. 128pp. 9¼ x 10¾. 27430-6

PHOTOGRAPHIC SKETCHBOOK OF THE CIVIL WAR, Alexander Gardner. 100 photos taken on field during the Civil War. Famous shots of Manassas Harper's Ferry, Lincoln, Richmond, slave pens, etc. 244pp. 10⅝ x 8¼. 22731-6

FIVE ACRES AND INDEPENDENCE, Maurice G. Kains. Great back-to-the-land classic explains basics of self-sufficient farming. The one book to get. 95 illustrations. 397pp. 5⅜ x 8½. 20974-1

SONGS OF EASTERN BIRDS, Dr. Donald J. Borror. Songs and calls of 60 species most common to eastern U.S.: warblers, woodpeckers, flycatchers, thrushes, larks, many more in high-quality recording. Cassette and manual 99912-2

A MODERN HERBAL, Margaret Grieve. Much the fullest, most exact, most useful compilation of herbal material. Gigantic alphabetical encyclopedia, from aconite to zedoary, gives botanical information, medical properties, folklore, economic uses, much else. Indispensable to serious reader. 161 illustrations. 888pp. 6½ x 9¼. 2-vol. set. (Available in U.S. only.) Vol. I: 22798-7
Vol. II: 22799-5

HIDDEN TREASURE MAZE BOOK, Dave Phillips. Solve 34 challenging mazes accompanied by heroic tales of adventure. Evil dragons, people-eating plants, blood-thirsty giants, many more dangerous adversaries lurk at every twist and turn. 34 mazes, stories, solutions. 48pp. 8¼ x 11. 24566-7

LETTERS OF W. A. MOZART, Wolfgang A. Mozart. Remarkable letters show bawdy wit, humor, imagination, musical insights, contemporary musical world; includes some letters from Leopold Mozart. 276pp. 5⅜ x 8½. 22859-2

BASIC PRINCIPLES OF CLASSICAL BALLET, Agrippina Vaganova. Great Russian theoretician, teacher explains methods for teaching classical ballet. 118 illustrations. 175pp. 5⅜ x 8½. 22036-2

THE JUMPING FROG, Mark Twain. Revenge edition. The original story of The Celebrated Jumping Frog of Calaveras County, a hapless French translation, and Twain's hilarious "retranslation" from the French. 12 illustrations. 66pp. 5⅜ x 8½.
22686-7

BEST REMEMBERED POEMS, Martin Gardner (ed.). The 126 poems in this superb collection of 19th- and 20th-century British and American verse range from Shelley's "To a Skylark" to the impassioned "Renascence" of Edna St. Vincent Millay and to Edward Lear's whimsical "The Owl and the Pussycat." 224pp. 5⅜ x 8½.
27165-X

COMPLETE SONNETS, William Shakespeare. Over 150 exquisite poems deal with love, friendship, the tyranny of time, beauty's evanescence, death and other themes in language of remarkable power, precision and beauty. Glossary of archaic terms. 80pp. $5\frac{3}{16}$ x 8¼. 26686-9

THE BATTLES THAT CHANGED HISTORY, Fletcher Pratt. Eminent historian profiles 16 crucial conflicts, ancient to modern, that changed the course of civilization. 352pp. 5⅜ x 8½. 41129-X

THE WIT AND HUMOR OF OSCAR WILDE, Alvin Redman (ed.). More than 1,000 ripostes, paradoxes, wisecracks: Work is the curse of the drinking classes; I can resist everything except temptation; etc. 258pp. 5⅜ x 8½. 20602-5

SHAKESPEARE LEXICON AND QUOTATION DICTIONARY, Alexander Schmidt. Full definitions, locations, shades of meaning in every word in plays and poems. More than 50,000 exact quotations. 1,485pp. 6½ x 9¼. 2-vol. set.
Vol. 1: 22726-X
Vol. 2: 22727-8

SELECTED POEMS, Emily Dickinson. Over 100 best-known, best-loved poems by one of America's foremost poets, reprinted from authoritative early editions. No comparable edition at this price. Index of first lines. 64pp. 5³⁄₁₆ x 8¼. 26466-1

THE INSIDIOUS DR. FU-MANCHU, Sax Rohmer. The first of the popular mystery series introduces a pair of English detectives to their archnemesis, the diabolical Dr. Fu-Manchu. Flavorful atmosphere, fast-paced action, and colorful characters enliven this classic of the genre. 208pp. 5³⁄₁₆ x 8¼. 29898-1

THE MALLEUS MALEFICARUM OF KRAMER AND SPRENGER, translated by Montague Summers. Full text of most important witchhunter's "bible," used by both Catholics and Protestants. 278pp. 6⅝ x 10. 22802-9

SPANISH STORIES/CUENTOS ESPAÑOLES: A Dual-Language Book, Angel Flores (ed.). Unique format offers 13 great stories in Spanish by Cervantes, Borges, others. Faithful English translations on facing pages. 352pp. 5⅜ x 8½. 25399-6

GARDEN CITY, LONG ISLAND, IN EARLY PHOTOGRAPHS, 1869–1919, Mildred H. Smith. Handsome treasury of 118 vintage pictures, accompanied by carefully researched captions, document the Garden City Hotel fire (1899), the Vanderbilt Cup Race (1908), the first airmail flight departing from the Nassau Boulevard Aerodrome (1911), and much more. 96pp. 8⅞ x 11¾. 40669-5

OLD QUEENS, N.Y., IN EARLY PHOTOGRAPHS, Vincent F. Seyfried and William Asadorian. Over 160 rare photographs of Maspeth, Jamaica, Jackson Heights, and other areas. Vintage views of DeWitt Clinton mansion, 1939 World's Fair and more. Captions. 192pp. 8⅞ x 11. 26358-4

CAPTURED BY THE INDIANS: 15 Firsthand Accounts, 1750-1870, Frederick Drimmer. Astounding true historical accounts of grisly torture, bloody conflicts, relentless pursuits, miraculous escapes and more, by people who lived to tell the tale. 384pp. 5⅜ x 8½. 24901-8

THE WORLD'S GREAT SPEECHES (Fourth Enlarged Edition), Lewis Copeland, Lawrence W. Lamm, and Stephen J. McKenna. Nearly 300 speeches provide public speakers with a wealth of updated quotes and inspiration—from Pericles' funeral oration and William Jennings Bryan's "Cross of Gold Speech" to Malcolm X's powerful words on the Black Revolution and Earl of Spenser's tribute to his sister, Diana, Princess of Wales. 944pp. 5⅜ x 8⅜. 40903-1

THE BOOK OF THE SWORD, Sir Richard F. Burton. Great Victorian scholar/adventurer's eloquent, erudite history of the "queen of weapons"—from prehistory to early Roman Empire. Evolution and development of early swords, variations (sabre, broadsword, cutlass, scimitar, etc.), much more. 336pp. 6⅛ x 9¼.
25434-8

AUTOBIOGRAPHY: The Story of My Experiments with Truth, Mohandas K. Gandhi. Boyhood, legal studies, purification, the growth of the Satyagraha (nonviolent protest) movement. Critical, inspiring work of the man responsible for the freedom of India. 480pp. 5⅜ x 8½. (Available in U.S. only.) 24593-4

CELTIC MYTHS AND LEGENDS, T. W. Rolleston. Masterful retelling of Irish and Welsh stories and tales. Cuchulain, King Arthur, Deirdre, the Grail, many more. First paperback edition. 58 full-page illustrations. 512pp. 5⅜ x 8½. 26507-2

THE PRINCIPLES OF PSYCHOLOGY, William James. Famous long course complete, unabridged. Stream of thought, time perception, memory, experimental methods; great work decades ahead of its time. 94 figures. 1,391pp. 5⅜ x 8½. 2-vol. set.
Vol. I: 20381-6   Vol. II: 20382-4

THE WORLD AS WILL AND REPRESENTATION, Arthur Schopenhauer. Definitive English translation of Schopenhauer's life work, correcting more than 1,000 errors, omissions in earlier translations. Translated by E. F. J. Payne. Total of 1,269pp. 5⅜ x 8½. 2-vol. set.
Vol. 1: 21761-2   Vol. 2: 21762-0

MAGIC AND MYSTERY IN TIBET, Madame Alexandra David-Neel. Experiences among lamas, magicians, sages, sorcerers, Bonpa wizards. A true psychic discovery. 32 illustrations. 321pp. 5⅜ x 8½. (Available in U.S. only.) 22682-4

THE EGYPTIAN BOOK OF THE DEAD, E. A. Wallis Budge. Complete reproduction of Ani's papyrus, finest ever found. Full hieroglyphic text, interlinear transliteration, word-for-word translation, smooth translation. 533pp. 6½ x 9¼. 21866-X

MATHEMATICS FOR THE NONMATHEMATICIAN, Morris Kline. Detailed, college-level treatment of mathematics in cultural and historical context, with numerous exercises. Recommended Reading Lists. Tables. Numerous figures. 641pp. 5⅜ x 8½. 24823-2

PROBABILISTIC METHODS IN THE THEORY OF STRUCTURES, Isaac Elishakoff. Well-written introduction covers the elements of the theory of probability from two or more random variables, the reliability of such multivariable structures, the theory of random function, Monte Carlo methods of treating problems incapable of exact solution, and more. Examples. 502pp. 5⅜ x 8½. 40691-1

THE RIME OF THE ANCIENT MARINER, Gustave Doré, S. T. Coleridge. Doré's finest work; 34 plates capture moods, subtleties of poem. Flawless full-size reproductions printed on facing pages with authoritative text of poem. "Beautiful. Simply beautiful."–Publisher's Weekly. 77pp. 9¼ x 12. 22305-1

NORTH AMERICAN INDIAN DESIGNS FOR ARTISTS AND CRAFTSPEOPLE, Eva Wilson. Over 360 authentic copyright-free designs adapted from Navajo blankets, Hopi pottery, Sioux buffalo hides, more. Geometrics, symbolic figures, plant and animal motifs, etc. 128pp. 8⅜ x 11. (Not for sale in the United Kingdom.) 25341-4

SCULPTURE: Principles and Practice, Louis Slobodkin. Step-by-step approach to clay, plaster, metals, stone; classical and modern. 253 drawings, photos. 255pp. 8⅛ x 11. 22960-2

THE INFLUENCE OF SEA POWER UPON HISTORY, 1660–1783, A. T. Mahan. Influential classic of naval history and tactics still used as text in war colleges. First paperback edition. 4 maps. 24 battle plans. 640pp. 5⅜ x 8½. 25509-3

THE STORY OF THE TITANIC AS TOLD BY ITS SURVIVORS, Jack Winocour (ed.). What it was really like. Panic, despair, shocking inefficiency, and a little heroism. More thrilling than any fictional account. 26 illustrations. 320pp. 5⅜ x 8½.
20610-6

FAIRY AND FOLK TALES OF THE IRISH PEASANTRY, William Butler Yeats (ed.). Treasury of 64 tales from the twilight world of Celtic myth and legend: "The Soul Cages," "The Kildare Pooka," "King O'Toole and his Goose," many more. Introduction and Notes by W. B. Yeats. 352pp. 5⅜ x 8½.
26941-8

BUDDHIST MAHAYANA TEXTS, E. B. Cowell and others (eds.). Superb, accurate translations of basic documents in Mahayana Buddhism, highly important in history of religions. The Buddha-karita of Asvaghosha, Larger Sukhavativyuha, more. 448pp. 5⅜ x 8½.
25552-2

ONE TWO THREE . . . INFINITY: Facts and Speculations of Science, George Gamow. Great physicist's fascinating, readable overview of contemporary science: number theory, relativity, fourth dimension, entropy, genes, atomic structure, much more. 128 illustrations. Index. 352pp. 5⅜ x 8½.
25664-2

EXPERIMENTATION AND MEASUREMENT, W. J. Youden. Introductory manual explains laws of measurement in simple terms and offers tips for achieving accuracy and minimizing errors. Mathematics of measurement, use of instruments, experimenting with machines. 1994 edition. Foreword. Preface. Introduction. Epilogue. Selected Readings. Glossary. Index. Tables and figures. 128pp. 5⅜ x 8½.
40451-X

DALÍ ON MODERN ART: The Cuckolds of Antiquated Modern Art, Salvador Dalí. Influential painter skewers modern art and its practitioners. Outrageous evaluations of Picasso, Cézanne, Turner, more. 15 renderings of paintings discussed. 44 calligraphic decorations by Dalí. 96pp. 5⅜ x 8½. (Available in U.S. only.)
29220-7

ANTIQUE PLAYING CARDS: A Pictorial History, Henry René D'Allemagne. Over 900 elaborate, decorative images from rare playing cards (14th–20th centuries): Bacchus, death, dancing dogs, hunting scenes, royal coats of arms, players cheating, much more. 96pp. 9¼ x 12¼.
29265-7

MAKING FURNITURE MASTERPIECES: 30 Projects with Measured Drawings, Franklin H. Gottshall. Step-by-step instructions, illustrations for constructing handsome, useful pieces, among them a Sheraton desk, Chippendale chair, Spanish desk, Queen Anne table and a William and Mary dressing mirror. 224pp. 8⅛ x 11¼.
29338-6

THE FOSSIL BOOK: A Record of Prehistoric Life, Patricia V. Rich et al. Profusely illustrated definitive guide covers everything from single-celled organisms and dinosaurs to birds and mammals and the interplay between climate and man. Over 1,500 illustrations. 760pp. 7½ x 10⅛.
29371-8